The Power of My Spirit

Reading Scripture Through the Lens of The Holy Spirit

Lost In Translation
Bible Study Series
#4

Energion Publications
Cantonment, Florida
2024

Copyright © 2016, updated 2019, 2022, 2023, 2024 Deborah L. Roeger All rights reserved worldwide. No part of this book may be reproduced or used in any manner without the written permission of the copyright owner except for the use of quotations in a book review.

Unless otherwise noted, Scripture throughout this study is quoted from New American Standard Bible (NASB 1995) Copyright © 1960, 1962, 1963, 1968, 1971, 1972, 1973, 1975, 1977, 1995 by The Lockman Foundation. Used by permission. All rights reserved www.lockman.org

Scripture quotations marked MSG or "The Message" are from THE MESSAGE, copyright © 1993, 2002, 2018 by Eugene H. Peterson. Used by permission of NavPress, represented by Tyndale House Publishers. All rights reserved.

Scripture quotations marked NLT are from the Holy Bible, New Living Translation, copyright ©1996, 2004, 2015 by Tyndale House Foundation. Used by permission of Tyndale House Publishers, Carol Stream, Illinois 60188. All rights reserved.

Scripture quotations marked MIT are from MacDonald Idiomatic Translation, translated by William G. MacDonald. Copyright (c) William G. MacDonald.

Scripture quotations marked NET are from the NET Bible® copyright ©1996, 2019 by Biblical Studies Press, L.L.C. http://netbible.com. Scripture quoted by permission. All rights reserved.

Scripture quotations marked HCSB are from the Holman Christian Standard Bible®, Used by Permission HCSB ©1999, 2000, 2002, 2003, 2009 Holman Bible Publishers. Holman Christian Standard Bible®, Holman CSB®, and HCSB® are federally registered trademarks of Holman Bible Publishers.

Scripture quotations marked AMP are from the Amplified® Bible (AMP), Copyright © 2015 by The Lockman Foundation. Used by permission. www.lockman.org.

Scripture quotations marked CJB are from the *Complete Jewish Bible*, Copyright © 1998 and 2016 by David H. Stern. Used by permission. All rights reserved worldwide.

Scripture quotations marked KJV are from The Authorized (King James) Version. Rights in the Authorized Version in the United Kingdom are vested in the Crown. Reproduced by permission of the Crown's patentee, Cambridge University Press.

Scripture quotations marked ESV are from the ESV® Bible (The Holy Bible, English Standard Version®), copyright © 2001 by Crossway, a publishing ministry of Good News Publishers. Used by permission. All rights reserved.

ISBN: 978-1-63199-910-9

eISBN: 978-1-63199-911-7

Library of Congress Control Number:

Lost in Translation – 1241 Conference Rd - Cantonment, FL 32533 – pubs@energion.com

An Imprint of Energion Publications

The *Lost in Translation* series of Bible Studies is dedicated to Henri Louis Goulet and Messianic Studies Institute located in Gahanna, Ohio. You taught us that an inherently Jewish perspective of the Messianic worldview and way of life is the principle that all learning is for living. Through your teaching and encouragement my husband and I became lifelong learners!

Disclaimer: In this Bible Study I will cite a wide variety of references. While I am comfortable citing the identified source for the specific point referenced, that does not mean that I have read, understand, or necessarily agree or disagree with that source on other points of theology or doctrine. Therefore, referencing various authors or Study Bibles is not intended to be a blanket endorsement of either. On this point I appreciate the wisdom of Trevin Wax, Vice President, Research and Resource Development at the North American Mission Board, who rightly noted that "authors who may be wrong in some ways may be reliable and even helpful in other areas. We can benefit from their works as long as we read carefully."[1]

Note: The presentation of Hebrew and Greek words I have used is designed to make those words easier to read and pronounce. As a result, some letters are not precisely represented

---

[1] Wax, Trevin, *After You Believe by N.T. Wright: A Review*, March 22, 2010. Retrieved from https://www.thegospelcoalition.org/blogs/trevin-wax/after-you-believe-by-n-t-wright-a-review/ (last accessed June 16, 2023)

Table of Contents

Introduction To Lost In Translation Series ix
Preface xiii

1 Who is The Holy Spirit? Part 1 1
2 Who is The Holy Spirit? Part 2 29
3 God's Power to Create.. 53
4 Jesus the Perfect Example 77
5 Resurrection Power at Work 93
6 The Spirit's Power at Work in Paul 111
7 Power to Set the Captive Free 127
8 Power to Maintain Freedom 149
9 The Powerful Fruit of the Holy Spirit 169
10 The Power-Filled Gifts of the Holy Spirit 191
11 Understanding the Paraclete as Our Advocate 215
12 Creating the New Heaven and New Earth 233

How to do basic WORD STUDIES
when you don't read Hebrew or Greek 251
Index to the Word Studies 265
Meet the Author: Deborah L. Roeger 267

Acknowledgements

I can't think of a study I've written that has benefited more from my goal to be a life-long learner than this one. The first version of this study was written in 2016. Since that time, I've taught the study a number of times and given permission to other women to teach it as well. Each time the study has been taught I've made significant edits, additions and improvements to the content because God has continued to teach me about His amazing Spirit. This version of the study has stretched my learning curve once again and I have to say "Thank you Holy Spirit" for being the perfect Teacher!

The manuscript for this study has benefited from the careful read of Kelly Russell who volunteered her time and turned lessons around with lightning speed. The end result is most certainly an improvement over the original manuscript. Thanks so much Kelly!

The prayer partnership and encouragement of Diane Daniels remains steadfast. I continue to be immensely grateful for her seemingly inexhaustible supply of encouragement. She continues to stay the course month after month, year after year as I have written draft upon draft of this study and many others. She never fails to inspire with her words, her love and her prayers! We've marveled many times over the years as we have reflected on the friendship God has graciously given us. Again I say, "I wouldn't be me if I didn't have you as a friend."[1]

---

[1] I don't take credit for this friendship quote. However, the author is unknown.

Gratitude abounds for the faithful prayers of our growing number of other prayer partners. I have absolute confidence that I remain standing because you are on your knees praying!

My continued respect and gratitude also belong to Henry Neufeld and Energion Publications. Henry's knowledge of original Hebrew and Greek remains my safety net in the studies I write. I would not have the confidence to publish these studies without that safety net! Thank you, Henry for graciously sharing your gifts for the benefit of our readers.

This is the fourth study Energion Publications has released in the Lost in Translation series. Publishing that first study became a marathon as we experienced nothing short of an all-out spiritual battle. Each study thereafter has presented its own challenges. Henry and Jody consistently stay the course with patience and grace. Your persistence in addressing every detail in the first study set the course for every study to follow. For that I am humbled and thankful.

And lastly to my husband, Derf, my best friend, the love of my life for more than 50 years and my ministry partner for the last 24 years. You alone know the depth of my gratitude when I say, "Thank you!"

To God be the glory, great things He has done

Introduction To Lost In Translation Series

God instilled in me a love for digging deep into His Word. He added to that a passion for "getting it right" and the ability to assimilate a wealth of diverse material into an understandable lesson. Those gifts have enabled me to write well-researched meaningful studies. Each one incorporates numerous "Word Studies" along the way to ensure that original word meanings which have been largely lost in translation are brought to life again. The end result is a series of Bible Studies that have a scholarly emphasis on rightly dividing God's Word while highlighting personal application for spiritual growth and transformation. When asked, I succinctly describe *Lost in Translation* as connecting biblical scholars with the rest of us who sit in the church pews. However, I have come to understand that these studies also move toward providing a bridge between conservative evangelicals and pentecostal/charismatics. An explanation of that last statement will be helpful.

Through my research mentor I am able to reach into the best and most current scholarship of the subject matter of the study. With diligent research I become equipped to culturally and historically contextualize Bible passages. Doing so provides relevant background to aid the reader in their understanding of original language word meanings and concepts. My goal is never about increasing intellectual knowledge. My orientation is always a right understanding of God's Word with a focus on personal application and discipleship.

At times God adds to my research with revelation and understanding that does not come directly from the pages of the Commentaries, Bible Dictionaries or other sound scholarly materials I customarily reference. At those times, He simply speaks His heart to me on the matter. Often what He says answers a question I had been pondering but had been unable to draw to a satisfactory conclusion.[1] It wasn't until I started fine-tuning the manuscripts to begin the publication process that I caught a glimpse of what God had been doing through this combination of research and revelation. Here I'll need to insert a bit of background information.

In 2014 R. T. Kendall released *Holy Fire: A Balanced, Biblical Look At The Holy Spirit's Work In Our Lives*. In it, Kendall wrote about an unplanned "divorce" that had silently taken place in the church between God's Spirit and God's Word.[2] Using broad brushed descriptive strokes he defined two separate and distinct categories of churches.

- Denominations majoring on the written Word of God. Their focus is on the inerrancy of the written Word, expository preaching and sound doctrine. They may be virtually silent about the Holy Spirit. Generally, these congregations are labeled: *conservative evangelical* – strong in Word, much less emphasis on Holy Spirit.
- Other congregations seeking to experience the power that was present in the book of Acts. Their desire to see the gifts of the Spirit operating in the church today leads to an active pursuit of signs, wonders and miracles. Gener-

---

[1] In our international teaching/discipling ministry I have been asked to deliver sermons during a Sunday morning worship service. I imagine my preparation for those messages most likely happens in a way that is similar to those who are called to be Preacher/Pastors. The end result from sound prayerful preparation is a combination of searching out the Word through other resources and the divine guidance of Holy Spirit to bring greater understanding. It's a good example of the way in which God has led me to write Bible Studies.

[2] I had already come to recognize an invisible but distinct separating line between groups of Christ-followers. Thankfully Kendall's book equipped me with a way to articulate what I had observed.

ally, these congregations are labeled: *charismatic/pentecostal* – major emphasis on power manifestations of the Spirit, often much less emphasis on God's written Word.

There is nothing in what Kendall says that intends to indict either evangelicals or charismatics for their respective passionate pursuits. Kendall's point is that Scripture presents a clear and compelling picture of the early church as being *simultaneously strong in both Word and Power*. He credits some congregations with having found that proper balance between Word and Spirit which existed in the early church. Kendall stresses the need for that to be the goal of *every* church.

In his first epistle to the Corinthians, Paul identifies two groups of people but the distinction he makes is *not within* the body of Christ it is between those who are *in Christ* and those who are *outside of Christ*. To all of those *in Christ* Paul urged unity in the midst of their diversity.[3] The encouraging conclusion of Kendall's book is that he envisions a day when God will sovereignly *remarry* His Word and His Spirit. As that happens, proper first-century balance will be restored to the body of Christ.

It occurs to me that the *Lost in Translation* Bible Study series works towards that coming remarriage. To that end, the reader may find the series somewhat unique in its orientation – a well-researched Bible Study inseparably joined with Holy Spirit inspired counsel and revelation.

---

3   "For even as the body is one and *yet* has many members, and all the members of the body, though they are many, are one body, so also is Christ. For by one Spirit we were all baptized into one body ... God has placed the members ... just as He desired.... now there are many members, but one body. And the eye cannot say to the hand, 'I have no need of you'; or again the head to the feet, 'I have no need of you.'... But God has so composed the body, giving more abundant honor to that *member* which lacked, so that there may be no division in the body, but that the members may have the same care for one another." 1 Corinthians 12:12-25, italics in original

To God be the glory for what He has done, is doing and will yet do!

> [B]ut just as it is written, "Things which eye has not seen and ear has not heard, And which have not entered the heart of man, All that God has prepared for those who love Him." For to us God revealed them through the Spirit; for the Spirit searches all things, even the depths of God. 1 Corinthians 2:9-10

In His Service by His Grace,

Deborah L. Roeger

Preface

A Word from the Author: My goal for this study is to enable participants to have a life-transforming encounter with God. Our Western culture values *knowledge* for the sake of knowledge, but the culture of the Bible valued knowledge for the sake of guiding righteous behavior. J. I. Packer who is considered to be among the most influential evangelicals in North America has asserted that attempts to interpret God's Word without personal application do not deserve the title "Interpretation."[1] In the world of the ancient Hebrew, the goal of *every* student of *every* rabbi was to go well beyond learning what the rabbi knew and to be like the rabbi – to walk the way the rabbi walked through life. The purpose of education was not to gain head knowledge and become more intelligent but to inform perspective which would transform behavior. May the cry of your heart with every page of this study be, "O God, change me from the inside out, let me be more like you!" As your cry ascends and joins with my prayers for you, I am trusting God will hear and answer in unimaginable ways! Let the change begin!

Use of Yahweh: In the study I may use "Yahweh"– the most frequent Name for God in the Hebrew Bible. It is composed of four Hebrew letters: Yud (Y), Hey (H), Vav (V) and Hey (H) which combine as *Yahweh* or *YHVH*.

---

1 "…. Exegesis without application should not be called interpretation at all." J.I. Packer quoted by Dr. Grant C. Richison, Website Homepage *Verse-By-Verse Commentary by Dr. Grant C. Richison*. Retrieved from https://versebyversecommentary.com/ (last accessed September 15, 2021)

Yahweh is the personal Covenant Name by which the ancient Hebrews knew God. The first biblical reference is found in the exodus story.

> Moshe said to God, "Look, when I appear before the people of Isra'el and say to them, 'The God of your ancestors has sent me to you'; and they ask me, 'What is his name?' what am I to tell them?" God said to Moshe, "*Ehyeh Asher Ehyeh* [I am/will be what I am/will be]," and added, "Here is what to say to the people of Isra'el: '*Ehyeh* [I Am *or* I Will Be] has sent me to you.'" God said further to Moshe, "Say this to the people of Isra'el: '*Yud-Heh-Vav-Heh* [Adonai], the God of your fathers, the God of Avraham, the God of Yitz'chak and the God of Ya'akov, has sent me to you.' This is my name forever; this is how I am to be remembered generation after generation. Exodus 3:13-15 CJB, italics in original

With this answer, God announced His eternal Name to Moses. As noted in the *Complete Jewish Bible* translation quoted above, the Hebrew verb *'ehyeh* can be translated as "I Am" *or* "I Will Be." Notice in this more Jewish rendering of Exodus 3:13-15 how the four Hebrew letters mentioned above are used in this translation, "Say this to the people of Isra'el: '*Yud-Heh-Vav-Heh* [Adonai], the God of your fathers, the God of Avraham [Abraham], the God of Yitz'chak [Isaac] and the God of Ya'akov [Jacob], has sent me to you.'"

In context, the primary focus of God's answer to Moses is His promise *to be with* Moses and with the people Moses is sent to lead out of Egypt.[2] In the setting of the Old Testament, a name served a much greater function than simply an identification marker. A name communicated that which was essentially true of the one it

---

2   *ESV Study Bible* (Crossway Books 2008) study note Exodus 3:14, p. 149

identified.³ Yahweh equates His Name with His character as being "absolute and unchanging. This immutability provides inflexible reliability that the [promises He makes] will be realized."⁴ To the Hebrew mind, Yahweh above all else meant the God who faithfully keeps His Covenant with His people.⁵

Yahweh (often translated as Jehovah or LORD in most modern Bible translations) is the most intensely sacred Name to the Jewish people and many will not even pronounce it. In its place, they may say the four-letters Yud-Hey-Vav-Hey (YHVH) or will often simply use *Hashem* (literally "the Name"). Because of this sacredness, "God" is often written "G-d" in Jewish writings to avoid writing/saying the Name.⁶

Use of "the" Holy Spirit and Use of Holy Spirit: Throughout this study I will interchangeably refer to "the Holy Spirit" (His

---

3   Motyer, J. Alec, *The Prophecy of Isaiah: An Introduction & Commentary* (InterVarsity Press 1993) Isaiah 65:15-16d, p. 528

4   Sarna, Nahum M., *Exploring Exodus: The Origins Of Biblical Israel* (Schocken Books 1986, 1996) p. 52

5   "The verb form used here is אֶהְיֶה (*'ehyeh*) the Qal imperfect, first person common singular, of the verb הָיָה (*haya* 'to be').... [W]hen God used the verb to express his name, he used this form saying, 'I AM.' When his people refer to him as Yahweh, which is the third person masculine singular form of the same verb, they say 'he is.'... The idea of the verb would certainly indicate that God is not bound by time, and while he is present ('I AM') he will always be present, even in the future ...." *NET Bible Notes*, translator's note 47, Exodus 3:14. The source for this information is "*NET Notes*" however it will be descriptively cited as "*NET Bible Notes*" throughout the study. Unless otherwise indicated, the source of *NET Notes* in this study is BibleWorks 9, copyright 2013 BibleWorks LLC. As of June 15, 2018, BibleWorks ceased operation as a provider of Bible software tools.

6   The Jewish people understand Deuteronomy 12:4 as a prohibition against "erasing, destroying or desecrating the name of G-d." Jewish Community Center, *Writing G-d*. Retrieved from https://www.jccmb.com/templates/articlecco_cdo/aid/1333937/jewish/Writing-G-d.htm (last accessed August 9, 2021). As a result, many special precautions are taken both when writing the Name and when eliminating any documented format on which the Name has been written.

title) and "Holy Spirit" (His name). Because some might find that objectionable, an explanation will be helpful. It is noteworthy that in the original Greek of John 20:22, for example, the phrase "*pneuma hagion*" (translated Holy Spirit) could properly be a name or a title, depending on how one reads the Greek. Similarly, we find in Scripture references to "Jesus" as His name, while "Christ" (Messiah) is His title. We alternate between name and title often in the English language. For example, we say, "When Lincoln was the president" or "President Lincoln." If we are thinking of Holy Spirit as a name, it is already definite without the use of "the" because a name does not need to be preceded by a definite article. I suggest discomfort with a reference to "Holy Spirit" may be due to lack of familiarity with using His name. However, using His name rather than His title emphasizes the personal nature of the Holy Spirit. And that's my point.

Use of Hebrew word *Talmid* (singular) or *Talmidim* (plural): By the time of Jesus' earthly ministry, discipleship was well-established within the Jewish culture. All the great sages, rabbis and teachers of Torah had *talmidim* (disciples). A *talmid* (a disciple) was on a pilgrimage that was far more than an intellectual pursuit. The *talmid's* goal was to be *like* the rabbi – he wanted to assimilate the essence of who the rabbi was into his own life. This was radical discipleship – it was a complete re-making of the one who was being discipled so as to become like his rabbi in knowledge, wisdom and ethical behavior.

In other words, a *talmid's* deepest desire was to follow his rabbi so closely that he would start to think and act just like his rabbi. Jesus summed up the goal of discipleship this way: "*[A]fter [each disciple] has been fully trained, [he] will be like his teacher.*"[7] A *talmid's* behavior would be a reflection on their teacher's reputation – either positively or negatively.[8] That means perseverance

---

7 Luke 6:40
8 Keener, Craig S., *The Gospel Of John: A Commentary*, Volume Two (Hendrickson Publishers 2003) John 13:34-35, citing e.g., Aeschines Timarchus

was a standard requirement for every *talmid*.⁹ Once a *talmid* was fully trained, he would become a teacher and he would disciple *talmidim* of his own. What Jesus had begun by making *talmidim* of His first followers, the body of Christ now does as she makes new *talmidim* of Jesus. We see the apostle Paul following this established rabbinic pattern when he says, "*Imitate me, as I also imitate Christ. Now I praise you because you always remember me and keep the traditions just as I delivered them to you.*"¹⁰

When we understand disciple-making in its first-century context, most of us would have to admit that Jesus' (and likewise Paul's) idea of making disciples is vastly different than many self-designated "Christians" or what we often call a "follower," a "believer" or even a "disciple" today.

Throughout the study when I use the phrase "Christ-follower" or the word "Believer" I intend those word choices to be synonymous with the definition and culturally relevant understanding of a *talmid*.

About Word Studies: Hebrew scholar Tremper Longman refers to Bible translations as "commentaries with no notes."¹¹ I think he is spot on! Because no language easily and accurately translates word-for-word one to another, every translator makes judgment calls as to which word best fits the context as he sees it. Longman calls these "interpretive decisions" and that's why he suggests that any translation amounts to that translator's commentary on the text.¹² Even so, by the very nature of translation,

---

    171-173 among others, pp. 926-927
9 Keener, Craig S., *The Gospel Of John: A Commentary*, Volume Two (Hendrickson Publishers 2003) John 13:34-35, p. 926
10 1 Corinthians 11:1-2
11 Longman, Tremper III, *How To Read Proverbs* (InterVarsity Press 2002) p. 18
12 Longman, Tremper III, *How To Read Proverbs* (InterVarsity Press 2002) p. 18

the person translating typically leaves no notes behind for future readers to follow his line of reasoning.[13]

"Our sacred literature does not use obscure language, but describes most things in words clearly indicating their meaning. Therefore, it is necessary at all times to delve into the literal meaning of words to achieve complete understanding of what is actually meant."[14] To that end, from time to time in our lessons it will be advantageous to stop and do a "Word Study" which will allow us to consider the contextual meaning of that word from its original Hebrew or Greek language.

A diligent assessment of original word meanings relies on several factors. Both the authors and the original audience of the Scriptures lived in a different world than today's modern world. Politics, culture(s), ethics, worldview, theology as well as the realities of daily life were all radically different from what we know and experience. Those factors shaped the thoughts and expectations of the biblical writers which in turn shaped their words. An important task in biblical understanding is to discern, as much as possible, what any given word meant to the *original* author. Therefore, the more we are able to appreciate the ancient mindset of the Bible the better equipped we are to understand what God desires to communicate in a given text.

When we work to understand the Greek language of the New Testament, it is critical to realize just how much Hebrew thought impacted the New Testament authors. Most recent scholarship suggests *all* of those authors were Hebrew men who grew up in Jewish homes and were educated in the Old Testament writings.[15] As a result, the Hebrew thought-world of the Old Testament is

---

13   In my research experience, the *New English Translation* (NET) seems to be the exception to this rule in that according to netbible.com it contains 60,932 translator notes.

14   Rabbi Samson Raphael Hirsch (1808-1888). Retrieved from https://www.thiss.org/ (last accessed August 8, 2021)

15   According to Henri Louis Goulet, my research mentor, recent research suggests that absent evidence otherwise even Luke must be held to be Jewish.

the beginning source for proper understanding of New Testament Greek words. Although those men wrote in Greek, the thinking behind their writings was informed by their Hebrew heritage making the Old Testament the best starter dictionary we have for the New Testament.

To understand Greek words in the New Testament we may also need to consider ordinary everyday word usage in the first-century Greco-Roman world. Paul authored approximately 50% of the books in the New Testament. As an apostle to Greek-speaking Gentiles, he desired to shape those who had begun to follow Christ into new social communities. He understood that God's way is a whole new way to live, not a simple re-ordering of the *world's* way. Therefore, Paul was intent on providing direction to new Christ-followers about how they should re-orient their lives to walk out life according to their new identity *in* Christ.[16] To quote scholar Teresa Morgan, "New communities forming themselves within an existing culture do *not* typically take language in common use in the world around them and immediately assign to it radical new meanings.... This is all the more likely to be the case where the new community is a missionary one [as it was in Paul's case]. One does not communicate effectively with potential converts by using language in a way which they will not understand."[17] Paul "writes with what he assumes will be shared cultural assumptions regarding language and concepts that he uses without detailed explanation."[18] In other words, Paul, along with the other New Testament authors, would have chosen Greek words which already had common meaning to their audience. That cultural consideration may also supply important interpretive guidance

---

    Henri Louis Goulet, Email to Deborah Roeger March 27, 2022, citing the work of Isaac Oliver on Luke

16 Tucker, J. Brian, *Reading 1 Corinthians* (Cascade Books 2017) p. 4

17 Morgan, Teresa, *Roman Faith and Christian Faith: Pistis and Fides in the Early Roman Empire and Early Churches* (Oxford 2015) p. 4

18 Keener, Craig S., *Romans*, New Covenant Commentary (Cascade Books 2009) Introduction, p. 2

which will aid in our proper understanding of New Testament word meanings. When we fail to put biblical words in their proper historical, cultural context they end up getting lost in translation.

No matter what language we are discussing, it is common for words to have more than one meaning. The semantic range of a word is observed by its usage in various contexts. The more times a word is used in different ways, the broader its semantic range. As a result, scholars often advise that words do not mean anything outside of a context. My friend and research mentor Henri Goulet, shares this example he uses at the Messianic Studies Institute in Gahanna, Ohio. Take the English word "trunk: It could mean a host of things from an elephant's [nose], a suitcase, an ornamental chest, the rear compartment of a car, the main stem of a tree, the main part of a human body to which the head and appendages are connected, the principal channel of a tributary, or a circuit between two telephone exchanges."[19]

In the lessons in this study, Word Studies are not intended to explore the entire semantic range of a given word. Every author determines the meaning of a word by how he uses it within a context. The focus of each word studied will be narrowed by the specific context in which the author originally used that word in the particular passage we are studying. To that end, I will always seek to place Word Studies in original literary context as well as to add relevant cultural context where possible.

Refer to the supplement at the end of this study for helpful guidance on how to complete your own research of Hebrew and Greek words using free internet resources.

The Bible's Use of Ancient Near East Background: Because our lessons, where applicable, will seek to point out the historical context for Scripture, I will include references to ancient Near

---

19 Henri Louis Goulet, Academic Dean, Executive Director, & Faculty Messianic Studies Institute; Ph.D. Studies (Unfinished), University of Cape Town, Biblical Studies, 2007–2010; S.T.M., Capital University, Biblical Studies, 2007; M.A., Ashland University, Biblical Studies, 2003; B.S., The Ohio State University, Pharmaceutical Sciences, 1984

Eastern[20] beliefs as appropriate. As Jewish scholar Nahum Sarna points out: "modern scholarship has shown that the Torah made use of very ancient traditions which it adapted to its own special purposes."[21] For example, there are poems in Proverbs that clearly depict creation in imagery and expressions drawn from ancient pagan myths.[22] When a biblical author used ideas and concepts from the ancient culture around him the purpose was to borrow from the imagery to make his communication clear. That does not mean that the author endorsed the original pagan theology.[23] As Sarna noted, "the [pagan] materials used have been transformed so as to become the vehicle for the transmission of completely new ideas" which are entirely consistent with the nature and character of Yahweh.[24] In fact, some scholars believe that the very purpose of "borrowing" from ancient Near Eastern concepts was to demonstrate the absolute superiority of Yahweh over every false god.[25] According to Jewish scholar Joshua Berman, "For weak and oppressed peoples, one form of cultural and spiritual resistance

---

20 The ancient Near East is the region which includes modern Turkey, Syria, Lebanon, Israel, Palestine, Jordan, Egypt, Iraq and Iran. Important ancient civilizations in this region were the Egyptians, Arameans, Babylonians, Assyrians and Persians. Power, Cian, *Kingship in the Hebrew Bible*. Retrieved from https://www.sbl-site.org/assets/pdfs/TBv3i3_PowerKingship.pdf (last accessed August 8, 2021)

21 Sarna, Nahum M., *Understanding Genesis Through Rabbinic Tradition and Modern Scholarship* (The Jewish Theological Seminary 2015) p. 39

22 See for example: Proverbs 3:20; 8:29; 30:4; Waltke, Bruce K., *The Book of Proverbs: Chapters 1-15*, The New International Commentary on the Old Testament (Eerdmans 2004) *Theology*, p. 68

23 Waltke, Bruce K., *The Book of Proverbs Chapters 1-15*, The New International Commentary on the Old Testament (Eerdmans 2004) *Theology*, p. 68

24 Sarna, Nahum M., *Understanding Genesis Through Rabbinic Tradition and Modern Scholarship* (The Jewish Theological Seminary 2015) p. 4

25 See for example: Longman III and Garland, general editors, *The Expositor's Bible Commentary: Psalms*, Vol. 5, Revised edition (Zondervan 2008) *Reflections: Yahweh Is The Divine Warrior*, p. 734

is to appropriate the symbols of the oppressor and put them to competitive ideological purposes."[26]

It is worth noting that not all scholars embrace the use of ancient literature outside the Bible itself to assist in biblical interpretation. Some argue that it is a dangerous practice. I am inclined to agree with Professor Jon D. Levenson, Harvard Divinity School, who rightly warns on the one hand that historical criticism should never replace "the more traditional modes of study within religious communities." On the other hand, he advises that neither should modern research of the Bible's historical context be "disregarded or neutralized." Instead, he advocates: "[T]he worthiest course ... is one that combines the modern and the traditional modes of study in an intellectually honest and theologically sophisticated way."[27]

---

26   Berman, Joshua, *Ani Maamin: Biblical Criticism, Historical Truth, and the Thirteen Principles of Faith* (Maggid Book 2020) p. 55. Berman points out during much of its early history "ancient Israel was in Egypt's shadow." Ibid., p. 55

27   Levenson, Jon D., *The Shema and the Commandment to Love God In Its Ancient Contexts*, TheTorah.com, August 14, 2016, last updated June 20, 2021. Retrieved from https://www.thetorah.com/article/the-shema-and-the-commandment-to-love-god-in-its-ancient-contexts (last accessed June 29, 2021)

LESSON 1:

WHO IS THE HOLY SPIRIT? PART 1

> "And the Spirit of God was hovering over the surface of the waters." Genesis 1:2b ESV

THIS IS A study about the *power* of God's Spirit. From start to finish, the Bible contains references to the Spirit commonly known as the Holy Spirit or in older translations the Holy Ghost.[1] Our Key Scripture for this lesson is found in the opening words of the Bible recorded in Genesis 1:2. In those few words the author of Genesis provides us with our first glimpse of God's Spirit. In the very last chapter of the Bible, the author of Revelation provides us with our last biblical view of this Spirit, "The [Holy] Spirit and the bride (the church, believers) say, 'Come' … (Revelation 22:17 AMP)." In other words, from cover to cover the Bible speaks of the Holy Spirit. As we will soon see, however, He is not always identified that specifically on the pages of Scripture.

---

1 For example, Luke 1:35 is translated using the phrase "Holy Ghost" or similar in the King James Bible, Geneva Bible of 1587, Bishops' Bible of 1568, Coverdale Bible of 1535, Tyndale Bible of 1526 and the Douay-Rheims Bible published in 1582. Our English word "Ghost" comes from the old Anglo-Saxon word "gast." Included within its meanings was breath, soul and spirit. The term "spirit may be the modern word with the range of meanings closest to that of the Old English gast." *WORDORIGINS.ORG* entry for *ghost / give up the ghost*, October 30, 2020. Retrieved from https://www.wordorigins.org/big-list-entries/ghost-give-up-the-ghost (last accessed April 3, 2024)

In this study we are going to learn that the Spirit of God is not a separate entity or agent with an independent existence and autonomous action. God's Spirit is His divine power entering into action. It is through the Holy Spirit that God takes the initiative to enable, equip and empower every plan He has for us. We will also discover that it is through the Holy Spirit that God releases His power which "makes His church *willing* to live godly lives."[2] That means God, through His Spirit, not only endows us with power, He also endows every Christ-follower with the motivation to do those things He empowers us to do.[3] However, that's getting way ahead of ourselves.

Let's begin with first things first. I have heard it said that A. W. Tozer asserted the average church member's understanding of the Holy Spirit was so vague that it was nearly non-existent. So, a good place to begin our study is by exploring some basic concepts about God's Spirit. It may seem natural in a study of Holy Spirit[4] to dive right in to the New Testament. However, we are going to heed the advice of scholar Daniel Block and begin our discussion

---

2 MacArthur, John, *The MacArthur Study Bible* (Thomas Nelson 2006) study note Philippians 2:13 under *to will and to work*, p. 1793, italics added, citation omitted

3 "Christians are recipients of God's initiatives of motivation and empowerment." *Holman Christian Standard Bible*, Study Bible edition (Holman Bible Publishers 2010) study note Philippians 2:12-13 under *God … is working*, p. 2046

4 As noted in the Preface, at times in this study I will refer to "the Holy Spirit" (His title) simply as "Holy Spirit" (His name) emphasizing His personal nature. Refer to Preface for additional explanation. In fact, E. W. Bullinger points out that *pneuma hagion* (literally, spirit holy) occurs 52 times in the New Testament (without Articles). In every instance he contends that the phrase is "always wrongly rendered" when it is translated as "the Holy Spirit" (with the definite Article and capital letters). Bullinger, E. W., *Preface to Romans 8 - the Greek word for spirit in the N.T. from appendix 101 of the Companion Bible*, p. 1. Retrieved from https://www.hopeoftheglory.com/AFW/hotg_pdf/r8.pdf (last accessed December 18, 2023)

of God's Spirit in the Old Testament because that is where God begins the introduction of His Spirit. As Block advises:[5]

> When we are attempting to formulate a Biblical doctrine of the Holy Spirit we can ill afford to do so without paying more careful attention to the OT understanding than we have done heretofore. After all, the outlook of the theologians of the NT was determined primarily by [the Old Testament] their sacred Scriptures and not by prevailing Greek notions. This applied to their anthropology and their pneumatology [study of Holy Spirit] no less than their theology, their soteriology [doctrine of salvation] and their Christology [understanding of the person, nature and role of Christ].

In other words, *every* aspect of the beliefs held by the New Testament writers about God and His Spirit was shaped by the Old Testament. As recognized by scholar Richard Averbeck, "There are some things that are completely new about the work of the Holy Spirit in the New Testament compared to the Old Testament. The Holy Spirit as the agent of Jesus' conception through Mary springs to mind immediately. But much of what is there in the New Testament already has its roots sunk deep into the soil of the Old Testament."[6] To that end we're going to jump right in to the first reference to God's Spirit in the Bible. Generally speaking,

---

5   Block, Daniel I., *The Prophet Of The Spirit: The Use Of Rwh In The Book Of Ezekiel*, Journal of the Evangelical Theological Society, 32 no 1 Mar 1989, pp. 27-49, at p. 48. Retrieved from https://www.etsjets.org/files/JETS-PDFs/32/32-1/32-1-pp027-049_JETS.pdf (last accessed December 14, 2023)

6   Averbeck, Richard E., *The Holy Spirit in the Hebrew Bible and Its Connections to the New Testament* (2009). Retrieved from https://bible.org/seriespage/holy-spirit-hebrew-bible-and-its-connections-new-testament (last accessed January 22, 2024). This article is included in Wallace, Daniel B. and Sawyer, M. James, editors, *Who's Afraid Of The Holy Spirit? An Investigation Into The Ministry Of The Spirit Of God Today* (Biblical Studies Press 2013)

the very first occurrence of a word in the Bible will provide the natural foundation for the subsequent uses of that word. In the matter of the Spirit, this first mention is a necessary prerequisite "for a robust understanding of spirit."[7]

Keep in mind as we build our Old Testament understanding about God's Spirit, we need to apply caution so as not to read later New Testament understanding of Holy Spirit into these Old Testament references. "A primary principle in hermeneutics is that the meaning of a passage is found in what the original author intended it to mean [which means] . . . that meaning *must* be the meaning they could understand at the time, not the meaning we would determine based on our position of advanced historical developments.... [W]e must admit that the human author could not have intended in his or her message what we know only from subsequent revelation."[8] "Even ... the Gospels portray the spirit more in the already established pattern of the [Spirit of the Lord] in the OT than the yet undeveloped trinitarian doctrine to the HS [Holy Spirit], for in that time Christ had not yet ascended to send the [Holy Spirit]."[9] What the Old Testament does is lay "the conceptual groundwork . . . for the doctrine of the Holy Spirit later revealed in the NT."[10]

The quote below expands our Key Scripture for this lesson so as to put it into its biblical context. If we were reading this text in its original Hebrew, we would see that God's Spirit is introduced

---

7   Levison, Jack, *A Boundless God: The Spirit according to the Old Testament* (Baker Academic 2020) p. 20
8   Firth and Wegner, "Introduction," in *Presence Power And Promise: The Role of the Spirit of God in the Old Testament,* edited by Firth and Wegner (IVP Academic 2011) p. 18, quoting from Klein, Blomberg and Hubbard, Jr., *Introduction to Biblical Interpretation*, 2nd edition (Word 2004) p. 11, italics in original
9   Walton, John H., "The Ancient Near Eastern Background Of The Spirit Of The Lord In The Old Testament," in *Presence Power And Promise: The Role of the Spirit of God in the Old Testament,* edited by Firth and Wegner (IVP Academic 2011) p. 67
10 *NET Bible Notes*, study note 8, Haggai 2:5

with an active presence before the author of Genesis has written twenty words![11]

> In the beginning God created the heavens and the earth. The earth was without form and void, and darkness was over the face of the deep. **And the Spirit of God was hovering over the face of the waters**. And God said, "Let there be light," and there was light. And God saw that the light was good. And God separated the light from the darkness. God called the light Day, and the darkness he called Night. And there was evening and there was morning, the first day. Genesis 1:1-5 ESV, bold added

Initially we notice that at the very beginning of the account of creation God's Spirit (His *ruah* {roo'-akh}) was present and actively engaged. In that we learn the Holy Spirit is *not* created by God. Like God and Jesus, the Holy Spirit already existed before the first act of creation takes place. As one author suggested, "we might adapt the well-known phrasing [about the pre-existence of Jesus] to formulate an OT affirmation [about Holy Spirit]: 'In the beginning was the *rûah*, and the *rûah* was from God and the *rûah* was God. All things were made by him and nothing was made without him. In him was life and that life was the light of men.'"[12]

Now let's do a Word Study to see how the ancient Hebrews identified this pre-existing Spirit. Because this is our first Word Study, I think it is important to remind you of something I pointed out in the Preface. Word Studies are *not* intended to explore the entire semantic range of a given word. The focus of each word we

---

11 Jack Levison identifies the terms *rûah 'ĕlōhîm* as the sixteenth and seventeenth words of the original Hebrew text in Genesis. Levison, Jack, *A Boundless God: The Spirit according to the Old Testament* (Baker Academic 2020) p. 20

12 Walton, John H., "The Ancient Near Eastern Background Of The Spirit Of The Lord In The Old Testament," in *Presence Power And Promise: The Role of the Spirit of God in the Old Testament*, edited by Firth and Wegner (IVP Academic 2011) pp. 43-44

study will be narrowed by the specific context in which the author originally used that word.

> ## WORD STUDY
>
> In Genesis 1 the Hebrew word which is translated as **Spirit** is ruah {rooʻ-akh}(also transliterated as ruach or ruwach). In the Old Testament whenever ruah appears with reference to elohim (Hebrew word translated as "God"), it always refers to His Spirit.[13]
>
> Ruah is employed close to 400 times in the Old Testament with a wide range of meanings.[14] According to the Theological Dictionary of the Old Testament, the basic idea of ruah is "'air in motion.'"[15]

---

13 Walton, John H., Ed., *Zondervan Illustrated Bible Backgrounds Commentary*, Vol. 1 (Zondervan, 2009) Genesis 1:2 under *Spirit of God*, p. 15

14 Firth and Wegner, "Introduction," in *Presence Power And Promise: The Role of the Spirit of God in the Old Testament,* edited by Firth and Wegner (IVP Academic 2011) p. 16, reporting 394 uses. Scholar John Levison reports 378 references to *ruah* in the Old Testament, plus an additional eleven Aramaic references. Levison, John R., *The Holy Spirit Before Christianity* (Baylor University Press 2019) p. 77. Scholar Daniel Block also reports 378 uses of *ruah* in the Hebrew text of the Old Testament, attributing the eleven Aramaic references to the Aramaic parts of Daniel. Block, Daniel I., *The Prophet Of The Spirit: The Use Of Rwh In The Book Of Ezekiel*, Journal of the Evangelical Theological Society, 32 no 1 Mar 1989, pp. 27-49, at p. 28, citing R. Albertz and C. Westermann, "*rûah*," THAT, 2.727 for the tabulation of these and related forms. Retrieved from https://www.etsjets.org/files/JETS-PDFs/32/32-1/32-1-pp027-049_JETS.pdf (last accessed December 14, 2023). "[M]ore than a third of the nearly four hundred references to *rûah* in the Jewish Bible are to *rûah* understood as wind or breeze." Levison, Jack, *A Boundless God: The Spirit according to the Old Testament* (Baker Academic 2020) p. 19

15 Harris, Archer, and Waltke, editors, *Theological Wordbook of the Old Testament* (Moody Press 1999) # 2131a, p. 836

> *Four primary word meanings have been identified:[16]
> 1) wind, especially denoting wind created and controlled by God; 2) an influence outside of normal human experience which provides capacity and power; 3) the powerful and creative divine breath which gives life to living beings, both men and animals; and 4) the controlling cognitive element within a person that is the "seat of affection, emotions and passions, of the will, and of intellectual and moral life."[17]*
>
> *In addition to spirit [not divine] or Spirit [divine], ruah has also been translated as breath (Habakkuk 2:19), a breeze (Genesis 3:8), wind (Exodus 10:19), or even a violent storm (1 Kings 19:11).*

As an initial matter, let's take note of the fact that our Word Study does not provide us with any physical description of God's Spirit. Genesis 1:2 describes no material form by which the Spirit can be seen by the human eye. We could search the rest of the Old Testament and still find nothing at all about the form, shape, or composition of the Holy Spirit. By the same token, scholars

---

16 Hill, David, *Greek Words and Hebrew Meanings: Studies in the Semantics of Soteriological Terms*, Society for New Testament Studies Monograph Series 5 (Wipf and Stock 2000, previously published Cambridge University Press 1967) pp. 207,209,215,216,217

17 Hill, David, *Greek Words and Hebrew Meanings: Studies in the Semantics of Soteriological Terms*, Society for New Testament Studies Monograph Series 5 (Wipf and Stock 2000, previously published Cambridge University Press 1967) p. 215, citing H. W. Robinson, 'Hebrew Psychology,' *The People and the Book*, pp. 360f. Hill points out that this particular meaning of *ruah* "develops naturally from the close association observed between breathing and various feelings and emotions: in anger the breath [*ruah*] is hot (Ezek. 3:14); in impatience [*ruah*] become short (Micah 2:7; Exod. 6:9: Job 21:4); in terror [*ruah*] is excited or troubled (Gen. 41:8; Dan, [*sic*] 2:1,3). Given this usage, it is not surprising that the step was taken to the use of [*ruah*] to describe the dominant impulse or disposition of an individual (cf. Gen. 26:35; Ps. 32:2)." Ibid. p. 215

have astutely observed the absence in the Old Testament of any description whatsoever of God's divine physical appearance.[18] The fact of the matter is that ancient Israel did not need a physical description of God. They had God's self-revelation through His mighty deeds which made His invisibility visible to them.[19] As we will see throughout our study, the same might be said of God's Spirit. We will learn about Him from what He does. As a case in point, we notice that in Genesis 1:2 the Spirit is depicted as being engaged in activity.

In His biblical debut, God's Spirit is not presented as an inactive observer who is sitting on the sidelines. He is described as "hovering" or "brooding" upon the surface of the waters. The Hebrew verb here is *rachaph* {raw-khaf'}. It provides the first glimpse of the active nature of God's *ruah*. The same verb is used in Deuteronomy 32:11 to refer to an eagle stirring up its nest and hovering over its young. When a bird is hovering, it is preparing for whatever the next action is.[20] In general, the basic idea of this Hebrew verb stem is vibration, movement. Thus, in this first description of God's Spirit the author seems to be depicting the fact of *energy* which is being manifested by movement.[21]

In the original biblical text, *rachaph* is presented in a verb tense which informs us that this *hovering* or *brooding* over the surface is

---

18 "Eminently significant and characteristic of the whole genius [brilliance] of the Old Testament is the absence of any description of the divine appearance." MacLaren, Alexander, *Expositions of Holy Scripture*, Isaiah Vision and Service, Isaiah 6:1 – Isaiah 6:13 under *I. The Vision*. Retrieved from https://biblehub.com/commentaries/isaiah/6-3.htm (last accessed February 24, 2023)
19 Keener, Craig S., *The Gospel Of John: A Commentary*, Volume One (Hendrickson Publishers 2003) 2B. The Father's Witness ([John] 5:36-44) p. 658
20 Walton, John H., "The Ancient Near Eastern Background Of the Spirit Of the Lord In The Old Testament," in *Presence Power And Promise The Role of the Spirit of God in the Old Testament*, edited by Firth and Wegner (IVP Academic 2011) p. 41
21 Firth & Wegner, "Introduction," in *Presence Power And Promise: The Role of the Spirit of God in the Old Testament*, edited by Firth and Wegner (IVP Academic 2011) pp. 16-17

a non-stop continuous action of God's Spirit – it is not occasional nor is it an on-again / off-again or start-and-stop type of activity. It is persistent and continuous. The other notable aspect of this verb as seen in the original text is that the author is communicating intensive action. This verb stem always intensifies the action of the verb by describing action that is forceful or vigorous. For example, this verb stem takes the word "broke," as in he broke the vase, and intensifies it so that the idea of "smashed" becomes a more accurate word choice.

The author of the narrative is making it especially clear that the Spirit is not engaged in a restful type of hovering. This hovering action is very active – picturing the Spirit as being poised and ready to take some action, yet waiting for just the right moment to do so.[22] The expectation is set that through His Spirit God is about to do something important. As the narrative unfolds we learn that God's Spirit is prepared to transform the chaos that is present at the beginning of creation.[23] The result of the Spirit's forceful action is going to be a new condition – the chaos is going to be changed into something new because of this hovering activity! In this activity we not only learn about God's Spirit, we find the purpose of the Genesis creation account. According to Jewish scholars, the creation narrative was *not* written so we know *how* creation took place – it is written to give credit to Yahweh as the one who created all that we see.[24] "When Israel thought about the source of the forces that they saw affecting and influencing

---

22 Walton, John H., "The Ancient Near Eastern Background Of The Spirit Of The Lord In The Old Testament," in *Presence Power And Promise: The Role of the Spirit of God in the Old Testament*, edited by Firth and Wegner (IVP Academic 2011) p. 43

23 Beale, G. K., *A New Testament Biblical Theology: The Unfolding Of The Old Testament In The New* (Baker Academic 2011) p. 559

24 Sarna, Nahum M., *The JPS Torah Commentary: Genesis,* The Traditional Hebrew Text with the New JPS Translation Commentary (The Jewish Publication Society 1989) Genesis 1:1 under *create*, p. 5; *heaven and earth*, pp. 5-6

humankind in creation and in nature, they often pointed to the activity of the *rûah*."[25]

The *ruah* of God is first introduced as something which is made known by His silent, yet powerful, movement across the waters. He is presented in Genesis 1 as "the immanent manifestation of God the creator."[26] It is by the agency of this Spirit as the "active, creative, and vital presence of God"[27] that God speaks creation into being.

> It is evident that the *rûah 'elohim* [Spirit (of) God] is not only superintending the work of creation but in fact brings creation about through the word. [Genesis 1:2] is emphasizing the actual powerful presence of God, who brings the spoken work into reality by the Spirit. Thus, the Spirit and the word work together to present [that truth that] the one God is responsible for all that is seen in the physical universe.[28]

Although *ruah* is a noun, as we have learned it can be used to denote *moving* and *doing*. In the Old Testament we see God's

---

25 Hildebrandt, Wilf, *An Old Testament Theology of the Spirit of God* (Hendrickson 1995) p. 18, as quoted by John H. Walton, "The Ancient Near Eastern Background Of The Spirit Of The Lord In The Old Testament," in *Presence Power And Promise: The Role of the Spirit of God in the Old Testament*, edited by Firth and Wegner (IVP Academic 2011) pp. 39-40

26 Walton, John H., "The Ancient Near Eastern Background Of The Spirit Of The Lord In The Old Testament," in *Presence Power And Promise: The Role of the Spirit of God in the Old Testament*, edited by Firth and Wegner (IVP Academic 2011) p. 43

27 Hildebrandt, Wilf, *An Old Testament Theology of the Spirit of God* (Hendrickson 1995) p. 42, as quoted by John H. Walton, "The Ancient Near Eastern Background Of The Spirit Of The Lord In The Old Testament," in *Presence Power And Promise: The Role of the Spirit of God in the Old Testament*, edited by Firth and Wegner (IVP Academic 2011) p. 39

28 Hildebrandt, Wilf, *An Old Testament Theology of the Spirit of God* (Hendrickson 1995) p. 35, as quoted by John H. Walton, "The Ancient Near Eastern Background Of The Spirit Of The Lord In The Old Testament," in *Presence Power And Promise: The Role of the Spirit of God in the Old Testament*, edited by Firth and Wegner (IVP Academic 2011) p. 42

Spirit "rushes upon, is upon, pours out, empties upon, blows, clothes, rests upon, guides—along with a host of other actions."[29] Once Genesis introduces the *ruah* of God He does not exit from the scene. Rather we then witness Him fully participating in creation, "empowering, if not executing," the series of words God speaks – the Spirit is God's power ready to work.[30]

To show just how versatile the word *ruah* is, its' very next use in the Bible is just two chapters later in Genesis 3:8. But here we don't find *ruah* used to refer to God or Holy Spirit, the author employs it to refer the time of day or the conditions in which God was walking in the garden.

> Then [Adam and Eve] heard the sound of the LORD God [*Yahweh 'elohim*] walking in the garden at the time of the evening breeze [*ruah*, literally "at the wind of the day"],[31] and they hid themselves from the LORD God among the trees of the garden. Genesis 3:8 HCSB

As we jump to this example, we begin to see that a nicely laid out understanding of Holy Spirit in the Old Testament simply does not exist. Scholar Jack Levison observes that, "Neat and tidy categorization, as natural as it may seem, does not do justice to the mysterious world of *rûah* in Jewish Scriptures."[32] Based on his

---

29 Levison, John R., *The Holy Spirit Before Christianity* (Baylor University Press 2019) p. 77
30 Hubbard, Robert L., Jr., "The Spirit and Creation," in *Presence Power And Promise: The Role of the Spirit of God in the Old Testament*, edited by Firth and Wegner (IVP Academic 2011) p. 87
31 Genesis 3:8 HCSB, footnote a. Retrieved from https://www.biblegateway.com/passage/?search=gen+3%3A8&version=HCSB (last accessed December 20, 2023)
32 Levison, Jack, *A Boundless God: The Spirit according to the Old Testament* (Baker Academic 2020) p. 19

extensive research Levison concludes, "The mysterious world of the *rûah* defies easy classification."[33]

Even so, *Brown Driver Briggs*, a well-respected Hebrew and English lexicon, has broadly grouped together some common ways in which *ruah* is used in the Old Testament. The ones that are of particular interest to us in this study are those that relate to or refer to the *Spirit of God*. These types of references vary. Some use the phrase "spirit of God," others employ "spirit of the LORD" and three times the phrase "Holy Spirit" is employed. However, the vast majority of Old Testament references to God's Spirit are more general in nature and do not employ any of those exact phrases.[34]

Actually, His Spirit is mentioned by many different names, usually in reference to a particular role or function. Among some of those names are Breath of the Almighty (Job 33:4); Spirit of wisdom (Isaiah 11:2; Ephesians 1:17); Spirit of counsel (Isaiah 11:2); Spirit of might (Isaiah 11:2); Spirit of understanding (Isaiah 11:2); Spirit of knowledge (Isaiah 11:2); Spirit of the fear of the Lord (Isaiah 11:2); Spirit of judgment (Isaiah 4:4; 28:6); Spirit of truth (John 14:17; 15:26); Spirit of adoption (Romans 8:15); Spirit of life (Romans 8:2; Revelation 11:11) and Spirit of Christ (Romans 8:9; 1 Peter 1:11). This pattern of descriptive names follows quite consistently with the biblical pattern of Yahweh's changing names.[35] As we might expect, Jesus is also known by a

---

33 Levison, Jack, *A Boundless God: The Spirit according to the Old Testament* (Baker Academic 2020) p. 18
34 Walton, John H., "The Ancient Near Eastern Background Of The Spirit Of The Lord In The Old Testament," in *Presence Power And Promise: The Role of the Spirit of God in the Old Testament*, edited by Firth and Wegner (IVP Academic 2011) p. 39, citing Wilf Hildebrandt, *An Old Testament Theology of the Spirit of God* (Hendrickson 1995) p. 18; Firth and Wegner, "Introduction" in *Presence Power And Promise: The Role of the Spirit of God in the Old Testament*, edited by Firth and Wegner (IVP Academic 2011) p. 16
35 For example: *El Roi* "God of Seeing" (Genesis 16:13); *Yahweh-Jireh* "The Lord Will Provide" (Genesis 22:14); *Yahweh-Rapha* "The Lord Who Heals" (Exodus 15:26); *Yahweh-Shalom* "The Lord Our Peace" (Judges 6:24); Judge,

rich variety of names.[36] In ancient times there was a vital connection between a name and the person that name identified. Since a name had a close association with the person's character, every encounter with Yahweh, Jesus, or God's Spirit which resulted in a new experience resulted in a new name.

Brown Driver Briggs identifies a total of 94 references to the *ruah* as referring to God's Spirit in the Old Testament. These references can generally be grouped together as follows:[37]

1. an agent of creation, as in Genesis 1:2 and of sustaining creation, as in Psalm 104:29-30
2. an agent inspiring an elated state of prophecy, as in Numbers 11:17,25
3. an agent impelling prophets to speak instruction or warning, as in Numbers 24:2-3
4. to legitimize a leader selected by God, as in 1 Samuel 16:13
5. imparting gifts of administration and wisdom, as in Deuteronomy 34:9
6. imparting energy for war, as in Judges 3:10
7. resting upon the Messianic king, as in Isaiah 11:2
8. a sign of divine ownership and Covenant relationship, as in Ezekiel 39:29

Lawgiver, King (Isaiah 33:22); *Adonai-Tzva'ot* "King of Glory" (Psalm 24:7-10) and *Yahweh-Rohi* "Shepherd of Israel" (Psalm 80:1)

36 For example: Immanuel (Matthew 1:23); The Son of Man (Luke 19:10); The Bridegroom (John 3:29); The Word of God (John 1:1); The Lion of Judah (Revelation 5:5) and The Bright Morning Star (Revelation 22:16)

37 *Brown Driver Briggs* was used as a primary reference source to create this list, but what is written here is not an exact quote. *Brown-Driver-Briggs Hebrew and English Lexicon*, Unabridged, Electronic Database. Copyright © 2002, 2003, 2006 by Biblesoft, Inc. Retrieved from https://www.blueletterbible.org/lexicon/h7307/kjv/wlc/0-1/ (last accessed December 17, 2023). See also: Herrick, Gary, *4. Pneumatology: The Holy Spirit*, from the series: An Introduction To Christian Belief: A Layman's Guide, Bible.org, June 3, 2004. Retrieved from https://bible.org/seriespage/4-pneumatology-holy-spirit (last accessed December 18, 2023)

9. an agency which brings something to life, as in Ezekiel 37:5,6,10
10. endowing men with various gifts and augmenting technical skills, as in Exodus 31:3
11. creative motion or energy, as in Genesis 1:2
12. equated with the angel of Presence, as in Isaiah 63:10,11
13. abiding in the midst of Israel, as in Haggai 2:5
14. equaling God's omnipresence, as in Psalm 139:7

As we have pointed out, three different times authors in the Old Testament expressly referred to "Holy Spirit." The first specific reference is in Psalm 51:11. That particular psalm is believed to be written by King David after the prophet Nathan confronted him about his sin with Bathsheba.

> Cast me not away from your presence, and take not your Holy Spirit [*ruah qodseka*][38] from me. Psalm 51:11 ESV

According to Jewish rabbis and Jewish theology, "the Holy Spirit may be acquired by any individual who orders his life in accordance with the fear of God" for the purpose of causing that person to persevere in their Torah obedience.[39] The best of scholarship views David's reference to God's Spirit in Psalm 51 as an earnest desire for God's holiness[40] with the understanding that God's Holy Spirit is "the inward power which makes for holi-

---

38 Estes, Daniel J., "Spirit and The Psalmist in Psalm 51," in *Presence Power And Promise The Role of the Spirit of God in the Old Testament*, edited by Firth and Wegner (IVP Academic 2011) p. 131
39 Hill, David, *Greek Words and Hebrew Meanings: Studies in the Semantics of Soteriological Terms*, Society for New Testament Studies Monograph Series 5 (Wipf and Stock 2000, previously published Cambridge University Press 1967) p. 229. Hill reasons that "The idea of the possession of the 'spirit of holiness' in Ps. 51 may be moving in this direction." Ibid.
40 Estes, Daniel J., "Spirit and The Psalmist in Psalm 51," in *Presence Power And Promise The Role of the Spirit of God in the Old Testament*, edited by Firth and Wegner (IVP Academic 2011) p. 133

ness."[41] David understood that he was a sinful man and only the Spirit of the living God could solve that problem. "In the context, [he] stands before God fearing rejection, the loss of his salvation … and the sentence of death …. His continued acceptance in [God's] divine presence and the divine presence [of God] within him though his *rûah* represent his only hope."[42] David knows the distinction that exists between his sinfulness and God's holiness. He pleads for God's inward power which can lead him to holiness not to depart from him. The background for the concern that God's Spirit could be removed from a person is likely found in the story of King Saul. When Saul chose to please the people rather than obey God, the Spirit of the LORD that had been *in* him departed from him and was replaced with "an evil spirit from the LORD [that] terrorized him (1 Samuel 16:14)." If King David is in fact the author of Psalm 51 then what we have is the introduction of the written phrase *holy spirit* for the first time in the history of Israel's relationship with Yahweh. It is interesting to note that Jesus understood that it was the Holy Spirit who had divinely inspired David to write Psalm 110:1.[43]

---

41 Hill, David, *Greek Words and Hebrew Meanings: Studies in the Semantics of Soteriological Terms*, Society for New Testament Studies Monograph Series 5 (Wipf and Stock 2000, previously published Cambridge University Press 1967) p. 210 suggesting the phrase "thy holy spirit" refers to "that inward sense of the presence and power of God which both purifies and inspires to obedient and righteous living." Said differently, "the meaning of 'holy spirit' in Ps. 51 … is that inward sense of God's holiness and knowledge of his presence (cf. *v.* 22) which both purifies man and directs him in the way of holiness." Ibid. p. 246

42 Block, Daniel I., *The Book of Ezekiel: Chapters 25-48*, The New International Commentary on the Old Testament (Eerdmans 1998) *Excursus: The Infusion of The Spirit of Yahweh Under The Old Covenant*, p. 360

43 "David himself said in [or by] the Holy Spirit, 'The Lord said to my Lord, "Sit at My right hand, Until I put Your enemies beneath Your feet."' Mark 12:36. The alternative translation to employ the word "by" instead of "in" is noted in footnote a. the NASB 1995. Retrieved from https://www.biblegateway.com/passage/?search=Mark+12%3A36&version=NASB1995 (last accessed April 3, 2024)

The next two direct references to Holy Spirit are found in Isaiah 63 which were likely written during the era of Persian rule after Israel returned to their land following their exile to Babylon.[44] Here Isaiah equates the presence of God with His Spirit.[45]

> But [Israel] rebelled and grieved his Holy Spirit [*ruah qodso*];[46] therefore he turned to be their enemy, and himself fought against them. Then he remembered the days of old, of Moses and his people. Where is he who brought them up out of the sea with the shepherds of his flock? Where is he who put in the midst of them his Holy Spirit [*ruah qodso*].[47] Isaiah 63:10-11 ESV

While these verses in Isaiah 63 were probably written post-exile, Isaiah is referring back to the exodus narrative when God led the Hebrew people out of Egypt. Because the presence and work of "Holy Spirit" are attributed all the way back to Israel's foundation it means that, historically speaking, we have located what one scholar refers to as, "the headwaters" of the Holy Spirit in the life of Israel![48] He made His debut in the creation narrative, but He made His first appearance in the midst of Israel at their debut as God's special treasure (His *segullah*).[49] The exodus narrative in

---

44 Levison, John R., *The Holy Spirit Before Christianity* (Baylor University Press 2019) p. 60
45 Green, Michael, *I Believe in the Holy Spirit*, Revised edition (Eerdmans 2004) p. 128. Michael Green was a British theologian, Anglican priest and Christian apologist. After his retirement he became Senior Research Fellow and Head of Evangelism and Apologetics at Wycliffe Hall, Oxford University.
46 Childs, Brevard S., *Isaiah*, Old Testament Library Commentary (Westminster John Knox Press 2001) Isaiah 63:7-14 under *2. Exposition*, p. 524
47 Childs, Brevard S., *Isaiah*, Old Testament Library Commentary (Westminster John Knox Press 2001) Isaiah 63:7-14 under *2. Exposition*, p. 524
48 Levison, John R., *The Holy Spirit Before Christianity* (Baylor University Press 2019) p. 49
49 God said to Israel, "Now if you will pay careful attention to what I say and keep my covenant, then you will be my own treasure [*segullah*] from among all the peoples, for all the earth is mine (Exodus 19:5 CJB)." "All the

the Bible describes God leading Israel through various agents such as the cloud by day, the pillar of fire by night or an angel. The author of the book of Exodus makes no mention of Holy Spirit. His involvement in leading Israel only appears in the biblical text which was written after the Babylonian exile. "If the spirit takes on the role of the *angel* of God's presence [in the Exodus story], this spirit also takes on the role of *God*."[50] This post-exile understanding reveals Israel's new insight that God's Holy Spirit was an active presence among them during the exodus![51] According to scholar

---

nations belong to God, but Israel was to stand in a place of special privilege and enormous responsibility. See Deut 7:6; 14:2; 26:18; Ps 135:4; and Mal 3:17." *NET Bible Notes*, translator's note 13, Exodus 19:5

50 Levison, John R., *The Holy Spirit Before Christianity* (Baylor University Press 2019) p. 49, italics in original

51 However, it is important to clarify that "in the Jewish tradition the Holy Spirit referred to in the Hebrew Bible [the Old Testament] is not taken to be the third person of the 'Trinity' .... In general, the Jewish view is that 'the spirit of God referred to in the Bible alludes to His energy (Isa 40:13; Zech 4:6).' Accordingly, it is recognized that 'the divine origin of the spirit' is implied by the term 'his (the Lord's) spirit of holiness' (... *ruakh qadesho*), 'Yet this does not mean that the holy spirit was regarded as a [single person of the Trinity] distinct from the divine presence (*shekina*).' In other words, according to the Rabbis, although the 'spirit of God' is of divine origin, this does not mean that there is a 'Holy Spirit'" as a divine person. On the contrary, the holy spirit is a mode of the one and only God's self-expression in word and action." Averbeck, Richard E., *The Holy Spirit in the Hebrew Bible and Its Connections to the New Testament* (2009), footnotes omitted. Retrieved from https://bible.org/seriespage/holy-spirit-hebrew-bible-and-its-connections-new-testament (last accessed January 22, 2024). This article is included in Wallace, Daniel B. and Sawyer, M. James, editors, *Who's Afraid Of The Holy Spirit? An Investigation Into The Ministry Of The Spirit Of God Today* (Biblical Studies Press 2013). In Jewish understanding, *Shekina* (or *Shekinah*) refers to "the visible presence of God." Hill, David, *Greek Words and Hebrew Meanings: Studies in the Semantics of Soteriological Terms*, Society for New Testament Studies Monograph Series 5 (Wipf and Stock 2000, previously published Cambridge University Press 1967) p. 253

George Guthrie, this was Paul's understanding! In the words of Guthrie:[52]

> When Paul writes, "'The Lord' is the Spirit," [in 2 Corinthians 3:17] he .... points out that "the Lord" ... spoken of in the OT context (Exod. 34:34) actually is the Holy Spirit. Paul, therefore, understands the references to "the Lord" in the Exod. 34 narrative as being references to the Holy Spirit as present among the Israelites....Paul seems to understand God's descent onto Mount Sinai (Exod. 24:15-18), his traveling among and instructing the Israelites (e.g., Exod. 33:3,7-11; Neh. 9:20; Isa. 63:11), and his descent on the tabernacle in the cloud (Exod. 33:9-11) to be the [Holy] Spirit coming into the camp. Thus it makes sense that the person of the Holy Spirit met with Moses on the mountain.

Scholar Jack Levison astutely points out that, even before Christian creeds were written to express the core beliefs of the Christians who authored them and "long before Christians annexed [Greek] philosophy to grasp the nature of the spirit, Israel told stories of a mysterious presence that prompted remarkable feats in the public sphere."[53]

> Broadly speaking [the spirit of God in the Old Testament] is the divine presence experienced in terms of power for action .... The [spirit of God] is the means of expressing God's presence to, and action within the world: it is the divine, creative, energizing and renewing power in the lives of men and communities.[54]

---

52 Guthrie, George H., *2 Corinthians*, Baker Exegetical Commentary On The New Testament (Baker Academic 2015) 2 Corinthians 3:17-18, pp. 225-226
53 Levison, Jack, *A Boundless God: The Spirit according to the Old Testament* (Baker Academic 2020) p. 34
54 Hill, David, *Greek Words and Hebrew Meanings: Studies in the Semantics of Soteriological Terms*, Society for New Testament Studies Monograph Series

In the Old Testament, God's Spirit is not isolated to the private individual who is in right relationship with God. As Levison recognizes, God's Holy Spirit works and influences in the sphere of what is considered to be profane [what is common and not holy]– not the sphere of what is recognized as set apart to God and holy. In light of that observation, it is interesting to note that the only direct Old Testament references to Holy Spirit (Psalm 51:11, Isaiah 63:10,11) are in the context of sin that grieves Him. In fact, one highly respected British priest and theologian points out that in these passages of Scripture the authors were quite "conscious of the moral and ethical aspect of God's *ruach* .... The holiness of the Spirit of the Lord stands in sharp contrast to the unholiness of his fallible servants, and perhaps this is why the Spirit is here [in Isaiah 63 and Psalm 51] called Holy."[55]

Let's add to our understanding of Holy Spirit's identity by taking a look at a New Testament outline of references to God's Spirit. We begin with the fact that the men who translated the Old Testament into Greek frequently rendered the Hebrew word *ruah* by the term *pneuma* {pnyoo'-mah} even though the range of meanings for *pneuma* is not as broad as the meanings for *ruah*.[56]

Word Study

The root word for pneuma denotes "vital force acting as a stream of air."[57] *Three primary meanings of pneuma*

---

5 (Wipf and Stock 2000, previously published Cambridge University Press 1967) p. 212

55 Green, Michael, *I Believe in the Holy Spirit*, Revised edition (Eerdmans 2004) p. 35

56 Hill, David, *Greek Words and Hebrew Meanings: Studies in the Semantics of Soteriological Terms*, Society for New Testament Studies Monograph Series 5 (Wipf and Stock 2000, previously published Cambridge University Press 1967) p. 217

57 Bromiley, Geoffrey W., *Theological Dictionary of the New Testament*, Abridged in One Volume (Eerdmans 1985) entry for *pneúma* under *A. pneúma in the*

> *are found in Greek literature: 1) wind; 2) breath (air breathed in or out) by a living creature; and 3) life or breath of life.*[58]
>
> *In ordinary Greek usage pneuma was not used to refer to a human or divine spirit, however "in biblical Greek [pneuma] is employed to render [ruah] [even] when it bears this meaning."*[59] *Paul commonly used pneuma/ spirit to refer to the "interior expression of the human person"*[60]*– a person's" inner 'spirit'."*[61]

As we survey the New Testament uses, our primary focus once again will be on those biblical uses of *pneuma* which refer to the Spirit of God or the activity of His Spirit. Biblical scholar E. W. Bullinger has grouped these uses together as follows:[62]

1. God Himself, as in John 4:24. In the original Greek, there is no definite article, therefore Bullinger points out

---

Greek World, I. The Meaning of the Term, 1. Wind, p. 876

58 Hill, David, *Greek Words and Hebrew Meanings: Studies in the Semantics of Soteriological Terms*, Society for New Testament Studies Monograph Series 5 (Wipf and Stock 2000, previously published Cambridge University Press 1967) p. 218

59 Hill, David, *Greek Words and Hebrew Meanings: Studies in the Semantics of Soteriological Terms*, Society for New Testament Studies Monograph Series 5 (Wipf and Stock 2000, previously published Cambridge University Press 1967) p. 218

60 Fee, Gordon D., *The First Epistle To The Corinthians,* New International Commentary on the New Testament (Eerdmans 1987) 1 Corinthians 2:10b-11, p. 111

61 Verbrugge, Verlyn D., "1 Corinthians," *The Expositor's Bible Commentary: Romans - Galatians,* Vol. 11, Revised edition, edited by Longman III and Garland (Zondervan Academic 2006) 1 Corinthians 2:10b-11, p. 278

62 E. W. Bullinger was used as a primary reference source to create this list, but what is written here is not an exact quote. Bullinger, E. W., *Preface to Romans 8 - the Greek word for spirit in the N.T. from appendix 101 of the Companion Bible.* Retrieved from https://www.hopeoftheglory.com/AFW/hotg_pdf/r8.pdf (last accessed December 18, 2023)

God is not simply "a" spirit, the Greek text says He is Spirit.
2. Christ Himself, as in 2 Corinthians 3:17,18
3. the agency of the Holy Spirit to bestow spiritual gifts, as in 1 Corinthians 12:4-11
4. the new creation nature in someone who has been born from above, as in John 3:3-7
5. the Holy Spirit Himself (*ho pneuma*) which occurs a total of 93 times, such as in Romans 8:16. Notably, 52 of those are references are written without articles. The original Greek text is *hagios pneuma*, which is properly translated "Holy Spirit," as in Acts 1:5

Similar to Dr. Levison's point regarding the inability to draw neat and tidy Old Testament conclusions about Holy Spirit, Dr. Michael Green points out that "there is no tidy doctrine of the Spirit ... in the whole of the New Testament. He always retains that unpredictable, mysterious otherness of the *ruach adonai [spirit of God]*."[63]

From our study thus far, we might conclude that God's Spirit is an impersonal, immaterial influence, force, or power. There is in fact disagreement within Christian circles concerning the true nature of Holy Spirit. Is the Holy Spirit simply an impersonal *force* or is Holy Spirit a *person*? Is it proper to refer to Holy Spirit with the impersonal pronoun *it* or is the use the personal pronoun *He* more appropriate?

Let's first acknowledge the obvious. The very essence of arguing about such identity matters goes well beyond what the biblical writers apparently felt the need to discuss. Moreover, as we will see, in Hebraic thought there is room for understanding two seemingly opposing views without violating the reality of either one. In actuality, it is our Greek mindset in the Western world-

---

[63] Green, Michael, *I Believe in the Holy Spirit*, Revised edition (Eerdmans 2004) p. 80

view that forces us to pick only one as viable and discard the other false.

My friend and research mentor, Henri Goulet, provides an explanation of apparent contradictions in the biblical record by borrowing a term from philosophy. It is the word "antinomy" and it refers to a contradiction between two statements, both apparently obtained by correct reasoning. Henri explains that when we face apparent contradictions in the Bible, the word "antinomy" provides a good roadmap.[64] Let's take for example the question of whether the Abrahamic Covenant is conditional or unconditional? Or another example is the question whether Jesus is God or is He human? In each of our examples, Hebraic thought allows *both* viewpoints to be possible – there is no forced need to choose one over the other. In our Western worldview, such a choice is outside the realm of possibility because we think a contradiction between two apparent opposites *must* be resolved by choosing one or the other. In Greek-oriented thinking it *can't* be both, a choice must be made for one over the other. However, Hebraic thought viewed God quite differently from the systematic theological thinking of our [western culture]:[65]

> The Western-style treatment of the divine character attempts to explain inconsistencies and harmonize contradictions systematically. The Hebrew mind was filled with wonder at the mystery of God. The vastness of God and his inscrutable [uninvestigatible] ways left them awestruck. Inconsistencies and contradictions are intimately related to human, finite understanding of the infinite God. He is beyond human comprehension.... The fact that God is incomprehensible is very much a

---

64 Goulet, Henri Louis, *The Election of Israel*, MSI class, May, 2012
65 Lawrence, N'Tan, *Hebrew Thought Compared With Greek (Western) Thought, A Key To Understanding Scripture Through the Eyes of the Authors*, p. 8, quoting Brad Young, *Paul the Jewish Theologian* (Hendrickson Publishers 1997) p. 25. Retrieved from www.hoshanarabbah.org/pdfs/heb_grk.pdf (last accessed May 23, 2024)

part of Jewish thought processes. The Western mind, however, explains everything but understands so little of the divine nature. The Hebrew mind, on the other hand .... thrives on the inconsistencies and contradictions of the one awe-inspiring God.

This understanding of the Hebrew culture allows us to quickly resolve the debate over the Spirit's personhood. The proper answer is that at times God's Spirit does appear to function as an invisible power or influence which accomplishes God's will on earth. We have already noted that in the Old Testament God's Spirit is primarily viewed as "the power through which God works and manifests himself in the world."[66] Even as an impersonal power, however, the witness of the Bible is that God's Spirit is "God in action [His personal presence and influence] for the benefit of his people," bringing His creation into conformity with His divine will.[67]

In this regard, Holy Spirit is presented as God's agent with attributes that only a person could have. While this is much less clear in the Old Testament,[68] in the writings of the Jewish rabbis

---

66 Hill, David, *Greek Words and Hebrew Meanings: Studies in the Semantics of Soteriological Terms*, Society for New Testament Studies Monograph Series 5 (Wipf and Stock 2000, previously published Cambridge University Press 1967) p. 212, quoting Manson, T.W., *On Paul and John* (London 1963) p. 33

67 Green, Michael, *I Believe in the Holy Spirit*, Revised edition (Eerdmans 2004) pp. 24,36

68 One Old Testament example is found in Isaiah 30:1 which presents God's Spirit as a person who knows and conveys His will. When discussing the Spirit in the Old Testament, the abridged version of the *Theological Dictionary of the New Testament* asserts, without Scripture reference, "The Spirit's power is personal. It is no immanent force of nature; nature is de-deified in the OT." Bromiley, Geoffrey W., *Theological Dictionary of the New Testament*, Abridged in One Volume (Eerdmans 1985) entry for *pneuma* under B. *Spirit in the OT, II. The Spirit of God*, 2, p. 880. Scholar "A. R. Johnson ... interprets the Spirit acting upon man as an 'extension of Yahweh's personality'. 'God', he says, 'is thought of in terms similar to those of man as possessing an indefinable extension of the Personality, which enables him

the Holy Spirit is personified with some frequency as speaking, crying, lamenting, weeping, rejoicing, or comforting. Notably these actions are always associated in these ancient rabbinic writings with the Spirit introducing quotations from the Old Testament.[69] One scholar suggests that this type of personification in ancient Jewish writings is "Probably ... a graphic attempt to express the presence and involvement of God in the affairs of his people."[70]

When we turn our attention to the New Testament we find that the authors supply us with a wealth of evidence pointing to Holy Spirit's personhood. Even so, He is never presented as a person equal to God the Father with an independent will of His own. He always acts in the capacity of an agent who executes God's will on earth.

> [T]he Spirit makes choices (1 Cor 12:11), teaches (John 14:26), guides (John 16:13), reveals Jesus (John 16:14), convicts (John 16:8), seals believers (2 Cor

---

to exercise a mysterious influence upon mankind.' In its creative aspect this appears as 'blessing'; in its destructive aspect it makes itself felt as a 'curse' ..." Hill, David, *Greek Words and Hebrew Meanings: Studies in the Semantics of Soteriological Terms*, Society for New Testament Studies Monograph Series 5 (Wipf and Stock 2000, previously published Cambridge University Press 1967) p. 209, footnote 1, quoting A. R. Johnson, *The One and the Many in the Israelite Conception of God*, 2nd edition (Cardiff 1961) pp. 15ff

69 The Jewish rabbis thought of the Holy Spirit as the one who inspired and even composed the Old Testament. As a result, it is common to find in those writings a saying from the Old Testament recorded as a saying of the Spirit. For example: "Israel or a biblical character recites part of a verse and Holy Spirit responds by quoting the remainder of the same verse or a neighbouring verse...." Hill, David, *Greek Words and Hebrew Meanings: Studies in the Semantics of Soteriological Terms*, Society for New Testament Studies Monograph Series 5 (Wipf and Stock 2000, previously published Cambridge University Press 1967) p. 228, citations omitted

70 Hill, David, *Greek Words and Hebrew Meanings: Studies in the Semantics of Soteriological Terms*, Society for New Testament Studies Monograph Series 5 (Wipf and Stock 2000, previously published Cambridge University Press 1967) p. 229

1:21-22), can be grieved (Ep. 4:30), blasphemed (Matt 12:31),[71] possesses a rational mind (Rom 8:26-27; 1 Cor 2:11-13), can be lied to (Acts 5:3-4), quenched (1 Thess 5:19), resisted (Acts 7:51), and on numerous occasions is distinguished from, yet directly linked with the Father and the Son as co-worker and co-recipient of worship [all of these Scripture work together to argue] definitively for his personhood (Matt 28:19-20; 2 Cor 13:14).[72]

Scholar David Hill provides an excellent summary which illustrates for us precisely how, in Jewish thought, Holy Spirit can be both a force and a person.[73]

> [The writings of Paul in Galatians][74] leave no doubt that Paul considered the 'spirit' to be a *power* working within men, influencing the will and producing conduct of a moral kind in which personal relationships are of crucial importance ([Galatians] 5:26). But the power is not an impersonal force: nor, as the norm of life and conduct, is it a cold impersonal ideal. Both the standard and the power are grounded in something real and personal, because they are essentially related to Jesus Christ and men's continuing experience of him.

---

71 "Therefore I [Jesus] say to you … blasphemy against the Spirit shall not be forgiven…. (Matthew 12:31)." The general context of this statement provides a clear understanding that blasphemy refers to the accusation that Jesus was casting out demons through the use of evil powers rather than through God's power.

72 Herrick, Gary, *4. Pneumatology: The Holy Spirit*, from the series: An Introduction To Christian Belief: A Layman's Guide, Bible.org, June 3, 2004 under *The Personhood of the Holy Spirit*. Retrieved from https://bible.org/seriespage/4-pneumatology-holy-spirit (last accessed December 18, 2023)

73 Hill, David, *Greek Words and Hebrew Meanings: Studies in the Semantics of Soteriological Terms*, Society for New Testament Studies Monograph Series 5 (Wipf and Stock 2000, previously published Cambridge University Press 1967) p. 271, italics in original

74 Hill focuses specific attention on Galatians 2:20 and 5:25.

In the next lesson, we will continue with our basic introduction to God's Spirit. As you have been reading this lesson the Holy Spirit may have illuminated the eyes of your understanding with one of those *aha* moments – the kind where you say out loud, "I get it! Thanks, Holy Spirit." For others, however, you might better fit into the category which I've heard replayed repeatedly on a Christian talk radio station. For a long time, the promotional advertisement for Chuck Swindoll's radio program on WRFD880 AM in Columbus, Ohio came from a portion of his teaching in which he was acknowledging that not all truth is plain or easy to understand; not everything in the Bible can be grasped in a single read. In a voice that was unmistakably his, Swindoll exclaimed, "Well, welcome to the club, **no one gets it**!"[75] So, if that aptly describes you at this early juncture of our study, take courage. I am right there with you – one foot in the "I think I've got it" group and the other firmly in the "Ok, I think I know enough to still be confused" group. The good news for those of us in the *still confused* group is that the Bible never demands full and complete understanding of the Holy Spirit and His ways as a necessary prerequisite for Him to be actively at work in us and through us! That said, I'll end this lesson with a quote attributed to A. W. Tozer, "You can discover more of the Holy Spirit in five minutes on your knees in adoring worship than five years at a seminary."[76]

Hear What The Spirit is Saying to the Church: *Welcome to a study about the power of My Spirit. Learn from Me. Not all that man has taught has been rightly related to my Truth. Will you let me 'set the record straight?' When you*

---

75 The Word, 880, WRFD-AM, Columbus, Ohio; radio promotion for *Insight for Living* with Chuck Swindoll

76 Tozer, A. W., *The Mystery of The Holy Spirit* (Bridge-Logos 2007) edited by Rev. James L. Snyder, *Introduction* under *Mystery and Majesty*. Retrieved from https://spiritnerds.org/wp-content/uploads/2021/11/Tozer_-Mystery-of-the-Holy-Spir-A.-W.-Tozer-Spiritnerd.org_-1.pdf (last accessed April 3, 2024)

see, when you understand, then you will know of Me in a way that is without limit. Let me in these pages introduce you to who I really am that you may become all that I created you to be.

LESSON 2:

WHO IS THE HOLY SPIRIT? PART 2

"After being baptized, Jesus came up immediately from the water; and behold, the heavens were opened, and he saw the Spirit of God descending as a dove *and* lighting on Him, and behold, a voice out of the heavens said, 'This is My beloved Son, in whom I am well-pleased.'"
Matthew 3:16-17, italics in original

IN OUR FIRST lesson, we began to explore a biblical introduction to God's Spirit. This lesson continues to lay a foundational understanding of Holy Spirit before we move on to experience His power. We concluded our last lesson recognizing that God's self-existing Spirit sometimes appears in Scripture as an impersonal, immaterial force or power, but the Bible also presents Him as a person. In sum, "the Spirit is the Lord's mighty agency at work in the world, making real his personal presence in every place."[1] That is to say, God manifests His working presence on earth through the Holy Spirit. "The Spirit of God ... is God exercising power, communicating himself, or operating. This power may be simply vital power, physical life; or it may be intellectual, moral and religious life. These are all communicated by the Spirit or רוּחַ [*ruah*] of God."[2] However, "[t]he Holy Spirit is not just some

---

1 Motyer, J. Alec, *The Prophecy of Isaiah An Introduction & Commentary* (InterVarsity Press 1993) Isaiah 40:6-8, citing Psalm 139:7, p. 301
2 Hill, David, *Greek Words and Hebrew Meanings: Studies in the Semantics of Soteriological Terms*, Society for New Testament Studies Monograph Series 5 (Wipf and Stock 2000, previously published Cambridge University Press

divine force emanating from God but different from him, [nor is Holy Spirit] some sort of action at a distance or some kind of gift detachable from God, for God *is* Spirit."[3]

We made the point in our first lesson that God's Spirit is not always identified that specifically on the pages of Scripture. There are four prominent biblical symbols which identify the presence and work of the Holy Spirit: dove, fire, wind and water. The *Theological Wordbook of the Old Testament* points out, "Since Hebrew does not lend itself to the abstract," the Bible often uses earthly-oriented picturesque ways and parallel words to express otherwise abstract concepts.[4] Similarly, the writings of the Jewish rabbis "often conceived [of God's Spirit] in material terms, such as light, fire, sound, water or a dove....Conceptions like these ... are understandable as the attempts to give expression to mystical, visionary experiences, and should therefore be treated as metaphorical descriptions: the rabbis did not think of the Spirit as an

---

1967) p. 212, quoting A. B. Davidson, *Theology of the Old Testament* (Edinburgh 1904) p. 193

3 Torrance, Thomas F., *The Mediation of Christ* (Helmers & Howard Publishers 1992) p. 125. Scholar Craig Keener views John's statement that "God is Spirit" (John 4:24) as pointing to the fact that God is not physical, He is not flesh, His nature is spirit. Keener, Craig S., *The Gospel Of John: A Commentary*, Volume One (Hendrickson Publishers 2003) 7.G. God Is a Spirit ([John] 4:24) p. 618

4 Harris, Archer, and Waltke, editors, *Theological Wordbook of the Old Testament* (Moody Press 1999) word#1596b under *'ōz. Strength, power*, p. 660, noting that the idea of strength is abstract and is therefore biblically expressed in pictorial ways. For example, strength is depicted as the ability to stand like a mountain (Psalm 30:7); God's strength is a strong tower (Psalm 61:3); God's strength is a rock (Psalm 62:7). See also: David Hill "The thought of the Hebrew was imaginative: he expressed himself in the language of pictures drawn from sense impressions, and that language remained poor in abstract terms, being dominated by concrete images." Hill, David, *Greek Words and Hebrew Meanings: Studies in the Semantics of Soteriological Terms*, Society for New Testament Studies Monograph Series 5 (Wipf and Stock 2000, previously published Cambridge University Press 1967) p. 212, footnote 1

actual material object."⁵ In the arena of God's Spirit the imagery of wind, fire, water and dove are "personal action descriptors" which can help us understand His personal deeds and His qualities.[6]

These symbols function in a similar way as concrete images that are used in the Bible to refer to God or Jesus. For example, Proverbs 18:10 declares that God's name is a "strong tower" which a righteous man can run into and find safety. In ancient times fortified storehouses were built in the countryside and cities. Because of their strength and height, they were firmly fixed structures that could provide a stronghold against an enemy. When threatened these towers made a good place for people to seek safety (Judges 9:51). By referring to God's name as a strong tower, the proverb pictures God's protection and refuge for those who seek Him.[7]

We see the same type of symbolism used in reference to Jesus. In Revelation 22:16 Jesus refers to Himself as "the bright morning star" The morning stars are the ones that appear in the sky just before you see the sun rise in the morning. "They signal new life—a new day."[8] Jesus is the one who came to bring new life.

In a similar way the biblical symbols used for the Holy Spirit each communicate a different role of Holy Spirit. Ancient Jewish writings used these materialistic terms in their attempt to describe

---

5   Hill, David, *Greek Words and Hebrew Meanings: Studies in the Semantics of Soteriological Terms*, Society for New Testament Studies Monograph Series 5 (Wipf and Stock 2000, previously published Cambridge University Press 1967) p. 233, citing Abelson, J., *The Immanence of God in Rabbinical Literature* (London 1912) pp. 212ff

6   Davis, John Jefferson, *Is the Holy Spirit Really a "Person"—with a Distinct Personality?* Themelios, Volume 47, Issue 3 (The Gospel Coalition). Retrieved from https://www.thegospelcoalition.org/themelios/article/is-the-holy-spirit-really-a-person-with-a-distinct-personality/ (last accessed March 13, 2023)

7   Waltke, Bruce K., *The Book of Proverbs: Chapters 15-31*, The New International Commentary on the Old Testament (Eerdmans 2004) Proverbs 18:10, p. 76

8   Heiser, Michael S., *The Unseen Realm: Recovering the Supernatural Worldview of the Bible* (Lexham Press 2015) p. 24

the actions of God's Spirit.⁹ In this lesson we'll consider each symbol.

Dove

Probably the most recognizable symbol of the Holy Spirit is the form of a dove (or the dove-like manner of the Spirit) that descended and enters *into* Jesus when He was baptized.¹⁰ This event is so significant that it is recorded in all four gospel accounts of His baptism (Matthew 3:16; Mark 1:10; Luke 3:22; John 1:32). We'll look at Matthew's account which is our Key Scripture for this lesson.

> After his baptism, as Jesus came up out of the water, the heavens were opened and he saw the Spirit of God descending **like a dove** and settling on him. And a voice from heaven said, "This is my **dearly loved** Son, who brings me great joy." Matthew 3:16-17 NLT, bold added

Clearly, Matthew is not saying a literal "dove" descended from heaven at the baptism of Jesus. He is using the dove as a symbol

---

9   Hill, David, *Greek Words and Hebrew Meanings: Studies in the Semantics of Soteriological Terms*, Society for New Testament Studies Monograph Series 5 (Wipf and Stock 2000, previously published Cambridge University Press 1967) p. 174

10 Jack Levison notes that the description "like a dove" in Mark and Matthew is an adverbial clause meaning it describes the way in which the Spirit descended from heaven. Levison then differentiates Luke's description as referring to Holy Spirit descending "*in bodily form* as a dove." Levison, Jack, *An Unconventional God: The Spirit according to Jesus* (Baker Academic 2020) pp. 49,50, italics in original. R. T. France likewise notes, "It is sometimes rightly argued" that the original Greek in Matthew may not be a reference to the actual form of dove but to the way in which the Spirit descended. However, in the same footnote France points out that it is not easy to define a "dove-like manner." France, R. T., *The Gospel of Matthew*, New International Commentary on the New Testament (Eerdmans 2007) Matthew 3:16, footnote 22, p. 121 citing L. E. Keck, *NTS* 17 [1970/1] pp. 63-67 for the dove-like manner argument.

The Power of My Spirit 33

for God's Spirit which descended from above.[11] The Greek-based culture that developed after the conquests of Alexander the Great (and was the predominate culture in the days of Jesus) thought doves were divine birds.[12]

I was intrigued to learn that in the days of the Old Testament a dove could be viewed as a messenger of love.[13] In similar fashion, referring to someone as a *dove* was an endearing term.[14] For example, in Psalm 74:19 the psalmist called Israel *God's dove*.[15] This ancient dove symbolism supplies us with an interesting backdrop to the words God spoke from heaven at the time He sent His Spirit to descend on Jesus *like a dove*. Matthew, Mark and Luke all record the Father calling Jesus His *"dearly loved* Son."[16] It may well be that the dove-image in the baptism of Jesus intended to communicate in symbolic language the love God expressed for His Son in His spoken words!

In any event, a review of ancient Jewish literature reveals that the dove was an established Jewish metaphor for God's Spirit.[17] As you will recall, in the Genesis creation account Holy Spirit was viewed as *hovering* or *moving* (*rachaph*) over the chaos when God's

---

11 "In late Judaism the dove was a symbol of the Holy Spirit (cf. Targum to Cant 2:12) as well as for the community of Israel." Hill, David, *Greek Words and Hebrew Meanings: Studies in the Semantics of Soteriological Terms*, Society for New Testament Studies Monograph Series 5 (Wipf and Stock 2000, previously published Cambridge University Press 1967) p. 242, footnote 4
12 Gundry, Robert H., *Mark: A Commentary on His Apology for the Cross* (Eerdmans 1993) p. 4
13 Walton, Matthews, and Chavalas, *The IVP Bible Background Commentary: Old Testament* (InterVarsity Press 2000) Song of Songs 1:15, p. 577
14 Kidner, Derek, *Psalms 73-150: An Introduction and Commentary*, Tyndale Old Testament Commentaries (IVP Academic 1973) Psalm 74:19, p. 299
15 See translations such as: ESV, HCSB, CJB
16 Matthew 3:17 NLT; Mark 1:11 NLT; Luke 3:22 NLT, italics added for all three verses
17 Keener, Craig S., *The Gospel Of John: A Commentary, Volume One* (Hendrickson Publishers 2003) 3. Jesus and the Abiding Spirit ([John] 1:32-33) p. 460

spoken word provided order and function to the earth. *Rachaph* is also used in Deuteronomy 32:11 of the eagle fluttering over her nested young (newly created eaglets). It is the same Hebrew word used in other contexts to refer to the rapid fluttering of a bird's wings.[18] Influential Jewish writings such as the Qumran Scrolls[19] and the Talmud[20] perceived a likeness of the hovering action between God's Spirit and birds. Therefore, these authors associated the dove with God's Spirit in Genesis 1:2.[21]

In Jewish understanding, the dove is also a symbol of creation.[22] This dove symbolism connects back to Noah sending the dove from the Ark to determine whether the floodwaters had receded (Genesis 8). In that account a literal dove was flying over the chaos caused by the flood as "a harbinger of the new creation."[23] Noah was anticipating God's new creation.

---

18 *Holman Christian Standard Bible*, Study Bible edition (Holman Bible Publishers, 2010) study note to Matthew 3:16, p. 1615
19 Also known as "*The Dead Sea Scrolls*" these manuscript fragments were discovered in eleven caves along the northwest shore of the Dead Sea between the years 1947 and 1956. Fragments of every book of the Hebrew canon (Old Testament) have been discovered except for the book of Esther.
20 The *Babylonian Talmud*, which often cites the Old Testament, is the basic book of Jewish law. It is a large collection of doctrines and laws compiled and written before the 8th Century, A.D. by Babylonian Jews. Generally, a citation from the *Babylonian Talmud* is considered authoritative. Genesis 1:2 is explained in the *Talmud* as follows: "The Spirit of God was borne over the water **as a dove** which broods over her young" (*Chagigah*, 15 a)." Westcott, Brooke Foss, *The Gospel According to St. John: The Greek Text with Introduction and Notes*, Vol. I (John Murray Publishing Company 1908) John 1:31,32, footnote 32, p. 43, bold added
21 *Holman Christian Standard Bible*, Study Bible edition (Holman Bible Publishers, 2010) study note to Matthew 3:16, p. 1615
22 Keener, Craig S., *The Gospel Of John: A Commentary*, Volume One (Hendrickson Publishers 2003) 3. Jesus and the Abiding Spirit ([John] 1:32-33) p. 460
23 Keener, Craig S., *The Gospel Of John: A Commentary*, Volume One (Hendrickson Publishers 2003) 3. Jesus and the Abiding Spirit ([John] 1:32-33) p. 460

Given ancient association between the dove and creation, it is probable that the descending dove at Jesus' baptism also pictures a new creation that is to be accomplished by the Holy Spirit through Jesus, the Messiah of Israel.[24]

Fire

In the Old Testament fire is evidence of God's presence (Exodus 3:2; 14:19), purification (Isaiah 6:6-7), His judgment (Numbers 11:1,3; 2 Kings 1:10,12), or His power (Judges 13:20; 1 Kings 18:38). According to the Psalmist, Yahweh makes "flames of fire His servants."[25] In other words, God is pictured as employing fire to do His will and carry out His plans. "Where men at first see only material objects and forms of nature there God is present, fulfilling His will through His servants ...."[26] Thus fire, as with God's Spirit, is seen as a servant who is entirely under His command. Scholar J. Alec Motyer observes that beginning with Exodus 3:2 (God's appearance to Moses as a burning fire in a bush), the enduring biblical image of fire "is the symbol of active divine holiness."[27] That makes fire an especially appropriate symbol for God's Spirit.

It is not surprising then to find the Holy Spirit appearing as *tongues of fire* resting on the waiting disciples who had heard Jesus promise that His Father would send the Spirit.

---

24 Ryken, Wilhoit, and Longman III, editors, *Dictionary of Biblical Imagery* (Intervarsity Press 1998) entry for *Holy Spirit* under *Dove,* p. 392. See also *Holman Christian Standard Bible*, Study Bible edition (Holman Bible Publishers 2010) study note to Matthew 3:16, p. 1615; Davis, John Jefferson, *Is the Holy Spirit Really a "Person"—with a Distinct Personality?* Themelios, Volume 47, Issue 3, The Gospel Coalition. Retrieved from https://www.thegospelcoalition.org/themelios/article/is-the-holy-spirit-really-a-person-with-a-distinct-personality/ (last accessed March 13, 2023)

25 Psalm 104:4 HCSB

26 Perowne, John, general editor, *The Cambridge Bible for Schools and Colleges*, Psalm 104:4, quoting Westcott on Hebrews 1:7. Retrieved from Hill, Gary, *The Discovery Bible*, HELPS Ministries, Inc.

27 Motyer, J. Alec, *The Prophecy of Isaiah: An Introduction & Commentary* (InterVarsity Press 1993) Isaiah 26:10-11, p. 216

> When the day of Pentecost had come, they were all together in one place. And suddenly there came from heaven a noise like a violent rushing wind, and it filled the whole house where they were sitting. And there appeared to them tongues as of fire distributing themselves, and they rested on each one of them. And they were all filled with the Holy Spirit and began to speak with other tongues, as the Spirit was giving them utterance. Acts 2:1-4

The scene Luke describes has distinct parallels to the fire, smoke and sounds of Mt. Sinai where God had appeared to cut His Covenant with Israel.[28] Through the use of similar miraculous signs, God sent His Spirit in a manner that communicated in a fresh new way the connection between His Old Covenant with Israel and His New Covenant with those who followed Jesus, the Messiah.[29]

Wind/Breath

Ruah is used in the Old Testament more than one hundred times to denote wind.[30] As an initial matter, it is helpful to recognize that ancient cultures associated wind and breath with "unseen spiritual forces."[31] The Hebrew culture thought of the wind as being something God controlled and used as a "medium" through

---

28 Exodus 19:16-18
29 Stern, David, H., *Jewish New Testament Commentary* (Jewish New Testament Publications 1992) Acts 2:2-3, p. 221
30 Block, Daniel I., *The Prophet Of The Spirit: The Use Of Rwh In The Book Of Ezekiel*, Journal of the Evangelical Theological Society, 32 no 1 Mar 1989, pp. 27-49, at p. 29. Retrieved from https://www.etsjets.org/files/JETS-PDFs/32/32-1/32-1-pp027-049_JETS.pdf (last accessed December 14, 2023). Of the nearly 400 times *ruah* is employed in the Old Testament, more than one third are understood as a wind or a breeze. Levison, Jack, *A Boundless God: The Spirit according to the Old Testament* (Baker Academic 2020) p. 19
31 Elwell, Walter A., editor, *Evangelical Dictionary of Theology*, Second Edition (Baker Academic 1984, 2001) entry for *Holy Spirit* under *The OT.*, p. 568

which He could exercise His power.[32] "The wind is ... invisible, mysterious and impalpable; it knows no limits, yet no one knows it origin. To this extent, any mysterious, unpredictable power is akin to the wind."[33]

In a symbolic sense, wind and breath are closely related to each other in that they each involve the movement of air.[34] Wind, breath and spirit are all considered to be "invisible force or life energies whose sources cannot readily be observed but whose effects are transparent and sometimes even violent."[35] When breath or wind is used to refer to "the Lord's Spirit, there is constantly the suggestion of power to effect change, to impose the divine will and order on things."[36] So, even though it may not initially be transparent to us, we can see how this idea of *ruah* as wind/breath becomes a good symbol for Holy Spirit. We have already seen that He was used by God to set things in motion in Genesis.

In the Bible, "the breath of life [is] the life-force that animates all living creatures."[37] When the *ruah* enters a creature created

---

32   Hill, David, *Greek Words and Hebrew Meanings: Studies in the Semantics of Soteriological Terms*, Society for New Testament Studies Monograph Series 5 (Wipf and Stock 2000, previously published Cambridge University Press 1967) p. 206

33   Hill, David, *Greek Words and Hebrew Meanings: Studies in the Semantics of Soteriological Terms*, Society for New Testament Studies Monograph Series 5 (Wipf and Stock 2000, previously published Cambridge University Press 1967) p. 206

34   Averbeck, Richard E., *The Holy Spirit in the Hebrew Bible and Its Connections to the New Testament* (2009). Retrieved from https://bible.org/seriespage/holy-spirit-hebrew-bible-and-its-connections-new-testament (last accessed January 22, 2024). This article is included in Wallace, Daniel B. and Sawyer, M. James, editors, *Who's Afraid Of The Holy Spirit? An Investigation Into The Ministry Of The Spirit Of God Today* (Biblical Studies Press 2013).

35   Ryken, Wilhoit, and Longman III, editors, *Dictionary of Biblical Imagery* (Intervarsity Press 1998) entry for *Holy Spirit* under *Wind and Breath*, p. 391

36   Motyer, J. Alec, *The Prophecy of Isaiah: An Introduction & Commentary* (InterVarsity Press 1993) Isaiah 11:4, p. 123, citing Psalm 33:6 as an example

37   Block, Daniel I., *The Prophet Of The Spirit: The Use Of Rwh In The Book Of Ezekiel*, Journal of the Evangelical Theological Society, 32 no 1 Mar

by God that creature comes to life. A person needs to breath in order to be alive and if they stop breathing their body gives up their spirit. As a result, to the ancient Hebrews it is God's wind or breath that gives life.[38] For example, in Ezekiel's vision of the valley filled with dry bones, the life-giving breath of God comes as *wind* and fills those dead bodies with new life (Ezekiel 37:9). No other text in all of the Old Testament "portrays the vivifying, power" and energizing effect of God's Spirit as dramatically as Ezekiel's encounter with the dry bones.[39] The prophecy of the dry bones was well recognized as a promise of restoration which was associated with a New Covenant, new hope and new life – the time when a new Spirit would be given to God's people. The promise to put His Spirit within His people (Ezekiel 36:26) makes clear that God's Spirit has the power to transform people.

On the other hand, the Sovereign God who releases the breath of life can also send a *wind* that results in death. "The grass withers, the flower fades, When the breath [*ruah*] of the Lord blows upon it; Surely the people are grass (Isaiah 40:7)." Here the imagery of Yahweh's breath (*ruah*) acts like a destructive wind causing the grass of the field to fade. The fact that grass is employed as a metaphor for man indicates frailty and lack of permanence in human life.

When Jesus explains the new birth experience to Nicodemus He draws an analogy between the activity of wind and the Spirit's

---

1989, pp. 27-49, at p. 38. Retrieved from https://www.etsjets.org/files/JETS-PDFs/32/32-1/32-1-pp027-049_JETS.pdf (last accessed December 14, 2023)

38 Block, Daniel I., *The Prophet Of The Spirit: The Use Of Rwh In The Book Of Ezekiel*, Journal of the Evangelical Theological Society, 32 no 1 Mar 1989, pp. 27-49, at p. 35, italics added. Retrieved from https://www.etsjets.org/files/JETS-PDFs/32/32-1/32-1-pp027-049_JETS.pdf (last accessed December 14, 2023)

39 Block, Daniel I., *The Prophet Of The Spirit: The Use Of Rwh In The Book Of Ezekiel*, Journal of the Evangelical Theological Society, 32 no 1 Mar 1989, pp. 27-49, at p. 37. Retrieved from https://www.etsjets.org/files/JETS-PDFs/32/32-1/32-1-pp027-049_JETS.pdf (last accessed December 14, 2023)

involvement in spiritual birth. "The wind blows where it wishes and you hear the sound of it, but do not know where it comes from and where it is going; so is everyone who is born of the Spirit. (John 3:8)." Jesus tells Nicodemus that the spiritual new birth experience, which resembles a new creation, is not like a natural birth where you can physically *see* the baby being born. A spiritual birth happens in a way that is similar to hearing the wind. You know wind is present because you can hear its' sound. You can't see the wind, you don't know where it originates from and you don't know its future direction, but the fact that you can *hear* it allows you to identify its presence.[40] Because the winds' effects can be observed, Jesus uses it as a comparison for those born of the Spirit. Just as there are mysterious aspects of the wind even though it is a real force, the new birth which originates with God's Spirit is mysterious yet real. There will be visible, observable effect of His presence in the life of a Christ-follower.

Before we conclude our discussion of Jesus' encounter with Nicodemus it is worth noting that the biblical text makes clear Jesus assumed that Nicodemus, as a teacher of Israel, would have understood the role of the Spirit in providing new life (John 3:7,10). After all, Nicodemus would have been very familiar with the text of Ezekiel 36:25-29 (God's promise of the New Covenant) upon which Jesus' statements are based.[41] The fact that Jesus is seen as rebuking the ignorance of Nicodemus supplies scholar Daniel Block with fuel to suggest that Jesus was *not* introducing "an inno-

---

40 This would not have been a new concept to Nicodemus. Numerous references to the mystery of the wind's origin are contained in the Old Testament and ancient Jewish literature. Beale, G. K. and Carson, D. A., ed., *Commentary on the New Testament Use of the Old Testament* (Baker Academic 2007) John 2:17 under F. *Theological Use*, p. 435

41 "There can be little doubt that [Jesus'] statements here are based on Ezek 36:25-29, a text with which the rabbi [Nicodemus] should have been familiar." Block, Daniel I., *The Prophet Of The Spirit: The Use Of Rwh In The Book Of Ezekiel*, Journal of the Evangelical Theological Society, 32 no 1 Mar 1989, pp. 27-49, at p. 40. Retrieved from https://www.etsjets.org/files/JETS-PDFs/32/32-1/32-1-pp027-049_JETS.pdf (last accessed December 14, 2023)

vative description of the work of the Holy Spirit in the new era."[42] To Block, Jesus' surprise that Nicodemus lacked understanding works to undermine the suggestion that in the Old Testament the Holy Spirit only came *upon* people, whereas in the New Testament He *indwells* people who choose to follow Christ.[43]

Now let's wrap up our discussion of the use of "wind" as a symbol for God's Spirit. As we have seen, wind helps provide concreteness to the actions of an otherwise invisible power. In many respects, the characteristics of the wind are similar to those of God's Spirit. Wind is a mysterious and powerful force which we can use and benefit from. We cannot always predict what it is going to do. We are not able to make or send the wind. The Holy Spirit, like the wind, is exclusively under God's control.[44] Similarly, Holy Spirit is immaterial in form. He is powerful but not visible and He operates solely according to the sovereign purposes of God.[45]

---

42 Block, Daniel I., *The Prophet Of The Spirit: The Use Of Rwh In The Book Of Ezekiel*, Journal of the Evangelical Theological Society, 32 no 1 Mar 1989, pp. 27-49, at p. 40. Retrieved from https://www.etsjets.org/files/JETS-PDFs/32/32-1/32-1-pp027-049_JETS.pdf (last accessed December 14, 2023)

43 Blocks other arguments against this dichotomy between Old and New Testaments include the truth that Israel was always commanded to love God from her heart and that Psalm 51:12-13 provides an "explicit witness" to the fact that David understood that "[h]is continued acceptance in the divine presence [of God] and the divine presence [of God] *within him* in the form of the *rwh* [*ruah*] represent his only hope." Block, Daniel I., *The Prophet Of The Spirit: The Use Of Rwh In The Book Of Ezekiel*, Journal of the Evangelical Theological Society, 32 no 1 Mar 1989, pp. 27-49, at p. 40, italics added. Retrieved from https://www.etsjets.org/files/JETS-PDFs/32/32-1/32-1-pp027-049_JETS.pdf (last accessed December 14, 2023)

44 Averbeck, Richard E., "Breath, Wind, Spirit and The Holy Spirit in the Old Testament," in *Presence Power And Promise The Role of the Spirit of God in the Old Testament*, edited by Firth and Wegner (IVP Academic 2011) p. 36

45 Walvoord, John F., *The Holy Spirit A Comprehensive Study of the Person and Work of The Holy Spirit* (Zondervan Publishing House 1965) p. 24. Retrieved from books.google.com (webpage no longer available)

Water

It is well established that water is essential to sustain life. In fact, generally speaking a person cannot survive more than three days without water. This truth makes the "meaning and evocativeness [of water] universal. Yet the significance of water was heightened for biblical writers, who lived in a region where water was scarce and drought ... [was] a constant threat to life."[46] In these conditions, satisfying thirst with water would understandably be "one of the most delightful sensations that can be experienced"[47] and therefore provided a powerful biblical image of thirsting for God.[48] Water and water in its various forms such as floods, rivers, streams, dew, or rain, is often used in the Bible to denote overflowing blessing from God, "particularly the abundant influences of the Holy Spirit."[49]

The precedent for water as a symbol for the Holy Spirit is explicitly found two times in the Old Testament: Isaiah 44:3 and Ezekiel 36:25-27[50] and is naturally carried over to the New Tes-

---

46 Ryken, Wilhoit, and Longman III, editors, *Dictionary of Biblical Imagery* (Intervarsity Press 1998) entry for *Water*, p. 929
47 Unger, Merrill F., *The New Unger's Bible Dictionary* (Moody Press 1988) entry for *Water*, p. 1361
48 See for example: Psalm 42:1; 143:6
49 Barnes, Albert, *Barnes' Notes On The Old And New Testaments*, Isaiah 44:3. Retrieved from Hill, Gary, *The Discovery Bible*, HELPS Ministries, Inc. "'Water' is, in Isaiah, the common metaphor for Divine grace. Sometimes, as in [Isaiah 44:3] (and Isaiah 35:6; Isaiah 43:20; Isaiah 55:1), the simple maim, 'water' or 'waters,' is the word used. At other times we have instead, or in addition, 'rain' (Isaiah 5:6; Isaiah 30:23; Isaiah 55:10), or 'dew'(Isaiah 26:19), or 'rivers' (Isaiah 30:25; Isaiah 32:2; Isaiah 33:21; Isaiah 41:18; Isaiah 43:19, etc.), or 'streams' (Isaiah 30:25; Isaiah 35:6), or 'floods' (as in [Isaiah 44:3])." Spence-Jones & Exell, general editors, *The Pulpit Commentary*, Isaiah 44:3. Retrieved from Hill, Gary, *The Discovery Bible*, HELPS Ministries, Inc.
50 Writings from ancient Jewish rabbis also use water as a symbol for God's Spirit. See for example: *y. Sukkah* 5:1; *Gen. Rab.* 70:8; *Rab. 4:8* as noted in Köstenberger, Andreas J., "John," in *Zondervan Illustrated Bible Backgrounds*

tament (as in John 7:37-38). We will begin by looking at the two Old Testament references.

> For I will pour water on the thirsty land, and streams on the dry ground; I will pour my Spirit upon your offspring, and my blessing on your descendants. Isaiah 44:3 ESV

This is one of five times the Old Testament speaks of pouring out God's Spirit.[51] Pouring out water speaks in a figurative way about the gift of God's Spirit as "the Agent of ongoing *blessing*."[52] After the last of the Old Testament prophets left the scene, the Jewish Rabbis believed that God's Spirit had departed from Israel.[53] However, there was a strongly held hope that in the future God would once again pour out His Spirit.[54] It was expected that the coming Messiah would possess God's Spirit and in "the Last Age, the righteous also would receive the Spirit as the agent of

---

Commentary, Vol. 2, edited by Clinton E. Arnold (Zondervan 2002) By this he meant the Spirit ([John] 7:39), p. 79

51 See also: Isaiah 32:15; Ezekiel 39:29; Joel 2:28; Zechariah 12:10. In each occurrence, "[t]he poured-out Spirit represents Yahweh's mark of ownership .... The notion of 'pouring' the Spirit is rooted in the perception of the *rûah* as a sort of divine fluid that covers the object. In each of the five occurrences of the idea in the OT, the pouring out of Yahweh's Spirit signifies the ratification and sealing of the covenant relationship with his people." Block, Daniel I., *The Book of Ezekiel: Chapters 25-48*, The New International Commentary on the Old Testament (Eerdmans 1998) Ezekiel 39:29, p. 488

52 Motyer, J. Alec, *Isaiah*, Tyndale Old Testament Commentaries (IVP Academic 1999) Isaiah 44:3-5, p. 311, italics in original

53 Hill, David, *Greek Words and Hebrew Meanings: Studies in the Semantics of Soteriological Terms*, Society for New Testament Studies Monograph Series 5 (Wipf and Stock 2000, previously published Cambridge University Press 1967) p. 231

54 Hill, David, *Greek Words and Hebrew Meanings: Studies in the Semantics of Soteriological Terms*, Society for New Testament Studies Monograph Series 5 (Wipf and Stock 2000, previously published Cambridge University Press 1967) p. 232

regeneration" leading to national revival.[55] Foundational texts for this expectation include Ezekiel 36:26-27 and 37:14.

> Then I will sprinkle clean water on you, and you will be clean; I will cleanse you from all your filthiness and from all your idols. Moreover, I will give you a new heart and put a new spirit within you; and I will remove the heart of stone from your flesh and give you a heart of flesh. I will put My Spirit within you and cause you to walk in My statutes, and you will be careful to observe My ordinances. Ezekiel 36:25-27

> "… I will put My Spirit within you and you will come to life, and I will place you on your own land. Then you will know that I, the Lord, have spoken and done it," declares the Lord.'" Ezekiel 37:14

In Hebrew thought, only running, free-flowing water such as found in streams or fountains (called *living* water) could purify. The Bible contrasts free-flowing water with stored water such as that which is found in cisterns and stagnant water such as is found in pools or marshes. This type of water could not purify. In biblical language being physically purified by water "has a corresponding reality in the purification of the human spirit through the Holy Spirit."[56]

The work of the Spirit is often compared to taking what was once dry desert and turning it into fertile land, where water is

---

55 Hill, David, *Greek Words and Hebrew Meanings: Studies in the Semantics of Soteriological Terms*, Society for New Testament Studies Monograph Series 5 (Wipf and Stock 2000, previously published Cambridge University Press 1967) p. 232

56 See also: Matthew 3:11. Averbeck, Richard E., *The Holy Spirit in the Hebrew Bible and Its Connections to the New Testament* (2009). Retrieved from https://bible.org/seriespage/holy-spirit-hebrew-bible-and-its-connections-new-testament (last accessed January 22, 2024). This article is included in Wallace, Daniel B. and Sawyer, M. James, editors, *Who's Afraid Of The Holy Spirit? An Investigation Into The Ministry Of The Spirit Of God Today* (Biblical Studies Press 2013).

the key to that transformation. In fact, the Old Testament used "living water" as "a metaphor for the divine activity in quickening men to life."[57] Jesus clearly stood in Old Testament tradition when on the last day of a pilgrim feast He "cried out, 'If anyone is thirsty, let him come to Me and drink. He who believes in Me, as the Scripture said, 'From his innermost being will flow rivers of living water.'"[58] In his gospel account of this event, John then adds an editorial comment which makes certain that Jesus was talking about "the Spirit, whom those who believed in Him were to receive."[59] John's explanatory comment relies on his Jewish heritage which employed "living water" as a symbol for the Holy Spirit.[60]

In 1 Corinthians 12:13 Paul related "our drinking of Jesus [like we would take a drink of water] to our reception of the Holy

---

57 Hill, David, *Greek Words and Hebrew Meanings: Studies in the Semantics of Soteriological Terms*, Society for New Testament Studies Monograph Series 5 (Wipf and Stock 2000, previously published Cambridge University Press 1967) p. 291

58 John 7:37-38. Scholar Craig Keener points out that it is important to consider the question "from whom the rivers flow in this passage." His well-reasoned conclusion is that "the glorified Christ is the Spirit's source" not that the water's flow from the belly of the Christ-follower. Keener, Craig S., *The Gospel Of John: A Commentary*, Volume One (Hendrickson Publishers 2003) 1, Source of Rivers of Life ([John] 7:37-39) under *1D. From Whom Does the Water Flow?* pp. 728-729

59 John 7:39a. In John 7:39b the comment is added that "the Spirit was not yet *given*, because Jesus was not yet glorified (italics in original)." John 12:16 makes clear that Jesus is "glorified" by his death on the cross. "The request that the Father glorify the Son so that the Son might glorify the Father [John 17:1-5] was in effect a request that the Father now hasten the cross ... revealing the Son's love for, and devotion to, the Father." Keener, Craig S., *The Gospel Of John: A Commentary*, Volume Two (Hendrickson Publishers 2003) Reciprocal Glory of Father and Son ([John] 17:1-5), p. 1053

60 Hill, David, *Greek Words and Hebrew Meanings: Studies in the Semantics of Soteriological Terms*, Society for New Testament Studies Monograph Series 5 (Wipf and Stock 2000, previously published Cambridge University Press 1967) p. 291

Spirit."[61] In fact, the heart of Paul's teaching is that receiving the Holy Spirit is an absolute necessity to be a follower of Christ. Paul explained that the revelation provided by the Holy Spirit "is what essentially distinguishes the believer from the nonbeliever ([1 Corinthians] 2:10-14); the Spirit is what especially marks the beginning of Christian life (Gal. 3:2-3) [and] the Spirit above all is what makes a person a child of God (Rom. 8:14-17)."[62] In short, the very essence of the quality of life which we call "being born again" is an infilling of the Holy Spirit. His work of regeneration and transformation is "the hallmark of what it means to be a Christian."[63] Communication between God and those He created is only possible on a spiritual level.[64] It is only through Holy Spirit that we can understand the gospel for our own salvation (1 Corinthians 2:9-13) and then share it with others (Luke 24:49).

As symbols of the Holy Spirit, a dove, fire, breath/wind and water all display the nature, character and work of the Holy Spirit which is otherwise invisible. In true Hebraic fashion, they help us understand various functions of God's Spirit as they provide concreteness to an otherwise nonconcrete notion of God's Spirit. The following quote from scholar Daniel Block is a good way for us to summarize our discussion up to this point.[65]

---

61 Verbrugge, Verlyn D., "1 Corinthians," *The Expositor's Bible Commentary: Romans ~ Galatians*, Vol. 11, Revised edition, edited by Longman III and Garland (Zondervan Academic 2006) 1 Corinthians 12:13, p. 367

62 Fee, Gordon D., *The First Epistle To The Corinthians,* New International Commentary on the New Testament (Eerdmans 1987) 1 Corinthians 12:13, p. 603

63 Dr. Sandra Richter, Q & A Session following Wheaton College lecture, published on June 15, 2015. Retrieved from https://www.youtube.com/watch?v=VLnijooiFEc (last accessed December 24, 2023). Dr. Sandra Richter is an Old Testament scholar, author, international speaker and professor, at Westmont College in Santa Barbara, California

64 Verbrugge, Verlyn D., "1 Corinthians," *The Expositor's Bible Commentary: Romans ~ Galatians*, Vol. 11, Revised edition, edited by Longman III and Garland (Zondervan Academic 2006) 1 Corinthians 2:10b-11, p. 279

65 Block, Daniel I., *The Prophet Of The Spirit: The Use Of Rwh In The Book Of Ezekiel*, Journal of the Evangelical Theological Society, 32 no 1 Mar 1989,

It is clear that in the OT the word *rwh* [*ruah*] bears many different meanings. The nuances intended by the authors vary greatly, and the requirements of the context must determine the interpretation in each instance…. When we think in terms of the OT understanding of the *rwh* of Yahweh … we should think first and foremost of the divine presence on earth. It was on this basis that the psalmist could cry out: "Where can I escape from your *rwh*? / Where can I flee from your presence?" (Ps 139:7). The *rwh* is the agency through which God's will is exercised, whether it be in creation, his dispensing of life, his guidance and providential care, the revelation of his will, his salvation (Isaiah 63), his renewal of unregenerate hearts and minds, or his sealing of his covenant people as his own. The Spirit of Yahweh is not a self-existent agent operating independently. In the words of A. R. Johnson, the divine spirit is an "extension of Yahweh's personality" by which he exercises his influence over the world."[66] The *rwh* is the power of God at work among humankind. It is his creating, animating, energizing force. The *rwh* can hardly be identified as one other than God himself.

The remaining issue I would like to address as part of our Holy Spirit introduction is the fluid nature with which the New Testament speaks about the Spirit, the Father and the Son. A few New Testament verses will serve to highlight two specific questions

---

pp. 27-49, at pp. 48-49. Retrieved from https://www.etsjets.org/files/JETS-PDFs/32/32-1/32-1-pp027-049_JETS.pdf (last accessed December 14, 2023)

66 Johnson, A. R., *The One and the Many in the Israelite Conception of God*, second edition (Cardiff: University of Wales 1961) p. 36 as quoted by Daniel I. Block, *The Prophet Of The Spirit: The Use Of Rwh In The Book Of Ezekiel*, Journal of the Evangelical Theological Society, 32 no 1 Mar 1989, pp. 27-49, at p. 49. Retrieved from https://www.etsjets.org/files/JETS-PDFs/32/32-1/32-1-pp027-049_JETS.pdf (last accessed December 14, 2023)

for us. 1) Does the Son impart Holy Spirit, or does the Father send Him? 2) Is He the Spirit of the Father or the Spirit of the Son?

Jesus says He sends the Holy Spirit: "… And behold, I [Jesus] am sending forth the promise of My Father upon you [the Holy Spirit]; but you are to stay in the city until you are clothed with power from on high." Luke 24:49

John the Baptist says Jesus is the one who will baptize others with the Holy Spirit: "… 'He upon whom you see the Spirit descending and remaining upon Him, this is the One [referring to Jesus] who baptizes in the Holy Spirit' (John 1:33)." "I [Jesus] will ask the Father, and He will give you [the Holy Spirit], that He may be with you forever." John 14:16

Jesus says the Father will send the Holy Spirit: "But the Helper, the Holy Spirit, whom the Father will send in My name [referring to Jesus], He will teach you all things, and bring to your remembrance all that I said to you." John 14:26

Jesus says the Holy Spirit comes from the Father, but He will send Him: "When the [Holy Spirit] comes, whom I [Jesus] will send to you from the Father, that is the Spirit of truth[67] who proceeds from the Father, He will testify about Me." John 15:26

---

67 Dr. David Hill suggests that the best way to understand the phrase "Spirit of truth" is that it refers to "'the Spirit [who] mediates the truth as it is in Jesus.' The fact that [His] activity is to witness to Jesus within the Church and to convict of sin, righteousness and judgment suggests that the Johannine understanding of the Spirit is essentially the same as the Pauline: the Spirit is the powerful impact of the person, work and teaching of Jesus upon the hearts and lives of believers in every generation." Hill, David, *Greek Words and Hebrew Meanings: Studies in the Semantics of Soteriological Terms*, Society for New Testament Studies Monograph Series 5 (Wipf and Stock 2000, previously published Cambridge University Press 1967) p. 293. Notably throughout his work Dr. Hill refers to Holy Spirit with the impersonal

Jesus released the Holy Spirit to His disciples: "And when [Jesus] had said this, he breathed on them and said to them, 'Receive the Holy Spirit....'" John 20:22 ESV

Luke says Jesus receives the Holy Spirit from the Father and then Jesus poured out that Spirit at Pentecost: "Therefore having been exalted to the right hand of God, and having received from the Father the promise of the Holy Spirit, He [Jesus] has poured forth this which you both see and hear." Acts 2:33

Luke calls the Holy Spirit, the "Spirit of Jesus": "... and after they came to Mysia, they were trying to go into Bithynia, and the Spirit of Jesus did not permit them." Acts 16:7

Paul refers to both the Spirit of God and the Spirit of Christ: "However, you are not in the flesh but in the Spirit, if indeed the Spirit of God dwells in you. But if anyone does not have the Spirit of Christ, he does not belong to Him." Romans 8:9

As to our first question, "Who sends the Holy Spirit?" we see that the Bible asserts that it is Jesus who sends the Holy Spirit, but it also asserts that the Father sends Him. Dr. Gregory Lee, assistant professor of theology at Wheaton College, adds some clarity to the matter when he comments that the Spirit does proceed from both the Father and the Son, but not in the same way. He proceeds "derivatively" from the Son. To the extent that Holy Spirit is imparted by the Son it is because the Father has given Him to the Son such that the He can then proceed from the Son. That means the Holy Spirit is sent *derivatively* (we might think of Him as being

---

pronoun "it." His use of "it" is inconsistent with my understanding of Holy Spirit as a person. It is also inconsistent with repeated references to the Spirit in Bible translations using the masculine pronoun "Him." My edits to Dr. Hill's quote are made so as to be consistent with all my other references to the Spirit in this study.

"passed on") from the Son and He does so to complete the work that was started by the Son.[68] Scholar Raymond Brown refers to this as a "tandem relationship."[69] We see this type of relationship a few times in the Old Testament whereby God permitted a man who had been endued with His Spirit to pass it on to the man God designated as his successor. We find this type of tandem successor relationship between Moses and Joshua (Deuteronomy 34:9) and between Elijah and Elisha (2 Kings 2:9,10,15).

Scholar Craig Keener points out that John 15:26 emphasizes *the inseparable relationship between the Father and the Son*:[70]

> The Spirit 'proceeds' from the Father ... but is sent by the Son ... as well as by the Father ... yet even in sending the Spirit, Jesus first receives the Spirit from the Father .... John attempts no precise distinction between the roles of the Father and the Son here except in acknowledging the Father's superior rank; the Father often delegates his own roles to the Son in the Gospel ....Various other early Christian texts likewise appear unconcerned to make stark differentiations between the roles of Father and Son here; some portray the Spirit as from the Father (e.g., Acts 2:17; 5:32; cf. Ep. 1:17; Phil 3:3; 1 Pet 1:12), others perhaps from the Son (cf. Rom 8:2,9; Phil 1:19; 1 Pet 1:11). Early Christians probably regarded the alternatives as complementary rather than contradictory (see esp. Gal 4:6).

Notice that Dr. Keener, like Dr. Lee, refers to the Holy Spirit as *proceeding* from the Father and then as being *sent* by the Son

---

68 Dr. Gregory Lee, Q & A session following Wheaton College lecture, published June 15, 2015. Retrieved from https://www.youtube.com/watch?v=VLni-jooiFEc (last accessed December 24, 2023)

69 Green, Michael, *I Believe in the Holy Spirit*, Revised edition (Eerdmans 2004) p. 52, crediting Raymond Brown for the phrase "tandem relationship"

70 Keener, Craig S., *The Gospel Of John: A Commentary*, Volume Two (Hendrickson Publishers 2003) The World's Hatred ([John] 15:18-16:4) under *3. Witnesses against the World* ([John] 15:26-27) p. 1022

after He first receives the Spirit from the Father. Keener then goes on to point out that this distinction is not crisp and precise in the New Testament because apparently it wasn't the intention of those early Christ-followers "to make stark differentiations between the roles of Father and Son" in this regard.[71]

As to our second question, "Whose Spirit is He?" the Bible refers to Holy Spirit as the Spirit of Christ, but also identifies Him as the Spirit of God. In Paul's usage there is no difference in meaning between the two.[72] In biblical thought, "The Father and the Son are One, one in Being and one in Agency."[73] For clarification, I'll turn to Robert Gundry who comments, "the Spirit of God *is* the Spirit of Christ because Christ and God are one with each other, to have the Spirit in you is to have Christ in you because the Spirit and Christ are one with each other."[74] To Dr. Gundry's point, there is strong biblical emphasis that there is only **one** (*heis*) God[75] even though the Bible clearly refers to Father, Son and Holy Spirit individually. The biblical equation is: "the Spirit = the Spirit of God = the Spirit of Christ."[76] I like how one internet author explained the biblical math: it is $1 \times 1 \times 1 = 1$ not $1+1+1=3$.[77] None of the biblical relationships of "oneness"[78] mean that the related

---

[71] Keener, Craig S., *The Gospel Of John: A Commentary*, Volume Two (Hendrickson Publishers 2003) The World's Hatred ([John] 15:18-16:4) under *3. Witnesses against the World* ([John] 15:26-27) p. 1022

[72] Hill, David, *Greek Words and Hebrew Meanings: Studies in the Semantics of Soteriological Terms*, Society for New Testament Studies Monograph Series 5 (Wipf and Stock 2000, previously published Cambridge University Press 1967) p. 276

[73] Torrance, Thomas F., *The Mediation of Christ* (Helmers & Howard Publishers 1992) p. 23

[74] Gundry, Robert H., *Commentary on the New Testament* (Hendrickson Publishers 2010) Romans 8:9-11, p. 598, italics added

[75] See for example: Ephesians 4:6, 1 Timothy 2:5

[76] Keck, Leander E., *Romans*, Abingdon New Testament Commentaries (Abingdon Press 2005) The Power of the Spirit ([Romans] 8:1-17) p. 201

[77] *Can you explain the Trinity?* EveryStudent.com. Retrieved from http://www.everystudent.com/forum/trinity.html (last accessed December 18, 2021)

[78] In John 10:30 Jesus stated that He and His Father are one (*heis*) and in John 17:21 He prayed: "that [His disciples] may all be one [*heis*]; even as

parties are exactly the same without any distinction. "Within the Jewish vision of one God … we are to see different self-expressions – so different, yet so intimately related …."[79]

A study of the word "one" will be helpful because biblically it often means something other than the numeric number one.

> ### WORD STUDY
>
> *The Greek word heis {hice} is translated as* **one** *in the oneness relationship texts of the Bible (see for example: John 10:30; 17:21). Heis "describes that which is united as one in contrast to that which is divided or consisting of separate parts."*[80] *The biblical emphasis is on "essential unity (unity of essence)."*[81] *Heis can also be translated in a way that unambiguously indicates unity. See for example: John 11:52 HCSB (heis expressed as united) and Romans 15:6 HCSB (heis expressed as unite).*

As we can see, *heis* serves to underscore the fact of cohesive unity, rather than a division of parts. In the words of Keener, the New Testament authors most likely "regarded the alternatives as complementary rather than contradictory."

I acknowledged at the end of our first lesson that understanding the Spirit and His ways can be challenging. The Bible never promises us full and complete knowledge and thankfully our inability to comprehend biblical truths don't make them untrue.

You, Father, are in Me and I in You, that they also may be in Us, so that the world may believe that You sent Me."
79 Wright, N. T., *Paul for Everyone: The Prison Letters* (John Knox Press 2002, 2004) Philippians 2.5-11, p. 103
80 *Ephesians 4:4-6 Commentary*, Precept Austin. Retrieved from http://www.preceptaustin.org/ephesians_44-6.htm (last accessed December 18, 2021)
81 *NET Bible Notes*, translator's note 73, John 10:30

This study aims to help Christ-followers in their pursuit of greater comprehension. As you turn the pages of each lesson I believe your knowledge will grow. As it does, may I encourage you to apply those truths as you learn them? I have found that the best way to increase my Holy Spirit IQ is to actually put into practice the truth I have learned.

Hear What The Spirit is Saying to the Church: *For far too long have my people misunderstood and underestimated the power of My Spirit. I have come to set the record straight. In the days ahead there will be a powerful outpouring of My Spirit and the church will understand that My Word and My Spirit are inseparable in truth. So come learn from Me that you might prosper in the days ahead.*

Lesson 3:

God's Power to Create

 "In the beginning God created the heavens and the earth. The earth was formless and void, and darkness was over the surface of the deep, and the Spirit of God was moving over the surface of the waters." Genesis 1:1-2

WE HAVE ALREADY met God's Spirit as He hovers over the chaos in Genesis 1. You might recall in our first lesson we took note of the fact that, like the wind, the Holy Spirit has the power to set other things in motion. Our Key Scripture informs us that "God is about to transform the inert, disorganized matter, to affect it by His presence, to animate it with His Spirit."[1] Once the Spirit of God is introduced, the Bible never reports that He stopped moving in the earth realm. Recall that Jesus told Nicodemus God's Spirit is compared to the wind which is invisible to our eyes but is *always* in motion from one place to another.[2]

Because the very first activity we see the Spirit of God engaged in is creating, it will be helpful to understand what "create" means biblically.

---

1   Sarna, Nahum M., *The JPS Torah Commentary: Genesis,* The Traditional Hebrew Text with the New JPS Translation Commentary (The Jewish Publication Society 1989) Genesis 1:2 under *a wind from God*, p. 6
2   John 3:8

Word Study

The Hebrew word which is translated as **created** in Genesis 1:1 is bara' {baw-raw}. Its root denotes the concept of initiating a new thing and can refer to bringing something into existence.[3] Bara' can also stress to form something again, reform, or renew (Psalm 51:10; Isaiah 43:15, 65:17).[4] In the Bible it always refers to something which is not capable of being produced by human ability.[5] Therefore, its biblical use is reserved exclusively for "things so great or so novel that they demand God as their agent."[6]

Bara' is a reference to the completed product rather than the raw materials used.[7] The ordinary understanding of "the word lends itself well to the concept of creation ex nihilo [something out of nothing], although that concept is not necessarily inherent within the meaning of the

---

3 Harris, Archer, and Waltke, editors, *Theological Wordbook of the Old Testament* (Moody Press 1999) word #278, p. 127
4 *Psalm 51:10-19 Commentary*, Precept Austin. Retrieved from https://www.preceptaustin.org/psalm_5110-19_commentary (last accessed December 18, 2021)
5 Sarna, Nahum M., *The JPS Torah Commentary: Genesis,* The Traditional Hebrew Text with the New JPS Translation Commentary (The Jewish Publication Society 1989) Genesis 1:1 under *create*, p. 5; Harris, Archer, and Waltke, editors, *Theological Wordbook of the Old Testament* (Moody Press 1999) word #278, p. 127
6 Motyer, J. Alec, *The Prophecy of Isaiah: An Introduction & Commentary* (InterVarsity Press 1993) Isaiah 48:7, p. 378; Harris, Archer, and Waltke, editors, *Theological Wordbook of the Old Testament* (Moody Press 1999) word #278, p. 127
7 Sarna, Nahum M., *The JPS Torah Commentary: Genesis,* The Traditional Hebrew Text with the New JPS Translation Commentary (The Jewish Publication Society 1989) Genesis 1:1 under *create*, p. 5

> *word."*[8] *On the other hand, the idea of God creating de novo as a sole and free act of His own "determination that it should be so" is inherent in the meaning of* bara'.[9]

While God's creative ability is vast, the most frequent use of *bara'* refers to God's acts of the creation of the universe and the natural phenomena. For example, the Bible tells us that, among others things, He created heaven and earth – a merism (Genesis 1:1), humanity (Genesis 1:27), north and south – another merism (Psalm 89:12), righteousness and salvation (Isaiah 4:8), the heavenly host (Isaiah 40:26) and the ends of the earth (Isaiah 40:28). ("[A] merism is a Hebrew idiom which states polar opposites in order to highlight everything that lies in between those opposites").[10] These things "by their greatness or newness or both absolutely require a divine agent."[11]

However, we can't properly understand what it means to bring something into existence until we understand what it meant in the ancient world in which the Bible was written. In our modern Western worldview, we understand something to exist because it materially takes up space or has a form we can describe. In

---

8   Harris, Archer, and Waltke, editors, *Theological Wordbook of the Old Testament* (Moody Press 1999) word #278, p. 127. The idea that God created everything we see out of nothing appears to have its origin in 2 Maccabees, written in the late Second Temple period. Sarna, Nahum M., *The JPS Torah Commentary Genesis* (The Jewish Publication Society 1989) Genesis 1:1 under *create*, p. 5

9   Motyer, J. Alec, *The Prophecy of Isaiah: An Introduction & Commentary* (InterVarsity Press 1993) Isaiah 43:1, p. 330; Motyer, J. Alec, *Isaiah*, Tyndale Old Testament Commentaries (IVP Academic 1999) Isaiah 43:1-7, p. 301

10   Beale, G. K., *Revelation*, The New International Greek Testament Commentary (Eerdmans 1999) p. 199; Motyer, J. Alec, *The Prophecy of Isaiah: An Introduction & Commentary* (InterVarsity Press 1993) Isaiah 10:16, p. 116, totality is expressed by employing a contrasting pair

11   Motyer, J. Alec, *Isaiah*, Tyndale Old Testament Commentaries (IVP Academic 1999) Isaiah 4:5, p. 68

ancient cultures, creation was viewed quite differently. To the ancient people, "something existed when it had a function – a role to play."[12] So *bara'* is best understood as bringing something into functional existence. When we understand the act of creating the way the author of Genesis understood it, we can freshly read the Genesis creation account, focusing on the function of each created element. To illustrate the point, let's use the account of separating day and night:

> Then God said, "Let there be lights in the expanse of the heavens to separate the day from the night, and let them be for signs and for seasons and for days and years; and let them be for lights in the expanse of the heavens to give light on the earth" .... Genesis 1:14-15

God's Spirit brings order out of the chaos by differentiating various roles. For example, day is separated from night, signs are given for changing seasons and light is given on the earth. In Genesis 1:14-19, the function of light is distinguished from the role of darkness and the function of a day is defined differently than the function of night. Every ancient Near Eastern culture believed that "there was a precreation condition of non-functionality characterized by water and darkness."[13] That precreation condition of the universe which lacked function "was remedied by the creative acts that assigned functions by giving names, separating, and bringing functional order to the cosmos."[14]

---

12 Walton, John H., "Genesis," in *Zondervan Illustrated Bible Backgrounds Commentary*, Vol. 1, edited by John H. Walton (Zondervan 2009) Genesis 1:1, p. 11
13 Walton, John H., "Genesis," in *Zondervan Illustrated Bible Backgrounds Commentary*, Vol. 1, edited by John H. Walton (Zondervan 2009) Genesis 1:2, pp. 12-13
14 Walton, John H., "Genesis," in *Zondervan Illustrated Bible Backgrounds Commentary*, Vol. 1, edited by John H. Walton (Zondervan 2009) Genesis 1:2, p. 13

We see a perfect example of this in the Genesis creation narrative. In Genesis when God as King spoke, everything in His Kingdom came into proper order.[15] The chaos became functioning order through the agency of His Spirit thereby demonstrating the greatness of God's power.[16] Thus in the first chapters of the Bible, we are introduced to a power that is beyond compare. We learn that when God chooses to exchange His order for chaos, He employs the agency of Holy Spirit.

Likewise, if God wants to undue His created order so that it returns to a state of chaos, His Spirit is up to the task. Dr. John Currid noticed parallels between the Exodus plagues and the Genesis creation story and concluded that the chaos which resulted from those ten plagues reveals that God was actually undoing or "de-creating" Egypt one plague at a time.[17] According to Currid, "God took the creation order of Genesis 1 and reversed it in Exodus 7-12 for the purpose of reducing order to chaos and bringing judgment upon Egypt."[18] For example, in Genesis 1:1-5 we read that God separated light from darkness. However, in the ninth Egyptian plague, He made darkness prevail over light (Exodus 10:21-29). Or again, in Genesis 1:9-13 we learn that God created vegetation to grow on the land. On the other hand, He used the

---

15 To ancient people, "the cosmos is less like a machine [and] more like a kingdom." Walton, John H., "Genesis," in *Zondervan Illustrated Bible Backgrounds Commentary*, Vol. 1, edited by John H. Walton (Zondervan 2009) Genesis 1:1, p. 11
16 Harris, Archer, and Waltke, editors, *Theological Wordbook of the Old Testament* (Moody Press 1999) word #278, p. 127
17 Dr. Currid is on the faculty of the Reformed Theological Seminary. He has served as Chair of the Biblical Studies Division in Jackson, Professor of Old Testament in Charlotte and as Chancellor's Professor of Old Testament. He is an ordained minister in the Presbyterian Church in America and has served several churches throughout his career. He is also a trained archaeologist.
18 Currid, John D., *Ancient Egypt and the Old Testament* (Baker Books 1997) p. 115

seventh and eighth plagues to destroy Egypt's crops (Exodus 9:18-10:20).[19]

The Egyptians believed that Pharaoh had the power to maintain cosmic order, which they called *ma'at* (universal equilibrium, the cosmic force of harmony, order, stability and security). In their belief, it was Pharaoh's responsibility to maintain *ma'at* by controlling the climate, regulating the seasons and generally preserving order in the world. In ancient thought, if Pharaoh could not maintain *ma'at* in the world, then arguably he could not be the true god.[20] Thus the very process by which God proved His absolute power in Exodus challenged the foundation and the essence of the Egyptian world order. Their world was turned upside down as Yahweh, the God of Israel, demonstrated His unlimited power over all creation. God's Spirit is not mentioned by name anywhere in the Exodus plague narrative. However, because He is God's agent who manifests the will of God on earth it is plausible to conclude His acts of de-creation are simply another expression of His unlimited power – an extension of Himself through which He performs great and mighty deeds.[21]

---

19 See: Currid, John D., *Ancient Egypt and the Old Testament* (Baker Books 1997) p. 115, Figure 3 The Plagues as De-Creation comparing the Genesis creation narrative with the Egyptian plagues

20 "The Pharaohs claimed to be descended from the gods, and were worshipped as such even during their lifetime. The entire land with its population was owned by them." Graetz, H., Professor, *History Of The Jews Volume 1 From the Earliest Period to the Death of Simon The Maccabee (135 BCE)*, Egyptian Idolatry, Chapter 1 (The Jewish Publication Society of America 1891) p. 10. Retrieved from http://www.archive.org/details/historyofje01grae (last accessed April 6, 2024). "The Egyptian king is not merely a 'sacred image' of the deity, but he is a *living* image of the god." Beale, G. K., *We Become What We Worship* (IVP Academic 2008) p. 130, italics in original

21 "In the OT the spirit of the Lord (*rûah yhwh*; LXX, *to pneuma kyriou*) is generally an expression for God's power, the extension of himself whereby he carries our many of his mighty deeds (e.g., Judg. 14:6-20; 1 Sam 11:6)." Elwell, Walter A., editor, *Evangelical Dictionary of Theology*, Second Edition (Baker Academic 1984, 2001) entry for *Holy Spirit* under *The OT*, p. 568

Scholar Scot McKnight observed that in the same way God's Spirit hovered over the chaos in Genesis to bring forth an ordered creation, the Spirit hovers over us as Christ-followers to transform us into the likeness of Christ.[22] The clear witness of the New Testament is that Christ-followers are a "new creation." In short, "'[n]ew creation' means that the life of the future world [which God had promised] has begun in believers now."[23] In fact, Luke's depiction of the disciples receiving the Holy Spirit on Pentecost was "intended to create ... the conviction that the gift of the Spirit to the Church ... inaugurated a New Age, a new order of existence, a new Creation."[24] Let that sink in for a moment. We are not sitting around waiting for the new creation, we are part of the new creation! The first act of this new creation is recorded as Jesus *breathing* on His disciples and instructing them to receive the Holy Spirit. When He breathed on them the age that was to come had begun. "The Holy Spirit is the certain evidence, that the future has dawned, and is also the reliable guarantee of its final consummation."[25]

For those who can read Greek, it would be easy to see that this act of breathing (John 20:22), which inaugurated the new creation, is the same act of breathing which created life in Adam (Genesis 2:7) and restored life to the dead dry bones in Ezekiel 37:9.[26] We'll look at these three verses side-by-side making it easy

---

22 McKnight, Scot, *Open To The Spirit: God In Us, God with Us, God Transforming Us* (Waterbrook 2018) p. 83, noting that this transformation takes place as we gaze into the face of Jesus
23 Keener, Craig S., *The IVP Bible Background Commentary: New Testament* (Intervarsity Press 1993) Galatians 6:15, p. 537
24 Hill, David, *Greek Words and Hebrew Meanings: Studies in the Semantics of Soteriological Terms*, Society for New Testament Studies Monograph Series 5 (Wipf and Stock 2000, previously published Cambridge University Press 1967) p. 259
25 Green, Michael, *I Believe in the Holy Spirit*, Revised edition (Eerdmans 2004) p. 129
26 Most scholars "go on to conclude that because Genesis language first appeared in John 1:1 and now is recapitulated here [in John 20:22], Genesis must be

to see the common thread that runs through them. Of course, John 20:22 was originally written in Greek. On the other hand, when we refer to a Greek word in an Old Testament text which was originally written in the Hebrew language, the reference is to the Greek translation of the Old Testament, called the Septuagint or the LXX.

> And when [Jesus] had said this, He breathed [breathed = *emphusaō*; He breathed = *enephysēsen*] on [His disciples] and *said to them, "Receive the Holy Spirit [*pneuma*]...." John 20:22[27]

> Then the LORD God formed man of dust from the ground, and breathed into [breathed LXX Greek = *emphusaō*; breathed into LXX Greek = *enephysēsen*] into his nostrils the breath [LXX Greek = *pnoe*, a noun related

---

the point of origin for John here in [John] 20:22. Unfortunately, once these parallel motifs are noted, rarely do scholars consider other possible connections .... while the Gen. 2 link is correct to a degree, it fails to satisfy the context completely. The author of Gen 2:7 speaks of breathing the breath of life into humanity by using the term πνοὴν (*pnoēn*/'breath') not πνεῦμα (*pneuma*/'breath' or 'spirit'). It is only Ezek. 37:9 and John 20:22 that use εμφυσάω [*emphusao* {em-foo-sah'-o}] and πνεῦμα [*pneuma* {pnyoo'-mah}]! Also, most fail to make the simultaneous connection between the inbreathing of life and the comments about the covenant of peace found in Ezek. 37:26 (cf. Ezek. 34:25), something that is absent in the Genesis passage .... This seems to clarify for the reader which Old Testament text is being employed by John. Therefore, while connections can be made to the book of Genesis, I [referring to scholar Brian Neil Peterson] believe it was not the central focus of [John]. Yes, John wanted to draw the connection between Jesus and Yahweh as creator (John 1:1)—one who has authority to create both physical and spiritual life. But ... Ezek. 37 also needs to come into view, especially the context of instituting the new covenant of peace." Peterson, Brian Neil, *John's Use of Ezekiel: Understanding the Unique Perspective of the Fourth Gospel* (Fortress Press 2015) p. 173

27 See: Harris, W. Hall, "John," in *The Bible Knowledge Word Study: The Gospels*, edited by Eugene H. Merrill (Victor 2006) John 20:22, p. 382 for the Greek; Levison, John R., *Filled With The Spirit* (Eerdmans 2009) p. 371 for the Greek

to *pneuma*][28] of life; and man became a living being. Genesis 2:7[29]

> Then He said to me, "Prophesy to the breath [Hebrew = *ruah*, LXX Greek = *pneuma*], prophesy, son of man, and say to the breath [Hebrew = *ruah*, LXX Greek = *pneuma*], 'Thus says the Lord GOD, "Come from the four winds [Hebrew = *ruah*, LXX Greek = *pneuma*], O breath [Hebrew = *ruah*, LXX Greek = *pneuma*], and breathe on [LXX Greek = *emphysēson*] these slain, that they come to life."'"[30] So I prophesied as He commanded me, and the breath [Hebrew = *ruah*, LXX Greek = *pneuma*] came into them, and they came to life and stood on their feet, an exceedingly great army. Ezekiel 37:9-10

Thayer's Greek Lexicon indicates that the Hebrew word *ruah* is one of the primary meanings that *emphusaō* [*enephysēsen*] has in view.[31] After God formed Adam from the dust He "breathed into his nostrils the breath of life; and man became a living being."[32] On a much larger scale, centuries later, Ezekiel saw an entire valley of dry bones and heard God say He was about to fill them with breath so they could come to life.[33] Ezekiel then prophesied to God's Spirit, as he was instructed, commanding breath [God's *ruah*] to come forth. Ezekiel watched as the *ruah* of God entered the dead bones and with new life, they stood to their feet.[34] This

---

28 Henry Neufeld Email to Deborah Roeger January 12, 2024
29 See: Levison, John R., *Filled With The Spirit* (Eerdmans 2009) p. 371 for the Greek translation of the original Hebrew
30 See: Levison, John R., *Filled With The Spirit* (Eerdmans 2009) p. 371 for the Greek translation of the original Hebrew
31 *Thayer's Greek Lexicon*, entry for *emphusaó*. Retrieved from https://biblehub.com/thayers/1720.htm (last accessed December 22, 2023)
32 Genesis 2:7
33 Ezekiel 37:5
34 Ezekiel 37:9-10

was the same animated, life-giving breath that God had breathed into Adam.

The biblical stage was ready, the divine pattern had been set, for God to send forth His *ruah* and breathe life back into the crucified body of Jesus. Later Paul would affirm, "So also it is written, 'The first man, Adam, became a living soul.' The last Adam became a life-giving spirit."[35] The phrase "it is written" is the way New Testament authors alerted their readers that they were preparing to quote from the only Scripture they knew at that time – the Tanakh (what we call the Old Testament). So what Old Testament verse does Paul quote here? It is Genesis 2:7, the account of God breathing life into Adam during creation.

You may recall that in ancient Hebrew thought "breath" is another word for God's Spirit.[36] We can metaphorically imagine these two life-giving power events taking place in this way. At the creation of the first Adam, God exhaled His power. When Adam received God's power-filled breath in his nostrils, he inhaled God's Spirit-created life. As a result, his lifeless body took on life. In the tomb of His Son, God exhaled His power. When Jesus received His Father's power-filled breath in His nostrils, He inhaled God's Spirit-created life. As He did His lifeless body overcame death! What God did for His Son, His Son does for every one of His disciples. He breathes on them and they receive new life.[37] "The

---

35 1 Corinthians 15:45, uppercase text and italics omitted
36 The three terms "breath," "wind," and "spirit," are represented in the Hebrew by the word *ruah*.
37 John 20:21-22. Scholars see this as an unmistakable allusion to Genesis 2:7. See for example: "Most scholars concur that when Jesus breathes on the disciples, John is alluding to the creative, life-imparting act of God in Gen 2:7 …." Keener, Craig S., *The Gospel Of John: A Commentary*, Volume Two (Hendrickson Publishers 2003) 1E. Empower for the Mission ([John] 20:22) p. 1204. See also: Westcott, Brooke Foss, *The Gospel According to St. John: The Greek Text with Introduction and Notes*, Vol. II (John Murray Publishing Company 1908) John 20:22, p. 350 pointing out that "[t]he same image which was used to describe the communication of the natural

old creation began with the breath of God; now the new creation begins with the breath of God the Son."[38] The death, burial and resurrection of Christ has set the new creation in motion. "Now Christ, who is himself life-giving spirit, will thrive within believers."[39]

Having identified the power source behind new creation, let's look at the two explicit Scriptures establishing the fact that every true Messiah-follower is a *new creation*.[40]

> Therefore if anyone is in Christ, **he is a new** [*kainos*] **creature** [*ktisis*]; the old things passed away; behold, new things have come. 2 Corinthians 5:17, bold added

> Those who desire to make a good showing in the flesh try to compel you to be circumcised, simply so that they will not be persecuted for the cross of Christ. For those who are circumcised do not even keep the Law themselves, but they desire to have you circumcised so that they may boast in your flesh. But may it never be that I would boast, except in the cross of our Lord Jesus Christ, through which the world has been crucified to me, and I to the world. For neither is circumcision any-

---

life, is here used to express the communication of the new, spiritual life of re-created humanity."

38 *Spirit Filled Life Bible* (Thomas Nelson Publishers 1991) study note John 20:22 under *Receive the Holy Spirit*, p. 1613
39 Levison, John R., *Filled With The Spirit* (Eerdmans 2009) p. 316
40 Scholar John Grassmick points out that the only two uses of the phrase "new creation" are found in Galatians 6:15 and 2 Corinthians 5:17. (Note: the Grassmick entry cites 1 Corinthians 5:17 in error, the correct citation is 2 Corinthians 5:17). Grassmick, John D., "Galatians," in *The Bible Knowledge Word Study: Acts-Ephesians*, edited by Darrell L. Bock (Victor 2002) Galatians 6:15, p. 416

thing, nor uncircumcision, **but a new** [*kainos*] **creation** [*ktisis*]. And those who will walk by this rule, peace and mercy be upon them, and upon the Israel of God. Galatians 6:12-16, bold added

Let's first address the phrase "in Christ" which Paul used in 2 Corinthians 5:17, in addition to his other numerous uses of this expression as he wrote his epistles.[41] While Paul doesn't always employ this phrase in exactly the same way,[42] it is read-

---

41 By one author's count Paul employs the phrase "in Christ" or the similar expressions "in the Lord" or "in Him" 164 times. Stott, John R. W., *'In Christ': The Meaning and Implications of the Gospel of Jesus Christ*, C.S. Lewis Institute, June 3, 2007. Retrieved from https://www.cslewisinstitute.org/resources/in-christ-the-meaning-and-implications-of-the-gospel-of-jesus-christ/ (last accessed February 26, 2024)

42 See for example: Cohick, Linn H., *The Letter To The Ephesians*, The New International Commentary on the New Testament (Eerdmans 2020) *Excurses: "In Christ,"* pp. 91-94, quote from p. 94, citing Campbell, p. 69. Cohick points to the work of Constantine Campbell, *Paul and Union with Christ: An Exegetical and Theological Study* (Zondervan 2012), indicating she "focuses on the range of meanings within the [preposition *en*] used in the phrase. The preposition *en* has an extensive semantic range, including a locative or spatial ('in' or 'in the sphere of'), instrumental ('with'), and causal meaning ('because of' or 'on account of')." That means that context of the phrase "in Christ" is the determinative factor to understand its meaning. Campbell argues that in Ephesians 1:3 Paul employs "in Christ" in its instrumental sense to indicate that "God accomplishes redemption through Christ." Ibid, Cohick, p. 94. On the other hand, scholar William Klein suggests that while Paul's use of "in Christ" in Ephesians 1:3 may have an instrumental sense in that "the blessings comes through Christ," the rest of Ephesians points to the locative or spatial sense as dominant meaning referring to inclusion in Christ. Klein, William W., "Ephesians," in *The Expositor's Bible Commentary: Ephesians - Philemon*, Vol. 12, Revised edition, edited by Longman III and Garland (Zondervan Academic 2006) Ephesians 1:3, p. 48. See also: Fuller, Reginald, *Aspects of Pauline Christology*, Review and Expositor 71, no. 1 (1974) pp. 5-17 (identifying four different uses of the expression "in Christ" in Paul's writings) and Colijn, Brenda B., Paul's Use of the 'In Christ' Formula, Ashland Theological Journal 23 (1991) pp. 9–26 (identifying five different uses of this phrase). Both articles are quoted in *What does the phrase 'ἐν Χριστῷ' in the Pauline Corpus mean?* Biblical Hermeneutics Stack

ily recognized that this is a way Paul refers to a true *talmid* of Christ.[43] When the Apostle John used this phrase he appears to equate being "in Christ" with abiding in Him and He in us which is made possible "because He has given us of His Spirit (1 John 4:13)." When He is permitted to lead, the indwelling Holy Spirit ensures there is a shared common will, plan and purpose between Christ, the Father and the followers of Christ.

It will be helpful to consider both the word "new" and the word "creature/creation" as used in our Scripture quotes from 2 Corinthians 5 and Galatians 6. I have highlight both terms in bold text in the verses I've quoted. We will begin with the word "new" as used in the phrase *new creation*.

Word Study

*The Greek word which is translated as **new** in 2 Corinthians 5:17 and Galatians 6:15 is kainos {kahee-nos'}. When kainos is used to refer to something new as to its form, it means recently made, fresh, recent, unused, unworn. As a reference to a new substance, kainos means of a new kind, unprecedented, novel, uncommon, unheard of.*

Kainos contrasts what is new in kind and to what previously existed. In other words, it can denote something which takes the place of. Kainos is equivalent to "not yet

---

Exchange, greek. Retrieved from https://hermeneutics.stackexchange.com/questions/20035/what-does-the-phrase-%E1%BC%90%CE%BD-%CE%A7%CF%81%CE%B9%CF%83%CF%84%E1%BF%B7-in-the-pauline-corpus-mean (last accessed February 26, 2024)

43 Refer to the Preface where the Hebrew term *talmid* meaning disciple is described in detail.

having been."[44] *Something newly introduced which is implicitly better because it is different.*[45]

Neos is another Greek word translated as "new." *Neos* refers to something new in time, to something that recently has come into existence. By contrast, *kainos* refers to something that is new in quality and is distinguished from what has seen previous service, is worn out, consumed, depleted, or has been blemished in some way through age.[46] It denotes new as newly introduced or current, not known before.[47]

Let's add to our understanding with a Word Study on "creature/creation."

> ### WORD STUDY
>
> *The Greek noun translated as* **creature** *in 2 Corinthians 5:17 and* **creation** *in Galatians 6:15 is ktisis {ktis'-is}. The verb form of ktisis is ktizo which expresses the "basic act of will behind the bringing into being, foundation or institution of something."*[48]

---

44 "*Kainos* is new in kind and in contrast to what previously existed, so taking the place thereof. In that sense *kainos* looks backward, while its synonym *neos* looks forward. *Kainos* is equivalent to 'not yet having been': *neos* is 'not having long been.'" Omicron, T. Oliver, *The Two Word Aspects of "New,"* STEM Publishing, Magazines, Scripture Quarterly. Retrieved from http://www.stempublishing.com/magazines/SQ/NEW2ASPC.html (last accessed December 18, 2021)

45 Zodhiates, Spiros, *The Complete Word Study Dictionary: New Testament* (AMG Publishers 1992) word #2537, p. 804

46 Trench, R. C., *Trench's New Testament Synonyms*, entry for *new*. Retrieved from http://studybible.info/trench/New (last accessed December 18, 2021)

47 Zodhiates, Spiros, *The Complete Word Study Dictionary: New Testament* (AMG Publishers 1992) word #3501, p. 1007

48 *Romans 1:20-21 Commentary*, Precept Austin, quoting Gerald Cowen, *Salvation Word Studies From The Greek New Testament* (Broadman Press

> *Ktisis can denote bringing something into existence that did not exist before.*[49] *It can also refer to the act of creating and forming in a spiritual sense.*[50] *In the New Testament, ktisis is always connected with creative acts of God.*[51]

When the Old Testament was translated from Hebrew to Greek, *ktizo* – the verb form of *ktisis* –was chosen as one of the words to translate the Hebrew verb *bara'*.[52] *Ktisis* does not describe the finished product, nor does it describe the entire process. It is not an end in and of itself. *Ktisis* is the jumping-off point, the start of something new.

Just as God was the source of new life in the crucified body of Jesus, His new creation breath is the source of new life in everyone who chooses to follow Him. Rick Renner, the author of *Spiritual Gems from the Greek*, provides a creative way to describe what happens when breath enters its subject.[53]

> If I hold a deflated balloon that is without form to my lips and breathe into it, the balloon will inflate. The blowing of *my breath* . . . causes it to fill up so that its true

---

1990). Retrieved from http://www.preceptaustin.org/romans_1 (last accessed December 18, 2021)

49 *2 Corinthians 5:17 Commentary*, Precept Austin. Retrieved from https://www.preceptaustin.org/2corinthians_517_commentary (last accessed December 18, 2021)

50 Zodhiates, Spiros, *The Complete Word Study Dictionary: New Testament* (AMG Publishers 1992) word #2936, p. 896

51 *2 Corinthians 5:17 Commentary*, Precept Austin. Retrieved from https://www.preceptaustin.org/2corinthians_517_commentary (last accessed December 18, 2021)

52 *Sermon Index.net*, entry for *Greek Word Studies: Creation (2937) ktisis*. Retrieved from http://www.sermonindex.net/modules/articles/index.php?view=article&aid=33771 (last accessed December 18, 2021)

53 Renner, Rick, *Sparkling Gems from the Greek* (Harrison House Publishers 2003) May 2, p. 299, italics in original

form becomes visible. When the balloon is fully inflated, I tie a knot at the base to trap the air within. Now the air that filled up the balloon and caused it to take form is the same substance that empowers it to *sustain* its form. It was my breath that created its form, and it is my breath that now sustains it. And if the molecules inside the balloon were analyzed, it would be found that a part of me is held inside in the form of the air I breathed into it.

As we have already noted, after His resurrection, Jesus breathed on His first disciples and said, "Receive the Holy Spirit." When His disciples inhaled His breath, those *molecules* containing new life became a part of their DNA. The same Holy Spirit He had received from His Father now resided in them. That Spirit which had been derivatively imparted by the resurrected Christ[54] was life-giving and life-sustaining power capable of creating new life in them. The wonderful news is that what He did for His first disciples He has continued to do for every true disciple since then! The same power that breathed new life into Jesus' dead body breathes new life into every Christ-follower. Holy Spirit brings with Him all the work Christ accomplished in His life, His death, His burial and His resurrection to new life.[55] "The indwelling of the Spirit is, of course, metaphorical. If we [could see inside] our bodies we will not find the Holy Spirit visible there. He inhabits our human spirit, which is immaterial by nature, just as God is (John 4:24). This means that what he brings with him into our

---

54 Refer back to Lesson 2 for the concept that the Holy Spirit proceeds derivatively from Christ.

55 Averbeck, Richard E., *The Holy Spirit in the Hebrew Bible and Its Connections to the New Testament* (2009) under *Pouring, Drinking, And The "Indwelling" Of The Holy Spirit*. Retrieved from https://bible.org/seriespage/holy-spirit-hebrew-bible-and-its-connections-new-testament (last accessed January 22, 2024). This article is included in Wallace, Daniel B. and Sawyer, M. James, editors, *Who's Afraid Of The Holy Spirit? An Investigation Into The Ministry Of The Spirit Of God Today* (Biblical Studies Press 2013).

lives is the full force of 'the things freely given to us by God' in Christ Jesus (1 Cor 2:12)."[56]

So now that we understand more fully how new creation takes place, let's consider why it matters to us that we are new creatures in Christ. Redemption and creation are biblically interwoven.[57] *Kainos* is used to designate those "[t]hings brought into being by the redemptive work of Jesus."[58] The very idea of redemption implies that the redeemed subject was in bondage. That said, redemption in the Bible "refers primarily to man's subjection to the dominion and curse of sin . . . ."[59] Before Christ redeemed us we were being held captive to the bondage of Satan who is the ruler of the kingdom of darkness and to the bondage of death which is the penalty of sin. The new creation was initiated by the redemptive work of the cross which, as a practical matter means, there is a new King on the throne – His name is King Jesus.

In between the first coming of Christ and His return, the new creation overlaps the old creation. Theologians call this present age in which we live the "already and not yet" Kingdom of God. Some scholars suggest a more accurate term is, "already, not full."[60]

---

56 Averbeck, Richard E., *The Holy Spirit in the Hebrew Bible and Its Connections to the New Testament* (2009) under *Pouring, Drinking, And The "Indwelling" Of The Holy Spirit*. Retrieved from https://bible.org/seriespage/holy-spirit-hebrew-bible-and-its-connections-new-testament (last accessed January 22, 2024)

57 Ryken, Wilhoit, and Longman III, editors, *Dictionary of Biblical Imagery* (Intervarsity Press 1998) entry for *Creation* under *Redemption as Creation*, p. 181. G. K. Beale asserts that throughout the New Testament the overlapping ideas of new creation, resurrection to eternal life, temple and God's Kingship [His Kingdom] "are inextricably linked and are facets of one another." Beale, G. K., *A New Testament Biblical Theology: The Unfolding Of The Old Testament In The New* (Baker Academic 2011) pp. 741-742

58 Grassmick, John D., "Galatians," in *The Bible Knowledge Word Study: Acts-Ephesians*, edited by Darrell L. Bock (Victor 2002) Galatians 6:15, p. 416

59 Unger, Merrill F., *The New Unger's Bible Dictionary* (Moody Press 1988) entry for *Redemption*, pp. 1068-1069, Scripture references omitted in quote

60 I credit R. T. France with the phrase "already, not full." It speaks to an inaugurated invisible version of the kingship of God in Messiah, and the fact

That's because we are experiencing a *foretaste* of God's Kingdom now, as we await a *full taste* in the future.

> Jesus … vigorously proclaimed that he was launching the invasion of God's kingdom into human society. From now on the kingdom was inaugurated, but it was not yet consummated. And the first Christians caught on to this understanding with enthusiasm. The End had dawned with the coming of Jesus, his death, resurrection and gift of the Spirit. They lived now between the times. This present age, the age of the flesh, lay behind them. The coming age, the age of the Spirit, lay ahead of them. But not entirely ahead. Even now they experienced the Spirit, the gift of the end-time. Even now they knew God's salvation, even though that salvation was still to be experienced in all its fulness at the final coming of Christ. Even now they could anticipate the final verdict of 'acquitted', though they had to struggle to show forth that righteous character in their lives. Even now they knew Jesus had been raised from the dead, the firstfruit of a glorious crop to come, although they still had to face their own death.… The 'age to come' was no longer exclusively future. It had begun, and they were the people of the future living in the land of the present.… The Holy Spirit is the certain evidence that the future had dawned, and is also the reliable guarantee of its final consummation.… The Spirit is a 'first instalment, a down payment'.… and is, at the same time, the pledge of all the future holds in store.[61]

---

    that we are seeking and praying for the visible fullness of the kingship of God to come on earth, as it is in heaven. The essence of this phrase speaks the fact that we've had a "foretaste" of God's Kingdom, but we have not yet experienced the "full taste."

61 Green, Michael, *I Believe in the Holy Spirit*, Revised edition (Eerdmans 2004) pp. 128-129

Even though we are not yet delivered from the *presence* of evil in this age, every Christ-follower "can experience deliverance from the *power* of this present evil age right now."[62] In the words of Joni Eareckson Tada, "Yes, we all still deal with the presence of sin in our lives, but its sway over us has been destroyed. We no longer *must* sin."[63] The truth that we can presently experience deliverance from the "power" exerted by Satan's kingdom has everything to do with the fact that we are a new creation in Christ! We begin with the truth that:

> Now we have received, not the spirit of the world, but the Spirit who is from God, so that we may know the things freely given to us by God. 1 Corinthians 2:12

The following quote from scholar Murray J. Harris nicely summarizes the act of new creation in the life of a Christ-follower.[64]

> [Becoming a Christ-follower involves] a total restructuring of life that alters its whole fabric—thinking, feeling, willing, and acting. Anyone who is "in Christ" is "Under New Management" and has "Altered Priorities Ahead" ….

Throughout the New Testament, we frequently find *spirit* and *power* being associated making it clear that the Holy Spirit is the

---

62 Guzik, David, *Galatians 1 – Challenging a Different Gospel*, Enduring Word, bold in original has been omitted, italics in original has been retained. Retrieved from https://enduringword.com/bible-commentary/galatians-1/ (last accessed July 22, 2021)

63 Tada, Joni Eareckson, *The 'In Christ Alone' Stanza That Makes Joni Want to Leap*, The Gospel Coalition article, January 14, 2024, italics in original. Retrieved from https://www.thegospelcoalition.org/article/in-christ-alone-stanza/ (last accessed February 26, 2024)

64 Harris, Murray J., "2 Corinthians," in *The Expositor's Bible Commentary: Romans – Galatians*, Vol. 11, Revised edition, edited by Longman III and Garland (Zondervan Academic 2006) 2 Corinthians 5:17, p. 481

One who imparts power to us.[65] That creative power indwells every *talmid*[66] day in and day out equipping, enabling and empowering them to do all that God commands. Let me illustrate that truth this way. Imagine you have been asked to cross a very wide lake. The only thing you have is a row boat, but you no longer have the oars. So, you launch the boat and begin to paddle across the lake with your hands. You haven't gotten very far off shore when a friend comes by and loans you his speedboat with three large high-powered engines on the back. Without Holy Spirit's power our attempts to live an obedient life pleasing to God resemble being in that rowboat without oars. However, with His power we're like that speedboat with its high-powered engines!

Paul compares Christ-followers to worthless clay jars who are filled with God's power so as to highlight the fact that "this surpassing power [*dunamis*]" is *God's* power not their own (2 Corinthians 4:7)! By virtue of being a new creation in Christ, the power supplied by the Holy Spirit enables us to turn down every temptation from Satan to disobey King Jesus. Every act of obedience to Him further advances His Kingship and His Kingdom rule on earth as it is in heaven. As such, every act of obedience strikes another blow against Satan's rulership.

While there is overlap in the kingdoms at present, Paul makes it abundantly clear that as to the life of a Christ-follower "there is no neutral sphere between the old and new creations, no area of [commonality] between the spirit of the world and the spirit that is from God. There is no safe-zone in which [Christ-followers] can find refuge.... If [Christ-followers] attempt to hold on to [worldly] values while claiming to belong in a community of ultimate truths, they forfeit the latter and retain only the former ...."[67] Because Christ-followers really are the beginning of God's

---

65 *ESV Study Bible* (Crossway Books 2008) study note Luke 1:16-17 under *spirit and power*, p. 1944, citing Luke 4:14; Acts 1:8; 10:38; Romans15:13; 1 Corinthians 2:4; Ephesians. 3:16; 1 Thessalonians. 1:5; 2 Timothy 1:7

66 Hebrew word for disciple. See Preface for explanation of its use in this this study.

67 Levison, John R., *Filled With The Spirit* (Eerdmans 2009) p. 282

end-time new creation, "they must act the way new creatures act, which is to live for Christ by viewing all of reality from the perspective of his word and not from the viewpoint of the world."[68]

It's just a few days before Christmas as I am editing this particular lesson. Many excited children will soon be opening gifts that come in boxes with this warning label, "batteries not included." Unless the batteries are supplied, whatever is inside that box will not be able to do what it is designed to do. That's a pretty good analogy for the gift of the Holy Spirit.[69] "The Spirit [pours out] the love of God in our hearts to secure the indwelling of the Son and His love to such an extent that Christ may be formed within us, and our whole inner man will bear the imprint of His likeness."[70] However, the Spirit comes with an implicit warning label. Unless we permit Him to radically transform us from the inside out and allow Him to lead in the ordinary course of life, He will not be able to do what God intends Him to do!

> Every faculty of our nature, every moment of our life, and every religious work of our body, soul, and spirit must be surrendered to the power of the Spirit of God. In nothing can independent control or independent force have a place. Everything must be under the leading of the Spirit.[71]

> [To] be filled with the Spirit of God .... [d]emands inevitably that the present occupant and governor of the heart, our individual self, be cast out and everything be surrendered into the hands of the new inhabitant, the

---

68 Beale, G. K., *A New Testament Biblical Theology: The Unfolding Of The Old Testament In The New* (Baker Academic 2011) p. 303

69 Towns, Elmer, *The Names of the Holy Spirit*, Chapter 7 under *The Principle of Personal Power*. Retrieved from https://www.ntslibrary.com/PDF%20Books/The_Names_Of_The_HolySpirit[ETowns].pdf (last accessed April 10, 2024)

70 Murray, Andrew, *Experiencing The Holy Spirit* (Whitaker House 1984) p. 86

71 Murray, Andrew, *Experiencing The Holy Spirit* (Whitaker House 1984) p. 66

Spirit of God....He alone [must] be acknowledged as our Life and our Leader.[72]

By our own power we are only able to "reform (become *néos*), but by God's activity, [we become] *kainós*, qualitatively new."[73] Of course, that will require us to become very proficient at recognizing the conviction of the Holy Spirit and choosing to quickly align with whatever way He leads. As we do, we experience deliverance from the *power* of this present evil age right now, even though we are not yet delivered from the *presence* of evil in this age.

At our new creation, the work begins and it is the Holy Spirit who guides each new creature step-by-step in our vital regenerative work. Observable evidence of that transformative work is what scholar Scot McKnight calls "the surefire test to know the Spirit is at work in your life."[74] In the words of A. W. Tozer, "The Holy Spirit never enters a man and then lets him live like the world."[75] Because that is true, every Christ-follower's testimony should include a BC part (what life looked like before Christ) and an WC portion (what life looks like with Christ). As McKnight points out, as you grow toward Christlikeness, the change won't always be dramatic, nor will it always involve giants leaps from old nature (BC) to new nature behavior (WC). However, when the Spirit is at work in our life then there will be "visible change, shifts, movements, and growth."[76]

What the Holy Spirit began in new creation He intends to finish. The Apostle John was privileged to receive a vision of the

---

[72] Murray, Andrew, *Experiencing The Holy Spirit* (Whitaker House 1984) p. 56
[73] Zodhiates, Spiros, *The Complete Word Study Dictionary: New Testament* (AMG Publishers 1992) word #3501, p. 1008
[74] McKnight, Scot, *Open To The Spirit: God In Us, God with Us, God Transforming Us* (Waterbrook 2018) p. 80
[75] Tozer, A. W., *The Mystery Of The Holy Spirit*, edited by Rev. James L. Snyder (Bridge-Logos Foundation 2007) Chapter 1. Retrieved from file:///C:/Users/Deb/Downloads/Tozer_-Mystery-of-the-Holy-Spir-A.-W.-Tozer-Naijasermons.com_.ng_.pdf (last accessed December 18, 2023)
[76] McKnight, Scot, *Open To The Spirit: God In Us, God with Us, God Transforming Us* (Waterbrook 2018) p. 80

new heaven and earth while in exile on Patmos. The end-time fulfillment of the new creation is realized by the presence and work of the Holy Spirit.[77] That will be the subject of our last lesson in this study. Before we get there, we are going to learn that the new creation life that begins by the power of Holy Spirit can only be lived by means of Holy Spirit.[78]

Hear What The Spirit is Saying to the Church: *Yes, I create all things new and I have never stopped creating. By the power of My Spirit I create. Never underestimate the power of My Spirit to be at work in your life when you come to know Me. He is able to do exceedingly more than you can ask or imagine. Sadly, too few ask and too few imagine. Will you begin to ask and imagine today? My Spirit is waiting.*

---

77 Ferguson and Wright, editors, Packer, J. I., consulting editor, *New Dictionary of Theology* (InterVarsity Press 1988) entry for *New Testament Theology* under 2 Structure and Content, f. An analytic NT theology, p. 465, citing Romans 8:23; 2 Corinthians 1:22; 5:5; Ephesians 1:14

78 Rapa, Robert K., "Galatians," in *The Expositor's Bible Commentary: Romans - Galatians*, Vol. 11, Revised edition, edited by Longman III and Garland (Zondervan Academic 2008) Galatians 6:15, p. 638

LESSON 4:

JESUS THE PERFECT EXAMPLE

 "Jesus, full of the Holy Spirit, returned from the Jordan and was led around by the Spirit in the wilderness." Luke 4:1

SO FAR, WE have considered the power of God's Spirit operating in His role as the agent of God's creative and de-creative will at work in the cosmos. In this lesson, we want to shift gears a bit and move from the global display of power to the personal manifestation of power. Our Key Scripture for this lesson highlights the exercise of the kind of Spirit-power we want to explore in this lesson. Keep in mind it is the very *same* Spirit at work in each of the contexts we are exploring in this study. What differs is how God's power is revealed or demonstrated through His Spirit.

Paul told the church at Colossae that Jesus is the firstborn over all creation. The MIT[1] translation helps to clearly make the point I want to make here: "He is the image of the invisible God. He is *the prototype* of all creation."[2] As a prototype, Jesus serves as our model for the Spirit's creative power at work in and through the human spirit. The book of Hebrews refers to Jesus as the "author and perfecter of our faith"[3] where the word "author" is the Greek word *archegos* {ar-khay-gos'}. In the Greek language, it is a term

---

1 MacDonald, William Graham, *The Idiomatic Translation of the New Testament*, electronic version 2012. Retrieved from BibleWorks software
2 Colossians 1:15 MIT, italics added, asterisk omitted before beginning of second sentence
3 Hebrews 12:2

"used for. . . those *who cut a path forward for their followers* and whose exploits for humanity were rewarded by exaltation."[4] The Greek word translated as "perfecter" is *teleiotes* {tel-i-o-tace'}. It belongs to a word group denoting completion or reaching an intended goal, particularly when a prize is involved.[5] Jesus reveals what God's offspring looks like (acts like) in the flesh. Dallas Williard defines spiritual transformation as "basically [referring] to the Spirit-driven process of forming the inner world of the human self in such a way that it becomes like the inner being of Christ himself."[6] As sons and daughters of God we are called to be like Jesus. Through His perfect obedience, Jesus forged the path for His disciples. He has made a way for us to follow in His footsteps. We are equipped and enabled to do so because we have available to us the very same power He used to accomplish His Father's will. We will have more to say about that in our next lesson.

There are differences between Hebraic and Greek culture and language. As we learned in our first lesson, the Hebrew language does not easily lend itself to the abstract concepts.[7] On the other hand, if the Bible had been written by Greek-minded authors we would likely find its pages filled with long narratives containing lots of abstract words and ideas about the nature of God. However, since the biblical authors were Hebrew, those types of descriptions

---

4   Keener, Craig S., *The IVP Bible Background Commentary New Testament* (Intervarsity Press 1993) Hebrews 2:10, p. 654, italics added

5   Zodhiates, Spiros, *The Complete Word Study Dictionary: New Testament* (AMG Publishers 1992) word #5051, p. 1375

6   Williard, Dallas, *Renovation of the Heart: Putting on the Character of Christ* (NavPress 2002) p. 22 as quoted by Scot McKnight, *Open To The Spirit: God In Us, God with Us, God Transforming Us* (Waterbrook 2018) p. 81

7   Harris, Archer, and Waltke, editors, *Theological Wordbook of the Old Testament* (Moody Press 1999) word#1596b, p. 660, noting that the ideas of strength and security are abstract and are therefore biblically expressed in pictorial ways. For example, strength is depicted as the ability to stand like a mountain (Psalm 30:7); God's strength is a strong tower (Psalm 61:3); God's strength and ability to deliver and protect is pictured as a rock (Psalm 62:7).

are conspicuously and understandably absent.[8] Accordingly, the Bible never offers us doctrinal speeches or clear orderly descriptions of *how* the power of God's Spirit works. The biblical authors wrote about God's mighty deeds which *show* us in action what His power is like. It is in the framework of human experience that His power is revealed. As we pointed out in our last lesson, the Old Testament *always* makes Yahweh's nature known by His mighty deeds, His acts of power.[9]

The same can be said about the New Testament. In that regard, there are two such revealing narratives I want to explore in this lesson. Both provide us with an example of how Jesus was able to accomplish His Father's will by the power of Holy Spirit. The first is His wilderness temptation and the second is His struggle in the Garden of Gethsemane.

Victory in the Wilderness

To set the stage, you will recall that when Jesus was baptized by John the Spirit descended on Him like a dove and remained on Him.[10] Mark describes the descent of the Spirit using the Greek preposition *eis* (Mark 1:10). Because *eis* usually means "into" Mark may have intended his readers to understand that the Spirit descended *into* Jesus, not simply rested *upon* Him.[11] When John said the Spirit *remained* on Jesus, he used the Greek verb *meno* {men'-o} expressing a permanent relationship. In other words, Scripture makes clear that Jesus permanently possessed the Holy Spirit.[12]

As stated in our Key Scripture for this lesson, one of the first things the Spirit did was to lead Jesus into the Judean wilderness.

---

[8] Refer to Preface footnote 15 regarding latest research on Luke which contends that absent evidence otherwise even Luke must be held to be Jewish.
[9] Longman and Garland, editors, *The Expositor's Bible Commentary: 5 Psalms*, Revised edition (Zondervan 2008) *Reflections: The Praise of Yahweh*, p. 506
[10] John 1:32
[11] Levison, Jack, *An Unconventional God: The Spirit according to Jesus* (Baker Academic 2020) p. 49
[12] *NET Bible Notes*, study note 84, John 1:32

God had important work for Him to do there! After fasting for 40 days and 40 nights Jesus squared off against Satan in three recorded wilderness confrontations.[13] Luke describes these events to his readers in this way.

> Jesus, full of the Holy Spirit, returned from the Jordan and was led around by the Spirit in the wilderness for forty days, being tempted by the devil. And He ate nothing during those days, and when they had ended, He became hungry. And the devil said to Him, "If You are the Son of God, tell this stone to become bread." And Jesus answered him, "It is written, 'Man shall not live on bread alone.'"
>
> And he led Him up and showed Him all the kingdoms of the world in a moment of time. And the devil said to Him, "I will give You all this domain and its glory; for it has been handed over to me, and I give it to whomever I wish. Therefore if You worship before me, it shall all be Yours." Jesus answered him, "It is written, 'You shall worship the Lord your God and serve Him only.'" And he led Him to Jerusalem and had Him stand on the pinnacle of the temple, and said to Him, "If You are the Son of God, throw Yourself down from here; for it is written, 'He will command His angels concerning You to guard You,' and, 'On their hands they will bear You up, So that You will not strike Your foot against a stone.'"
>
> And Jesus answered and said to him, "It is said, 'You shall not put the Lord your God to the test.'" Luke 4:1-12

---

13 In Lesson 8 we'll take some time to consider the biblical origin of Satan and learn more about his adversarial characteristics.

The Power of My Spirit

Jesus emerged from the wilderness testing victorious.[14] He had met the adversary face to face and prevailed every time. We might be inclined to explain away His remarkable victories by insisting that He was, after all, God! But such a summary dismissal would cause us to miss one of the primary reasons God permitted these verbal assaults in the first place. In everything Jesus did, He modeled for us how to overcome the adversary. Paul informs us that when Jesus was born of the virgin Mary through the power of Holy Spirit He "emptied Himself, taking the form of a bond-servant, *and* being made in the likeness of men."[15] Emptying Himself does not mean Jesus ceased being God, the Greek word Paul used can be a metaphoric way to denote forfeiting "status and privilege."[16] Jesus retained His divinity, but took on the form of a servant in a human body with all of its limitations.[17] From the moment He was conceived in Mary's virgin womb His

---

14 Although the narrative of Jesus' experience in the wilderness is often referred to as "the temptation of Jesus," the key Greek verb *peirazo* {pi-rad'-zo} and its derivatives are neutral words. That word group can refer to either temptation or testing, depending on the focus of the author. Aligning with God's Spirit results in the experience being a *test* from God which has been successfully passed. On the other hand, aligning with the flesh that is being enticed by Satan results in *temptation* that is not resisted. Accordingly, some scholars make a case for referring to the wilderness portion of the gospel accounts as the "testing" of Jesus. See France, R. T., *The Gospel of Matthew*, New International Commentary on the New Testament (Eerdmans 2007) Matthew 4:1-11, pp. 126-127, crediting B. Gerhardsson with the title, *The Testing of God's Son* which France suggests seems to "sum up" the thrust of Gerhardsson's monograph on this portion of Scripture "admirably." Ibid. p. 127

15 Philippians 2:7, italics in original

16 *ESV Study Bible* (Crossway Books 2008) study note Philippians 2:7 under *Emptied himself*, p. 2283

17 For example: His birth is described as being human in form, Scripture provides Him with a human genealogy and speaks of His mother, father, brother and sisters. He had a human body that aged chronologically and grew physically. He experienced human conditions such as hunger, thirst, weariness and death. He experienced temptation and human emotions. He observed the law of Moses as a Jewish man.

divine nature united permanently with His human nature.[18] In His earthly ministry, He functioned in the human form with which He clothed Himself submitting Himself to the direction of Holy Spirit. The clearest example of His submission is one we have already noted, He was led into the wilderness by Holy Spirit. "To manifest His presence, indwelling, and glory in [us], Jesus counts it necessary that [we] should be filled with the Spirit."[19] In His humanity, He was modeling how God's sons and daughters should reflect His glory in human form (1 Peter 2:21; 1 John 2:6).[20]

The author of Hebrews acknowledged both the deity and the humanity of Jesus when he wrote, "Although He was a Son, [Jesus] learned obedience from the things which He suffered (Hebrews 5:8)." The wilderness testing was as much a classroom experience for Jesus as the wilderness experience between Egypt and the Promised Land was for Israel. "The Son's obedience revealed a dependence on God's power and assurance of his promises that was the antithesis of the wilderness generation's faithless disobedience."[21] The key to His victory was that He fully submitted Himself to His Father's plan and to the leading of the Holy Spirit. We are able to conclude from His victorious result that He had unwavering perfect submission to Holy Spirit. "[A]s the costliness of doing God's will increased, his readiness to obey rose to meet each challenge, even to the finale, the cursed death of the cross (Phil 2:8)."[22]

---

18 *ESV Study Bible* (Crossway Books 2008) *Biblical Doctrine: An Overview* under *The Humanity of Christ*, p. 2517
19 Murray, Andrew, *Experiencing The Holy Spirit* (Whitaker House 1984) p. 62
20 That is not to say that the *only* reason He took on human form was to reveal God's glory in human flesh. The entirety of Scripture makes clear that as a perfect sinless man He was qualified to be the perfect substitutionary sacrifice for sin.
21 Cockerill, Gareth Lee, *The Epistle to the Hebrews*, New International Commentary on the New Testament (Eerdmans 2012) Hebrews 5:8, p. 248, citations omitted
22 Johnson, Dennis, *Hebrews: A Commentary By Dennis Johnson*, Christ's Priesthood Surpasses Levi's and Aaron's ([Hebrews] 4:14–7:28) under *5:7–10*.

The Power of My Spirit 83

By His obedience Jesus not only revealed the powerful Kingdom success which results from completely submitting to the Father's will, He demonstrates for us how we can experience those same powerful results. But before we go there, let's jump ahead to the end of Jesus' earthly ministry. There we find another clear example of Holy Spirit at work providing Jesus, in the flesh, with the power to be obedient and fully aligned with His Father's will.

After Luke describes Satan's temptations of Jesus in the Judean wilderness, he shares something with us that we don't learn in the narratives provided by either Matthew or Mark. Luke alerts his readers to the fact that Satan's harassment of Jesus did not end in the wilderness. Luke writes, "When the devil had finished every [wilderness] temptation, he left [Jesus] until an opportune time."[23] A quick Word Study will help us understand what *time* Luke is referring to.

WORD STUDY

*The Greek word for the phrase **opportune time** in Luke 4:13 is kairos {kahee-ros}. Kairos could also be rendered "until a favorable time."*[24]

Kairos does not refer to time on a clock or a calendar. It refers to "the right time" or "the proper time" for something. The Theological Dictionary of the New Testament calls kairos time the "'decisive point'... often with a stress on the fact that it is divinely ordained."[25]

Retrieved from https://www.thegospelcoalition.org/commentary/hebrews/ (last accessed January 25, 2024)
23 Luke 4:13
24 *NET Bible Notes*, translator's note 44, Luke 4:13
25 Bromiley, Geoffrey W., *Theological Dictionary of the New Testament* (Eerdmans Publishing Co. 1985) entry for *kairos* under *C. Kairos in the NT*, p. 389

Victory in the Garden of Gethsemane

As we read the gospel accounts, we learn that the premiere *opportune time* Satan waited for was the road to the cross which included the crisis time Jesus spent in the Garden. Now to be sure, the devil did not completely disappear until this time. As a study note in the *New English Translation* points out, "the cosmic battle with Satan and all the evil angels is consistently mentioned throughout Luke."[26] That study note points to specific encounters Jesus had with demonic spirits.[27] However, Jesus also made clear that individual people can functionally do the work of Satan.[28] With this in mind, we can understand, for example, that those who opposed Jesus also represented *opportune time* for Satan who was functionally able to do the work of his kingdom through them.

As a matter of fact, one author refers to *kairos* time as "kingdom opportunities."[29] That characterization is impressively descriptive of the precise moment Satan chooses when Jesus is alone in the garden of Gethsemane. Let's review the battle from Matthew's account.

> Then Jesus came with them to a place called Gethsemane, and said to His disciples, "Sit here while I go over there and pray." And He took with Him Peter and the two sons of Zebedee, and began to be grieved and distressed. Then He said to them, "My soul is deeply

---

26 *NET Bible Notes*, study note 44, Luke 4:13, citations omitted here, but included in next footnote
27 See: Luke 8:26–39; 11:14–23
28 For example, when Peter strongly objected to the plans the Father had for His Son, Jesus rebuked Peter saying, Get behind me, Satan! (Matthew 16:23). Jesus was not saying Peter had actually become Satan but that Peter was aligning his thoughts and actions with the thoughts and actions of Satan and therefore Satan was able to use Peter to accomplish his objectives.
29 *Today in the Word* (Moody Bible Institute 1989) as quoted in *Galatians 6:10 Commentary*, Precept Austin. Retrieved from http://www.preceptaustin.org/galatians_610_commentary (last accessed December 21, 2021)

grieved, to the point of death; remain here and keep watch with Me." And He went a little beyond them, and fell on His face and prayed, saying, "My Father, if it is possible, let this cup pass from Me; yet not as I will, but as You will." And He came to the disciples and found them sleeping, and said to Peter, "So, you men could not keep watch with Me for one hour? Keep watching and praying that you may not enter into temptation; the spirit is willing, but the flesh is weak." Matthew 26:36-41 CJB (see also Luke 22:39-46; Mark 14:32-42)

Unlike the Judean wilderness narrative, the adversary is never mentioned by name in the Garden testing. However, we can draw well-reasoned conclusions based on the totality of Scripture about what is taking place in this time of conflict. Jesus understands the fate that awaits Him. He is familiar with the excruciating suffering of the Roman crucifixions of His day. In fact, since this method of torturous death was widely used by Rome at that time, it is most likely that He would have passed by Roman crosses every time He went up to Jerusalem.[30] Understandably in the natural, His flesh did not want to go to the cross. The Garden scene as Matthew, Mark and Luke describe it is in such poignant language we can almost hear Satan tempt Jesus by rehearsing each painful moment and then shrewdly suggesting another way, an easier way, *another cup*!

A key to our understanding of the Garden temptation is found in the way in which "cup" operates as a biblical metaphor. Let's look at Matthew 26:39:

---

[30] According to the *Encyclopedia Judaic*, "Crucifixion was the standard Roman mode of execution for non-Roman criminals and enemies of the state, and hence was practiced on a large scale in Judea under the Roman occupation." Skolnik, Fred, Editor in Chief, *Encyclopedia Judaic*, Second Edition, Volume 5 (Keter Publishing House Ltd. 2007) entry for *Crucifixion*, p. 309. Retrieved from https://ia903008.us.archive.org/12/items/EncyclopediaJudaica_201905/Encyclopedia%20Judaica.pdf (last accessed December 18, 2021)

> Going a little farther, he threw himself down with his face to the ground and prayed, "My Father, if possible, let *this cup* pass from me! Yet not what I will, but what you will." Matthew 26:39 NET, italics added

God blends "[a]ll of life's experiences ... into a cup for us.... The *cup* represents his personal decision and appointment."[31] In Old Testament imagery a "cup" could represent God's blessings, but it is most often employed as a symbol of God's judgment against sin.[32] The metaphor is also used in Scripture to denote suffering.[33] To *drink of a cup* refers figuratively to full participation in whatever that cup represented.[34] In keeping with this understanding, Jesus had previously referred to His impending death using cup imagery. For example:

> But Jesus said to them, "You do not know what you are asking. Are you able to drink *the cup* that I drink, or to be baptized with the baptism with which I am baptized?" Mark 10:38, italics added

> So Jesus said to Peter, "Put the sword into the sheath; *the cup* which the Father has given Me, shall I not drink it?" John 18:11, italics added

---

31 Motyer, J. Alec, *The Prophecy of Isaiah: An Introduction & Commentary* (InterVarsity Press 1993) Isaiah 51:17, p. 414, italics in original. "Throughout Scripture, as in the ancient Near East, the cup functions as a metaphor for an individual's fate." Elwell, Walter A., editor, *Baker's Evangelical Dictionary of Biblical Theology* (Baker Books 1996) entry for *Cup*. Retrieved from https://www.studylight.org/dictionaries/eng/bed/c/cup.html (last accessed April 13, 2024)

32 Ryken, Wilhoit, and Longman III, editors, *Dictionary of Biblical Imagery* (Intervarsity Press 1998) entry for *cup*, p. 186

33 France, R. T., *The Gospel of Matthew*, New International Commentary on the New Testament (Eerdmans 2007) Matthew 20:22-23, p. 758

34 *Forerunner Commentary*, What the Bible says about Drinking of the Cup, Bibletools.org. Retrieved from https://www.bibletools.org/index.cfm/fuseaction/Topical.show/RTD/cgg/ID/7635/Drinking-of-Cup.htm (last accessed December 16, 2021)

Drinking from a cup is done intentionally and voluntarily. According to the *Theological Dictionary of the New Testament* when someone refers to "drinking the cup" in the context of suffering they are indicating their willingness to acceptance that suffering.[35]

When Matthew records that Jesus prayed, "if possible, let this cup pass from me" he is alerting his readers that at that moment Jesus desired an alternative plan if possible. In the Greek language the phrase "let this cup pass from me" means "take away without touching."[36] In His prayer to His Father, Jesus was asking that the Father's will be accomplished in a way other than the cross. He knew all too well that the path to the cross would require so much more than He is capable of giving in the natural.

Even so, Jesus understood full well that to agree with Satan would mean stepping out of alignment with His Father's will. As Jesus prayed and waited in the Garden, His Father did *not* reveal another plan. The end result of the Garden struggle is captured in Jesus' firm resolve: "Yet not what I will, but what you will." By this statement, He makes clear His willing choice to become totally submissive to His Father's plan. He will drink the *cup* the Father has given Him to drink. By that resolute determination, the enemy stood defeated! At that very moment in time, just as at the very moment of time He had earlier rejected each of Satan's alternative offers in the wilderness, the power of Holy Spirit was released to walk Him through to obedience – even obedience to the cross! Holy Spirit will provide everything He now needs to obey His Father even to the last detail.[37] Because He has been

---

35 Bromiley, Geoffrey W., *Theological Dictionary of the New Testament* (Eerdmans Publishing 1985) entry for *pinō* under B. *The NT, 4. Figurative Use, a. Drinking the Cup of Wrath and Suffering*, p. 843

36 *NET Bible Notes*, translator's note 109, Luke 22:42

37 Matthew 27:50 says Jesus yielded up or gave up His spirit. In the Greek text this is active: Jesus "sends away" His breath/His spirit/the Spirit. It is clear, He is not abandoned, He takes the action Himself. Translators generally don't capitalize the word "spirit" in Matthew 27:50 suggesting they believe the reference is to Jesus sending away His human spirit/life/breath. R. T. France points out that Matthew uses an "unusual way to describe death."

given permission to act, the power of the Spirit at work in Jesus will now *transcend His human ability* and *transform His human inability*.[38]

Let's slow the process down a bit so we can review step-by-step the unique power that was working in Jesus when He obediently submitted to His Father's plan. As an initial matter, since there is no specific mention of Holy Spirit power at work in Jesus during these confrontations with the adversary how do we know God's Spirit was at work? Of course, as we have already mentioned, Jesus was aware that the Holy Spirit came on Him (entered into Him) and remained. As we have noted, the Greek verb *meno* {men'-o} (translated as "remained") makes clear that Jesus continuously possessed the Holy Spirit.[39] When He publicly announced the purpose of His earthly ministry He declared that Holy Spirit was upon Him and had anointed Him to fulfill the purpose for which He was sent.[40] In biblical language, anointing describes the pouring out of God's Spirit on someone symbolizing His power and divine intervention to perform the duties He assigned.[41]

Jesus was aware that it was by the Spirit's leading He went into the wilderness to be tested. Scripture also tells us that Jesus had

---

See: France, R. T., *The Gospel of Matthew*, New International Commentary on the New Testament (Eerdmans 2007) Matthew 27:50, p. 1078. Although it seems to be a minority opinion, I think it very possible that Matthew is cluing his readers into the fact that Jesus willingly released the Holy Spirit back to the Father before He took His last breath on earth in His human form. In the fullness of time the Father then sent the Holy Spirit to give new life to the crucified body of His Son who then breathed new creation life into His disciples through their receipt of the Holy Spirit.

38 McKnight, Scot, *Open To The Spirit: God In Us, God with Us, God Transforming Us* (Waterbrook 2018) p. 63, citing James D. G. Dunn, *The Acts of the Apostles*, Narrative Commentaries (Trinity Press International 1996) p. 12

39 *NET Bible Notes*, study note 84, John 1:32

40 Luke 4:18

41 For example, in connection with the anointing of both Saul and David we read that the Spirit of the Lord came upon them in power (1 Samuel 10:6; 1 Samuel 16:13).

The Power of My Spirit

self-awareness of the Spirit's power at work in Him and through Him. In Mark 5:30, for example, Jesus confronted the woman with the issue of bleeding who was healed simply by touching His garment. He knew that it was the power of Holy Spirit that had accomplished the healing by going out from Him to meet the woman's need. Mark says it this way, "Immediately Jesus, perceiving in Himself that the power proceeding from Him had gone forth, turned around in the crowd and said, 'Who touched My garments?'" In Luke 5:17 Luke makes specific mention of the power of God being present for healing to take place when Jesus was teaching. As one author notes, the dynamic power which is supplied by Holy Spirit is always "power in the sense of that which overcomes resistance or effects a change."[42] The very same power that performs miracles is the power that enabled Jesus to complete every act of obedience.

Now let's look at what enables this power to work. As a Jewish-born man, Jesus was under the Abrahamic Covenant which spelled out blessings for obedience and curses for disobedience. A covenant is an agreement, usually formal, between two or more parties. The covenant spells out the binding obligations of each party as well as the promised advantages or blessings that flow from covenant obedience.[43] There are two distinct, but interrelated, parts to the Abrahamic Covenant relationship. In the prescribed division of labor, there is a part God promises to do and there is a part Jesus must do. If Jesus does not do His part, God is not obligated to do His part. That's the very nature of how a covenant works.

Under covenant theology we could concisely separate Jesus' obligations from His Father's promises as follows:

---

42 *2 Timothy 1:7 Commentary*, Precept Austin. Retrieved from http://www.preceptaustin.org/2_timothy_17.htm#Power quoting Kenneth Wuest, *Word Studies from the Greek New Testament* entry for *dunamis* (last accessed December 21, 2021)

43 Unger, Merrill F., *The New Unger's Bible Dictionary* (Moody Press 1988) entry for *covenant* under *Application of the Term*, p. 259

Jesus' Part	**His Father's Part**
To seek His Father's will in every matter. Once He knew what God's will was He had a choice whether to do what His Father asked or substitute His own plan. As we see in the wilderness and the Garden, switching to a plan that appeals more to the flesh (it seems quicker, easier, more assured, etc.) is Satan's persistent temptation.	God's Spirit is ready, willing and able to release God's power and resource to complete every act of obedience. On the other hand, actions of disobedience/rebellion grieve Holy Spirit into silence and inaction.

Jesus always chose to submit to His Father's will. He fully understood that two opposing kingdoms could not co-exist, they cannot occupy the very same space in a human heart at the same time. So, in every instance of His earthly ministry, the Covenant obligations can be summarized as follows.

Jesus' Part	**His Father's Part**
Acting in a way that opposes what His flesh desired = dying to His flesh which enables power to be released to Him.	At the moment Jesus made a sincere decision to align His will with God's, the power of the Holy Spirit was immediately released to empower Him to complete the act He had chosen to do.

I like to say that God's power is released in less than a nanosecond[44] once Jesus resolved to align His will with His Father's will. But in reality, I think even one billionth of a second is longer

---

44 One billionth of a second

than it actually took for that power to begin to work in Him so that the will of the Father could be expressed through Him.

From the battle scenes in the wilderness and the Garden, we can draw several conclusions about the power of God's Spirit. First, because the Spirit remains in you that power is available every moment of every day. There is never a time when Spirit power is not available. A requirement for accessing the available power is complete and total submission to God's perfect will. Full submission and obedience provide access to God's unlimited power. His power will always accomplish His will.

Scholar Richard Averbeck compares accessing the power of Holy Spirit to be akin to a sailboat which is able to access the power of the wind when its sail is hoisted up. Averbeck writes, "we can 'put up the sails' in our lives and thereby take advantage of the blowing of the Spirit in and through our lives. We are empowered by the Holy Spirit as long as we have our sails up."[45] Christ-followers who have their *sails up* (a metaphor for receptivity and obedience),[46] immediately and joyfully welcome God's word with the intention of doing what that word says. They welcome it at a deep personal level to the exclusion of everything that would compete with that word. "The understanding that results from this kind of reception goes beyond the intellect to touch [their] conduct, commitment, and devotion [to God]."[47]

Jesus submitted Himself to His Father's plan not only to learn obedience but also to establish Himself as our teacher by becoming a model for us to follow. The gift of the Holy Spirit is the

---

45 Averbeck, Richard E., *The Holy Spirit in the Hebrew Bible and Its Connections to the New Testament* (2009). Retrieved from https://bible.org/seriespage/holy-spirit-hebrew-bible-and-its-connections-new-testament (last accessed January 22, 2024). This article is included in Wallace, Daniel B. and Sawyer, M. James, editors, *Who's Afraid Of The Holy Spirit? An Investigation Into The Ministry Of The Spirit Of God Today* (Biblical Studies Press 2013).

46 Green, Michael, *I Believe in the Holy Spirit*, Revised edition (Eerdmans 2004) p. 140

47 Gundry, Robert H., *Mark: A Commentary on His Apology for the Cross* (Eerdmans 1993) p. 206

means by which the ministry of Jesus continues on earth until He comes again.[48] It is also "the means by which we encounter or experience Christ here and now ... to experience the Spirit is to be in effective relationship with Christ."[49] The function of the Spirit is to effectuate both "the power and influence of the living Christ" which means that being led by the Spirit is "equivalent to having 'Christ within' as a living, guiding presence."[50]

Hear What The Spirit is Saying to the Church: *So much of My Kingdom comes down to choice. Too many people want to sit on the fence, staying in the shadows, living in the grey area. But I tell you that the grey area is not a safe place to be, nor is it the place of My Kingdom rule and power. My Kingdom is the Kingdom of Light so choose Light and you will walk in incomparable power and blessing.*

---

48 Hill, David, *Greek Words and Hebrew Meanings: Studies in the Semantics of Soteriological Terms*, Society for New Testament Studies Monograph Series 5 (Wipf and Stock 2000, previously published Cambridge University Press 1967) p. 288

49 Hill, David, *Greek Words and Hebrew Meanings: Studies in the Semantics of Soteriological Terms*, Society for New Testament Studies Monograph Series 5 (Wipf and Stock 2000, previously published Cambridge University Press 1967) p. 279

50 Hill, David, *Greek Words and Hebrew Meanings: Studies in the Semantics of Soteriological Terms*, Society for New Testament Studies Monograph Series 5 (Wipf and Stock 2000, previously published Cambridge University Press 1967) p. 277

LESSON 5:

RESURRECTION POWER AT WORK

"I pray that he will give light to the eyes of your hearts, so that you will understand . . . how surpassingly great is his power [*dunamis*] working in us who trust him. [His power] works with the same mighty strength he used when he worked in the Messiah to raise him from the dead and seat him at his right hand in heaven." Ephesians 1:18-20 CJB

IN OUR LAST lesson, we looked at two biblical accounts of God's power working in and through Jesus to resist and overcome Satan's temptations. Luke tells us that when Jesus returned to Galilee from the Judean wilderness He was armed with the Holy Spirit's power [*dunamis*] and news about Him spread (Luke 4:14). "Luke portrays Jesus as doing nothing without the Holy Spirit. Jesus is the example *par excellence* of a Spirit-filled, Spirit-led, Spirit-empowered human being ....."[1] In Acts 10 Luke summarizes the entirety of Jesus' earthly mission by acknowledging once again His anointing of power.

> . . . you yourselves know the thing which took place throughout all Judea, starting from Galilee, after the baptism which John proclaimed. You know of Jesus of Nazareth, how God anointed Him **with the Holy Spirit and with power** [*dunamis*], and how He went about

---

1   Gundry, Robert H., *Commentary on the New Testament* (Hendrickson Publishers 2010) Luke 4:14-15, p. 239, italics in original

doing good and healing all who were oppressed by the devil, for God was with Him. Acts 10:37-38, bold added

Notice that the power of Holy Spirit was for the purpose of defeating evil. The apostle Paul was well acquainted with the relentless attempts of Satan to exercise his power, often using human adversaries through whom he could functionally do his work, to accomplish his evil will. In Ephesians 6 Paul cataloged a variety of hostile spiritual powers that every Christ-follower faces.

> For our struggle is not against flesh and blood, but against the rulers, against the powers, against the world forces of this darkness, against the spiritual *forces* of wickedness in the heavenly *places*. Ephesians 6:12, italics in original

Jesus made no secret of the fact that after His resurrection His followers would face trouble in this world. He knew that tribulation would be instigated by the kingdom of darkness. However, in John 16:33 He assured His followers that they could "take heart" because He had conquered the world. He was referring to "the sum total of everything opposed to God."[2] The promise of John 16:33 is that these evil powers do not ultimately prevail over Christ-followers![3] However, until Christ's second coming, His followers will need to engage in spiritual battle with the types of evil forces Paul identifies.

Dr. Sandra Richter dispels what she calls "the good protestant work ethic" as the false belief that, "If I just peddle faster [in other words just work harder], then the Kingdom will come."[4] The wit-

---

2   Harris, W. Hall, "John," in *The Bible Knowledge Word Study: The Gospels*, edited by Eugene H. Merrill (Victor 2006) John 16:33, p. 361, citing *BAGD* 539

3   Keener, Craig S., *The Gospel Of John: A Commentary*, Volume Two (Hendrickson Publishers 2003) 2. Limited Faith ([John] 16:29-33) p. 1049

4   Dr. Sandra Richter, Q & A following Wheaton College lecture, published June 15, 2015. Retrieved from https://www.youtube.com/watch?v=VLnijooiFEc (last accessed December 24, 2023)

The Power of My Spirit

ness of the Bible is that no human power, no matter how hard they try, can stand against Satan.

The only way a Christ-follower can be used by God to successfully advance against Satan's kingdom on earth is by being equipped with God's power. We find that truth clearly stated in the last recorded words Jesus spoke to His disciples. They are found in the first chapter of Acts, spoken immediately before His ascension.

> Gathering [His disciples] together, [Jesus] commanded them not to leave Jerusalem, but to wait for what the Father had promised, "Which," *He said*, "you heard of from Me; for John baptized with water, but you will be baptized with the Holy Spirit not many days from now." … "[Y]ou will receive **power** [*dunamis*] when the Holy Spirit has come upon you; and you shall be My witnesses both in Jerusalem, and in all Judea and Samaria, and even to the remotest part of the earth." Acts 1:4-8, italics in original, bold added

Luke does not identify for us precisely what promise from His Father Jesus was referring to.[5] He does make clear that Jesus had previously told His disciples about this promise and that it related to the Holy Spirit coming upon them to empower them as witnesses.[6] In his first sermon, Peter relates the distribution of

---

5 Sam Storms suggests that the events which occurred at Pentecost are "the fulfillment of three prophetic words: first, the prophecy of Joel 2:28–32 (in accordance with the terms of the New Covenant); second, the prophecy of John the Baptist in Matthew 3:11–12; and third, the prophecy of Jesus himself in John 14–16 concerning the 'other Comforter.'" Storms, Sam, *The Gift of the Holy Spirit: An Essay by Sam Storms*. Retrieved from https://www.thegospelcoalition.org/essay/gift-holy-spirit/ (last accessed February 7, 2024). Dr. Sam Storms (ThM, Dallas Theological Seminary; PhD, The University of Texas at Dallas) is pastor emeritus at Bridgeway Church in Oklahoma City, founder of Enjoying God Ministries and a Council member of The Gospel Coalition.

6 "[O]ne thing is clear: the gift of the Spirit is understood as an endowment which enables the Apostles and other Christians to *communicate* with all

the Holy Spirit to the promise in Joel that in the latter days God's Spirit would be poured out on all flesh. Scholar Darrell Bock refers to the Pentecost impartation as "the gift of the Spirit, which enables God *to direct his people from within.*"[7] Holy Spirit is "experienced within man as a power operative in his heart."[8] That said, it seems plausible to me that Jesus might also have had in mind the New Covenant His Father had promised through the prophets Jeremiah and Ezekiel.[9] The New Covenant was essentially a promise of a new type of power which would operate *from within a person's purified heart.*[10] The Spirit was expected to create a new heart, the

---

people: it makes possible and effective the preaching of the word and works of God." Hill, David, *Greek Words and Hebrew Meanings: Studies in the Semantics of Soteriological Terms*, Society for New Testament Studies Monograph Series 5 (Wipf and Stock 2000, previously published Cambridge University Press 1967) p. 260. Moreover, Holy Spirit "gives direct instructions for concrete action in the expansion of the mission" God has given to the followers of Christ. Ibid. p. 261

7 Bock, Darrell, "Acts," in *The Bible Knowledge Word Study: Acts - Ephesians*, edited by Darrell L Bock (Victor 2006) Acts 1:4, p. 40, italics added

8 Hill, David, *Greek Words and Hebrew Meanings: Studies in the Semantics of Soteriological Terms*, Society for New Testament Studies Monograph Series 5 (Wipf and Stock 2000, previously published Cambridge University Press 1967) p. 279

9 On the night He was betrayed Jesus explained to His disciples that His shed blood would be the blood which would establish the promised New Covenant. See: Matthew 26:28; Mark 14:24; Luke 22:20. See also: Beale and Carson, editors, *Commentary on the New Testament Use of the Old Testament* (Baker Academic 2007) Luke 22:17-20, pp. 381-383; Averbeck, Richard E., *The Holy Spirit in the Hebrew Bible and Its Connections to the New Testament* (2009) who concludes that being baptized in, with or by the Holy Spirit is "based on the combination of divine promises in Ezek 36:25-28." Retrieved from https://bible.org/seriespage/holy-spirit-hebrew-bible-and-its-connections-new-testament (last accessed January 22, 2024)

10 See: Jeremiah 31:33; Ezekiel 36:26-27. God had also promised a *pouring out* of His Spirit in Isaiah 32:15; 44:3 and Joel 2:28. In other words, Judaism held a strong hope that there would be a future outpouring of God's Spirit. Hill, David, *Greek Words and Hebrew Meanings: Studies in the Semantics of Soteriological Terms*, Society for New Testament Studies Monograph Series 5 (Wipf and Stock 2000, previously published Cambridge University Press 1967) p. 232

center of motives and decisions, in God's people.[11] In any event, the power [*dunamis*] encounter Jesus promised conveyed the idea of being endowed with Holy Spirit[12] and the fulfillment of that promise was put on public display in Jerusalem 50 days later.[13]

> When the day of Pentecost[14] had come, they were all together in one place. And suddenly there came from heaven a noise like a violent rushing wind, and it filled the whole house where they were sitting. And there appeared to them tongues as of fire distributing themselves, and they rested on each one of them. And they were all filled with the Holy Spirit …. Acts 2:1-4

---

11 Dr. David Moffit asserts, and I agree, that dispatching the Holy Spirit is proof that the recipients have been purified and have therefore become "fit receptacles of the Spirit." The implication is that the indwelling presence of God's Holy Spirit could only inhabit a purified vessel. This conclusion seems to be supported by the statements of Jesus. Before his crucifixion He assured His disciples that it was to their benefit He depart so He could send them the Holy Spirit (John 16:7). As we have just read, when He appeared to them after His resurrection He told them to wait in Jerusalem until they received power from on high, referring to the Spirit He promised to send. Apparently, the Holy Spirit could not be sent until Jesus had completed His atoning act through His death, burial, resurrection and ascension permitting purification to be accomplished. See: Moffit, David M., *Atonement at the Right Hand: The Sacrificial Significance of Jesus' Exaltation in Acts*, p. 17. Retrieved from https://research-repository.st-andrews.ac.uk/bitstream/handle/10023/7776/Moffitt_2015_NTS_Atonement_AM.pdf (last accessed July 9, 2024). Dr. Moffitt is Senior Lecturer in New Testament Studies at University of St Andrews, St Mary's College in England.

12 Hill, David, *Greek Words and Hebrew Meanings: Studies in the Semantics of Soteriological Terms*, Society for New Testament Studies Monograph Series 5 (Wipf and Stock 2000, previously published Cambridge University Press 1967) p. 259

13 The Old Covenant had been initiated at Mt. Sinai when God came down in fire on Mt. Sinai.

14 Pentecost (translation of the Greek word *pentēkostē* {pen-tay-kos-tay'} meaning 50) was one of Israel's three pilgrim feasts. It was celebrated in Jerusalem fifty days after the Passover Sabbath (Leviticus 23:15-16).

Luke informs us those tongues of fire "rested on each one of them." It seems to me he points that out so as to highlight the fact that this initial Spirit endowment happened to all of them at once, but it was at the same time an individual experience. Each one was personally filled with God's Spirit. They have received the "present power of the living Lord"[15] and the "authority for the continuation of the ministry of Christ."[16]

About three years before, the public ministry of Jesus had been initiated with a very visible endowment of power from God's Spirit. We looked at that when we discussed the dove symbol in Lesson 3. In a similar fashion, the public ministry of His disciples was launched with a visible power endowment from God's Spirit. As Jewish men they would have understood their public ministry to include not only verbally sharing the good news of the Gospel, but living their life in a way that accurately RE•presented[17] Christ to the world around them.[18] Neither task could be accomplished successfully except through the power of the Holy Spirit. In fact, for Paul the ethical aspects of life as a follower of Christ are

---

15 Hill, David, *Greek Words and Hebrew Meanings: Studies in the Semantics of Soteriological Terms*, Society for New Testament Studies Monograph Series 5 (Wipf and Stock 2000, previously published Cambridge University Press 1967) p. 293

16 Hill, David, *Greek Words and Hebrew Meanings: Studies in the Semantics of Soteriological Terms*, Society for New Testament Studies Monograph Series 5 (Wipf and Stock 2000, previously published Cambridge University Press 1967) p. 287

17 I am intentionally repurposing the word "represent" at times in this study by making a clear separation between the prefix "re" and the remainder of the word "present." The prefix "re" indicates repetition and has an ordinary meaning of "again" or "back." My goal in showing the word in this unique form is to highlight the truth that one who is God's representative does not act on his own accord, that representative is actually commissioned by God to repeat what God has done, to show again who God is. I have placed the prefix "re" in all caps to indicate the emphasis on that syllable when pronouncing the word.

18 Stern, David, H., *Jewish New Testament Commentary* (Jewish New Testament Publications 1992) Acts 1:8, p. 216

entirely dependent on the activity of Holy Spirit.[19] What was true for those first followers of Christ is true for every other disciple of Christ down through the centuries. We are called to not only share the Gospel message, but to live it loud and clear by our lifestyle. Of course, that means we will need to avail ourselves of the regenerative transforming power of the Holy Spirit, as well as His empowerment for ministry. That brings us to our Key Scripture for this lesson. I'll restate it here using the NASB 1995 translation. As I do, I will point out the variety of power words Paul used.

> *I pray that* the eyes of your heart may be enlightened, so that you will know what is the hope of His calling, what are the riches of the glory of His inheritance in the saints, and what is the surpassing greatness of His **power** [*dunamis*] toward us who believe. *These are* in accordance with the **working** [*energia*] of the **strength** [*kratos*] of His **might** [*ischus*] which He **brought about** [*energeo*] in Christ, when He raised Him from the dead and seated Him at His right hand in the heavenly *places*. Ephesians 1:18-20, italics in original, bold added

In his prayer, Paul identifies power as one of the three aspects of salvation. The first is hope, the second is the guarantee of a rich inheritance and the third is the receipt of *dunamis* power which energizes. We'll focus here on the power aspect of salvation. Paul prays for followers of Christ to be *enlightened* to the incredible supernatural power [*dunamis*] of God which is readily available to all who trust Him. It is the same power that raised Christ from the dead! In the original Greek, Paul uses a form of the word "enlighten" which indicates his prayer is "not for a moment's

---

19 Hill, David, *Greek Words and Hebrew Meanings: Studies in the Semantics of Soteriological Terms*, Society for New Testament Studies Monograph Series 5 (Wipf and Stock 2000, previously published Cambridge University Press 1967) p. 269

insight, but that [Christ-followers] live enlightened lives."[20] Paul is speaking of enlightenment which has already been received and is now their permanent condition.[21] His prayer could be accurately reworded as, "since the eyes of your heart [meaning the control center of your life] have been enlightened,"[22] I am praying that you come to understand more and more "the absolutely unique and superior power exerted by God in the resurrection of Christ."[23] For Paul, knowledge and understanding typically refer to that which can be gained by experience.

To describe this resurrection power of Holy Spirit Paul employs four common Greek power terms all within a few words of each other. His redundant power language is not an attempt to distinguish between various types of power. Paul's objective is to use these words in a cumulative way such that they amplify the strength and effectiveness of God's power.[24]

To further understand the nature of this power, it will be helpful to define the Greek words found in Ephesians 1:18-20. We will begin with a Word Study on *dunamis*. I have been pointing out the repetitive use of *dunamis* throughout this lesson. Not only is it the power Paul refers to in his prayer, it is also the power of the

---

20 Klein, William W., "Ephesians," in *The Expositor's Bible Commentary: Ephesians - Philemon*, Vol. 12, Revised edition, edited by Longman III and Garland (Zondervan Academic 2006) Ephesians 1:18, p. 58

21 Hill, Gary, *The Discovery Bible*, HELPS Ministries, Inc., explanation of *Greek Perfect*

22 *NET Bible Notes*, translator's note 48, Ephesians 1:18. Reference to a person's heart as being "the command center of their lives" is found in Klein, William W., "Ephesians," in *The Expositor's Bible Commentary: Ephesians - Philemon*, Vol. 12, Revised edition, edited by Longman III and Garland (Zondervan Academic 2006) Ephesians 1:18, p. 58

23 Barth, Markus, *Ephesians Translation and Commentary on Chapters 1-3*, The Anchor Bible Vol 34 (Doubleday 1974) *Notes On Ephesians 1:19-20,20-23* under *19. How exceedingly great is his power ... that mighty strength is at work*, p. 152

24 Klein, William W., "Ephesians," in *The Expositor's Bible Commentary: Ephesians - Philemon*, Vol. 12, Revised edition, edited by Longman III and Garland (Zondervan Academic 2006) Ephesians 1:19, p. 59

Spirit which Luke says Jesus was armed with when He came out of His wilderness testing (Luke 4:14), the power with which God had anointed Jesus for His earthly work (Acts 10:37-38) and the power Jesus promised to send to His disciples (Acts 1:4-8).

> **WORD STUDY**
>
> *As noted, the Greek word translated as* **power** *in our Key Scripture is dunamis {doo'-nam-is} which refers especially to "achieving power," the "power or ability to carry out some function." It is power that is "capable for the task."*[25]
>
> *It is frequently employed in ancient literature to reference "military might or the ability to conquer" and over 200 times the New Testament authors use dunamis in a similar way to refer to "strength and conquering ability."*[26]
>
> *In the New Testament, dunamis is sometimes translated as "miracle." It always refers to an effective power that accomplishes things. It is by its manifestation dunamis can be recognized at work.*[27]

As we will see, all of the additional power words employed by Paul in our Key Scripture are so closely related to *dunamis* and to

---

[25] Hoehner, Harold W., "Ephesians," in *The Bible Knowledge Word Study: Acts-Ephesians*, edited by Darrell L. Bock (Victor 2002) Ephesians 1:19 under *Power (dynameōs)*, p. 429

[26] Renner, Rick, *Sparkling Gems from the Greek Volume II* (Harrison House Publishers 2016) October 17, p. 945, italics in original

[27] Barclay, William, *The Daily Study Bible*, rev. ed (John Knox Press 1975) John 2:23-25 under *The Searcher Of The Hearts Of Men*. Retrieved from https://www.studylight.org/commentaries/eng/dsb/john-2.html (last accessed December 22, 2021)

each other that they overlap.[28] To begin with, the Greek noun *energeia* {en-erg'-i-ah} is used exclusively in the New Testament to refer to supernatural power.[29] When referencing God, it is *"the [effective] supernatural ability to get something done."*[30] The related verb *energeo* {en-erg-eh'-o} denotes a force that is energizing, power that is actively at work and produces an outcome.[31] Electrical current flowing through a wire to illuminate a light bulb provides a good analogy.[32] Or as scholar Lynn Cohick offers, we can think of *energeia* as the energy produced as dynamite is exploding.[33] Before the wick is lit the dynamite only has potential power (*dunamis*),

---

28 Hoehner, Harold W., "Ephesians," in *The Bible Knowledge Word Study: Acts-Ephesians*, edited by Darrell L. Bock (Victor 2002) Ephesians 1:19 under *According to the mighty working of his power* (*kata tēn energeian tou kratous tēs ischyos autou*), p. 430

29 *NET Bible Notes*, study note 54, Ephesians 1:19. In the New Testament, *energeo* always describes supernatural energizing activity which is attributed to God. *Philippians 2:13 Commentary*, Precept Austin, citing William Barclay. Retrieved from https://www.preceptaustin.org/philippians_213 (last accessed July 8, 2021)

30 Renner, Rick, *Sparkling Gems from the Greek Volume II* (Harrison House Publishers 2016) July 10, p. 634, italics in original. As pointed out by William Barclay, *energeo* always refers to the action of God that is "effective" meaning it can neither be frustrated nor only half-done. When God exercises *energeo*, His action will always fully accomplish His will. *Philippians 2:13 Commentary*, Precept Austin, citing Barclay, W., *The Daily Study Bible Series*, Rev. ed. (The Westminster Press). Retrieved from https://www.preceptaustin.org/philippians_213 (last accessed May 14, 2024)

31 Bromiley, Geoffrey W., *Theological Dictionary of the New Testament*, Abridged in One Volume (Eerdmans 1985) entry for *ergon* under *energéō, enérgeia, enérgēma, energēs*, p. 254; Renner, Rick, *Sparkling Gems from the Greek* (Harrison House Publishers 2003) January 31, p. 59; The Greek energy words (*energeo, energes, energeia* and *energema*) all "have to do with the active operation or working of power and its effectual results." *Spirit Filled Life Bible* (Thomas Nelson 1991) *Word Wealth [1 Thessalonians] 2:13 effectively, energeo*, p. 1827

32 Hill, Gary, *The Discovery Bible*, HELPS Ministries, Inc., [G]1754 *energéō*

33 Cohick, Linn H., *The Letter To The Ephesians*, The New International Commentary on the New Testament (Eerdmans 2020) Ephesians 1:17-19, p. 121

however when it explodes that hidden power is made visible (*energeia*). Scholar Harold Hoehner is quick to point out that even though the word "dynamite" actually derives from the Greek word *dunamis*, "there is no suggestion [in Ephesians 1:19] or anywhere in the Bible that God's power has an explosive quality. Rather, it has the idea of 'power, ability, capability of acting.'"[34]

The last two words, *kratos* {krat'-os} and *ischus* {is-khoos'} function as additional descriptive synonyms.[35] As a power word, *kratos* includes the idea of rule/victory. One source refers to it as "power that brings dominion."[36] *Ischus* is part of a Greek word group that overlaps with *dunamis* but "with greater stress on the power implied."[37] *Ischus* denotes endowed strength or power (mental or moral).[38] Peter exhorted Christ-followers to serve not by their own strength but "by the strength [*ischus*] which God supplies."[39]

> By looking at power, one senses its inherent strength (*ischys*), but when its engine roars and it begins to move, its power of mastery becomes obvious (*kratos*). However, when it approaches a tree and knocks it over, one sees the activity of its power (*energeia*).[40]

---

34 Hoehner, Harold W., "Ephesians," in *The Bible Knowledge Word Study: Acts-Ephesians*, edited by Darrell L. Bock (Victor 2002) Ephesians 1:19 under *Power (dynameōs)*, p. 429, quoting Aristotle, *Metaphysica* 9.5.1 §1047b.31; 8.5 §1049b.24; 9.1 §1051a.5; Plato, *Respublica* 5.21 §477c-d

35 Cohick, Linn H., *The Letter To The Ephesians*, The New International Commentary on the New Testament (Eerdmans 2020) Ephesians 1:17-19, p. 121

36 Hill, Gary, *The Discovery Bible*, HELPS Ministries, Inc., [G]2904 *kratos*

37 Bromiley, Geoffrey W., *Theological Dictionary of the New Testament*, Abridged in One Volume (Eerdmans 1985) entry for *ischýō* under *1.*, p. 378

38 Zodhiates, Spiros, *The Complete Word Study Dictionary: New Testament* (AMG Publishers 1992) word #2479, p. 787

39 1 Peter 4:11

40 Hoehner, Harold W., "Ephesians," in *The Bible Knowledge Word Study: Acts-Ephesians* (Victor 2002), edited by Darrell L. Bock, Ephesians 1:19 under *According to the mighty working of his power (kata tēn energeian tou kratous tēs ischyos autou)*, p. 430

Because of the overlapping meanings of Paul's power words, a more literal translation of Ephesians 1:19b-20a would be "according to the power of the power of his power."[41] This heaping up of Greek power words is intended to emphasize the unrestrained unimaginable greatness of God's power whether it is at work in Christ or His followers.[42]

In Ephesians 1:18-20 Paul equates the power God used to resurrect Christ with the power at work in every Christ-follower. It is not the only time he used this equation. To the church meeting in Corinth he explained that the power that was working among the Corinthians is "ultimately resurrection power."[43] Scholar Frank Matera concludes that Paul's explanation of resurrection power is *not* referring to an after-death experience. "Rather, he has in view that resurrection life that is [a present-day] reality for those who are alive in Christ. It is precisely this [present-day] life that enables [Paul] to make the power of Christ present to the community despite weakness."[44] The point Paul is making is that through the indwelling Holy Spirit God supplies a consistent source of effective, energetic power to each Christ-follower. It is that supernatural resurrection power at work in a Christ-follower which we want to consider in this lesson.

Let's look at this from a very practical point of view. Every Christ-follower has two ways in which they can deal with sin. "One is to endeavor to ward it off with all his might, seeking his strength in the Word and in prayer. In this form of conflict, we

---

41 Hoehner, Harold W., "Ephesians," in *The Bible Knowledge Word Study: Acts-Ephesians* (Victor 2002), edited by Darrell L. Bock, Ephesians 1:19 under *According to the mighty working of his power (kata tēn energeian tou kratous tēs ischyos autou)*, p. 429
42 Bromiley, Geoffrey W., *Theological Dictionary of the New Testament*, Abridged in One Volume (Eerdmans 1985) entry for *ischýō* under *3.c.*, p. 379
43 2 Corinthians 13:4; Bromiley, Geoffrey W., *Theological Dictionary of the New Testament*, Abridged in One Volume (Eerdmans 1985) entry for *dýnamai* under *D. The Concept of Power in the NT, 4. The Community*, p. 191
44 Matera, Frank J., *II Corinthians: A Commentary* (Westminster John Knox Press 2003) 2 Corinthians 13:4, p. 308

The Power of My Spirit 105

use the power of [our own] will. The other [option] is to turn at the very moment of the temptation to the Lord Jesus in the silent exercise of faith" and rely on the power readily available through the Holy Spirit.[45] Paul was advocating the second option. He passionately expressed his earnest desire to *know* Christ and to *know* this power by which Christ had been resurrected.[46] Note that in our Key Scripture Paul did not pray that the Christ-followers in Ephesus might be *given* divine power, but that they might experientially *understand* the divine power they *already possessed*. They had not received a junior level of God's Spirit and neither do we. The resurrection power they have readily available through the Holy Spirit is power of such strength that no one, not even Satan, is able to overcome it.

British scholar N. T. Wright points to the fact that, "Far too many Christians today . . . are quite unaware that [the Holy Spirit's] power is there and is available."[47] Absent a life lived through Holy Spirit power Christ-followers are rendered ineffective and powerless in the work God has prepared in advance for them to do. They are unable to overcome evil, the enemy wins by default!

Paul considered resurrection to be "the supreme proof of [God's] power."[48] His resurrection power knows no limit whether it is at work in Christ or at work in you and me. It is vitally important for Christ-followers to understand and acknowledge this power because the kingdom of God is demonstrated not in idle talk but with the [*dunamis*] power of God put on display through the Holy Spirit (1 Corinthians 4:20).

In His humanity, Jesus understood the need in the wilderness to submit Himself completely to the Father so that in deny-

---

45 Murray, Andrew, *Experiencing The Holy Spirit* (Whitaker House 1984) p. 88
46 Philippians 3:10
47 Wright, Tom., *Paul for Everyone: The Prison Letters* (Westminster John Knox Press 2002, 2004) Ephesians 1:15-23, p. 16
48 Barclay, William, *The Daily Study Bible*, rev. ed (John Knox Press 1975) Ephesians 1:15-23 under *Paul's Prayer For The Church*. Retrieved from https://www.studylight.org/commentaries/eng/dsb/ephesians-1.html (last accessed December 22, 2021)

ing Himself His Father could provide the power needed to *begin* the work He had been sent to do. Likewise, He understood perfectly the need in the Garden to submit Himself completely to the Father so that in denying Himself His Father could provide the power He needed to *finish* the work He had been sent to do.[49] Sufficient power to do the will of God likewise flows freely every time a Christ-follower denies the greatest desire of his flesh.

Andrew Murray, a South African writer, teacher and Christian pastor of the 1800's, points out that every person faces "two great enemies by whom the devil tempts him and with whom he has to contend. The one is the world without, and the other is the self-life within. This last, the selfish ego, is much more dangerous and stronger than the first. It is quite possible for a man to have made much progress in forsaking the world while the self-life retains full dominion within him."[50] In sum, "Your own life and the life of God cannot fill the heart at the same time."[51]

As we have noted, the power that is released for obedience is not a watered-down version of God's power; it is power strong enough to resurrect a dead body. What does that mean for us as a practical matter? Upon our salvation, we are spiritually transferred out of the bondage of the kingdom of this world and become eternal citizens in the Kingdom of God. In the spiritual sense, those who follow Christ have been set free from the captivity of sin and have a new traceable family tree. It is a fundamental fact that, "[a] tree always lives according to the nature of the seed from which it grew. Every living being is always guided and governed by the nature which it received at its birth."[52] The very instant we are transferred from the kingdom of darkness to the Kingdom of Light we are born again and have this new family tree. However, at that point of rebirth we are just infants, babes in Christ. Just as

---

49 Journal Entry dated September 2, 2007
50 Murray, Andrew, *Experiencing The Holy Spirit* (Whitaker House 1984) p. 35
51 Murray, Andrew, *Experiencing The Holy Spirit* (Whitaker House 1984) pp. 53-54
52 Murray, Andrew, *Experiencing The Holy Spirit* (Whitaker House 1984) p. 31

The Power of My Spirit

in the natural infants grow to be toddlers and toddlers grow to be children, children to adolescents, adolescents to young adults and finally to mature adulthood, so it is in the Spirit. In fact, growth in the natural which we can see helps to figuratively explain the supernatural growth that we can't see.

If we give ourselves over to the control of our own flesh rather than the Spirit of God, we will not be able to enjoy the influence and rule of Christ in our hearts as we wait for the Kingdom of God to be revealed in all of its fullness.[53] Generally speaking, God's power does not work in an unwilling, unreceptive heart. The biblical truth is that no man can be liberated from his own flesh nature except through "death—that is, by first dying to it and then living in the strength of the new life that comes from God."[54] Only a heart that desires the things God desires can operate in His power. God will not empower the flesh because our flesh "sets itself in the place of God. It seeks, pleases and honors itself more than God."[55] On the other hand, by denying our flesh we can presently experience resurrection power.

As I journaled one summer morning I came to understand the concept of resurrection power in a whole new way.[56]

> One of the schemes of the enemy in this season is to tempt me to eat junk food when I'm not hungry. [I have heard it called] "stress eating." The amazing truth about stress eating is that it **never** satisfies! You only long for more. I think God showed me some time ago why that is – the emptiness, that hollow feeling, that sense of yearning, longing restlessness inside can only be satisfied

---

53 Galatians 5:21; DeHaan, Mark, *Already But Not Yet,* Been Thinking About It with Mark DeHaan and Friends, May 22, 2008. Retrieved from http://www.beenthinking.org/2008/05/22/already-but-not-yet/ (last accessed December 19, 2021). Webpage no longer available.
54 Murray, Andrew, *Experiencing The Holy Spirit* (Whitaker House 1984) pp. 35-36
55 Murray, Andrew, *Experiencing The Holy Spirit* (Whitaker House 1984) p. 58
56 Journal Entry July 17, 2009 9:10 a.m.

with more of Him! The "food" He offers is spiritual food to satisfy spiritual hunger. Satisfaction is found in Him alone and He will not compete with the flesh. If I choose to fill the void with physical food, the void remains and never seems satisfied. However, when I choose to deny my flesh and press into Him, I find satisfaction and that "empty feeling" that I tried to fill with food goes away! In other words, when I refuse to feed the flesh in that way, my flesh stops demanding to be fed in that way. Wow! What an amazing principle. I have seen this at work before – when I exercise my willpower over food, I have more power over food. But I never understood why. Now I see the truth that as I rely on God for the strength I need, He releases that strength to me and I am no longer *in need*.

Maybe another way to think about this process and why it works this way is to think in terms of spiritual warfare. When I experience a spiritual void (often recognized in my body as fear, anxiety, stress), Satan tempts me to fill the void with physical food. He knows it does not meet the existing need, but he also knows by giving in to the temptation I block the power of the Holy Spirit to minister to me in that moment! When over time, I have denied the flesh the "junk food" it craves, and in the process received power/strength/ministry from the Holy Spirit, I find I am no longer craving the physical food. There is a greater sense of peace* within and the cycle is broken (at least for the time being).

*It makes perfect sense that there would be greater peace within, which is always the result of the ministry of the Holy Spirit. The physical food that we eat beyond our need grieves the Holy Spirit! When He is grieved we cannot receive His power in the same way. We made our choice and fed the physical man rather than waiting on God to feed our Spirit!

I then added this note to my Journal Entry, "I believe this principle works with any other way we try to satisfy our inner need – drugs, alcohol, pornography, gambling, worry, etc." We can deny ourselves food or lusts of the flesh (like shopping, watching movies, reading certain types of literature). We can choose to deny our "rights" – for example, rights we think we have to judge, to get even, or to complain. In every case, when we exercise our choice to deny our flesh we gain victory over that which the flesh demands. The power then that is immediately available to us is the same power as the resurrection power that raised Christ from the dead. The more we die to our flesh (deny what the flesh wants) the more we walk in the fullness of the power of Christ that is within us.

Until recently I have lived my life as a Christ-follower under the false assumption that because the Holy Spirit indwelt me His leadership was consistently automatic. By automatic I mean it is involuntary, guaranteed, with no action or input from me. What I've come to understand from practical experience is that there are aspects of the Holy Spirit that are consistently automatic. For example, His conviction is continuously automatic, so is His reminder of truth we have heard and His willingness to help us understand Scripture. On the other hand, while His *desire to lead* is automatic, His *leadership* is not guaranteed. It is a moment-by-moment, situation-by-situation choice which can be overruled by the desires of my flesh. Very practically I have begun the habit when faced with temptation of any sort to simply say, "Right now I want to die to my flesh. Holy Spirit I need you to lead me." That may sound radical or maybe it sounds overly simplistic, but it works! I become aware at that moment that I have two choices – one leads to life, the other leads to death. In order to evidence Christ at work in me and through me I want to deny the natural reactions of my flesh and be confident that Holy Spirit is supernaturally leading every thought, word and action.

In the last lesson we looked at the covenant relationship Jesus had with the Father in His humanness and discovered there was a part for Jesus and a part for God. We experience the same division of labor. There are two parts of our covenant relationship with God - His part to do and our part to do.

Our Responsibility	**God's Responsibility**
The choice is always ours to make. Acting in a way that opposes what our flesh desires means dying to our flesh which enables resurrection power to be at work in us.	As soon as we make a sincere decision to align our will with God's, the power of the Holy Spirit will begin to flow immediately to empower us to complete the obedient act we have chosen to do.

Because God is a covenant-making and covenant-keeping God, His faithfulness never changes. That means when we do our part, we can trust God to do what He promises to do! This is always how a covenant works and God never forgets His covenant.

Hear What The Spirit is Saying to the Church: *The time has come to put My power back in My church!*

LESSON 6:

THE SPIRIT'S POWER
AT WORK IN PAUL

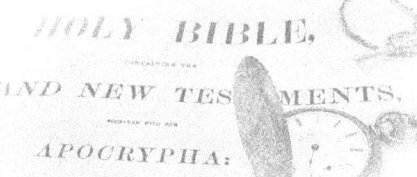

"We proclaim Him, admonishing every man and teaching every man with all wisdom, so that we may present every man complete in Christ. For this purpose also I labor, striving according to His power, which mightily works within me." Colossians 1:28-29

IN OUR PREVIOUS two lessons, we took note that Jesus accomplished His earthly Kingdom assignment by the *dunamis* which worked in Him and through Him. In this lesson, we want to look further into that power at work in ordinary Christ-followers like you and me. Rather than using Jesus as our model, we'll focus in this lesson on another prototype God has given us – the Apostle Paul. Why Paul? First, because he is the clearest biblical example, aside from Jesus, we have. Moreover, Paul invited Christ-followers to follow the example he set for them. "Be imitators of me, just as I also am of Christ (1 Corinthians 11:1)."

We've learned that after the resurrection of Christ, the Holy Spirit transformed His disciples from fearful bereaved men to bold and dynamic powerhouses. Infused with God's power they were used in mighty ways to advance His Kingdom on earth. Paul considered himself to be "abnormally born"[1] among those first Apos-

---

[1] 1 Corinthians 15:8. One internet source suggests "most scholars believe [Paul's meeting with Christ on the road to Damscus] was between 33 – 36 A.D." The dating suggests Paul's commission as the Apostle to the Gentiles happened about 6 to 8 years after the death of Christ. Shirley, Steve, *Q: #520. How long was it from the time of Jesus' death until He appeared to Paul*

tles. In fact, when we first meet Paul in Scripture he was among those attempting to stop the spread of the gospel! However, God's power met Paul on the road to Damascus and permanently overruled Paul's agenda.[2] Three days later God sent Ananias to Paul so that his sight could be restored and he could be filled with the Holy Spirit.[3]

"Meeting Jesus [on the road to Damascus] saved Paul …. Meeting the Holy Spirit empowered him for Kingdom ministry."[4] Following Paul's baptism, he immediately began to proclaim the good news of the gospel.[5] The same power that temporarily blinded him was the power that transformed him from a zealous persecutor to a zealous disciple.

Knowing of his unique commission, Paul admonished those he taught to imitate him. On at least six occasions Paul either approves of those who are following his example as he follows Christ's example or he commands Christ-followers to follow his example.[6] Some might call this arrogance of the worst sort. On the contrary, the serious student of Paul will recognize Paul's confidence was not in his flesh, but in God's power at work in him such that he could present himself as their example. No one had yet written the New Testament. As a matter of fact, Paul would be used by Holy Spirit to write almost half of the New Testament books in the Bible we read today. Because there were no written instructions that documented a post-resurrection experience of

---

on the road to Damascus? JesusAlive. Retrieved from https://jesusalive.cc/timeline-jesus-death-pauls-conversion/ (last accessed December 27, 2021)

2   R. T. Kendall provides this definition of what it means to overrule: "to disallow by exercising one's superior authority." Kendall, R. T., *40 Days with the Holy Spirit* (Charisma House 2014) pp. 31-34
3   Acts 9:9,17-18
4   Carrin, Charles, "Part Three: Power" in *Word Spirit Power: What Happens When You Seek All God Has to Offer* (Chosen 2012) authored by Kendall, Carrin and Taylor, p. 201
5   Acts 9:15,20; 11:25-26
6   Deere, Jack, *Surprised By The Power Of The Spirit: Discovering How God Speaks and Heals Today* (Zondervan 1993) p. 113. See 1 Corinthians 4:16-17; 11:1; Philippians 3:17; 4:9; 1 Thessalonians 1:6; 2 Thessalonians 3:9

discipleship for the early church, God provided living examples through His apostles, including Paul.

Our Key Scripture for this lesson speaks clearly about Paul's methodology and power source. Paul told the Colossians that because he desired every disciple to reach maturity he labored with determination. Then he made clear that the source of his untiring energy was "according to [Christ's] power [*dunamis*], which mightily works [*energeo*] within" him.

You may recognize two power words that we studied in our last lesson, *dunamis* and *energeo*, the verb form of the word *energeia*. Paul is especially fond of complementing the word *dunamis* with the word *energeia*. Let's do a quick review of what we learned about these two important words in Lesson 6. As it relates to Christ-followers, *dunamis* is power that resides in us with the potential and capacity to produce a change. On the other hand, Paul's recurring references to God "actively at work in" people and circumstances are captured most consistently with the words in the *energein* word group.[7] All of the words in the *energein* word group refer to actively putting available power to work. In other words, it is the difference between power made available and power put to use. When God's power is put to work, the result is that which had the *potential, ability, capacity* for change [*dunamis*] has actually experienced [*energeia*] the desired change.

This descriptive relationship between *dunamis* (potential power) and *energeia* (actual or realized power) dates at least as far back as the days of Plato (427-347 B.C.) and Aristotle (384-322 B.C.).[8] It has been recognized that this ancient Greek distinction

---

7   Perkins, Larry, *115. God at work–Paul's Concept of the Verb energein and Cognates (Philippians 2:12-13)*, Internet Moments with God's Word, posted June 30, 2011, nbseminary.com. Retrieved from http://moments.nbseminary.com/archives/115-paul%E2%80%99s-concept-of-the-verb-energein-and-cognates-%E2%80%93-god-at-work-philippians-212-13/ (last accessed December 27, 2021). Dr. Perkins is Professor Emeritus of Biblical Studies, Northwest Baptist Seminary.

8   Hoehner, Harold W., "Ephesians," in *The Bible Knowledge Word Study: Acts-Ephesians*, edited by Darrell L. Bock (Victor 2002) Ephesians 1:19

between the potential of *dunamis* power and the actual expression of power as *energeia* is maintained by the authors of the New Testament epistles.[9] Because Paul lived and ministered in a society heavily impacted by Greek philosophy he could use the language of the day to communicate an important Kingdom principle. Paul understood that *dunamis* alone wouldn't meet the need. *Energeia* had to be released by the Holy Spirit and when *energeia* was applied to *dunamis* God's grace and power were sufficient to meet every need.

"Paul saw the [Holy] Spirit as the key to everything in the Christian life."[10] He taught that the entire life of a Christ-follower "is about *living* in the Spirit, *walking* in the Spirit, and *marching in step* with the Spirit."[11] Moreover, Paul freely admitted that the Holy Spirit was the source of *all* the power at work in his life. If we had the opportunity to personally interview the Apostle Paul he would undoubtedly tell us that he would not have been able to accomplish anything of Kingdom value without the power of God's Spirit at work in him and through him. Paul knew from first-hand experience that it was in his human weakness that God's power was perfected. He understood what too few Christ-followers understand today:

> … God proclaims that his true power, and thus authentic ministry, does not work from a power orientation, but rather from a position of weakness.[12]

---

under *According to the mighty working of his power (kata tēn energeian tou kratous tēs ischyos autou)*, p. 429

9 Shelke, Christopher, editor, *Apostle Paul: The Mission to Nations and Peoples* (Gregorian & Biblical Press 2010) p. 136. Retrieved from books.google.com (last accessed 2016). Webpage no longer available

10 Fee, Gordon D., *The First Epistle To The Corinthians*, New International Commentary on the New Testament (Eerdmans 1987) 1 Corinthians 12:14, p. 607

11 McKnight, Scot, *Open To The Spirit: God In Us, God with Us, God Transforming Us* (Waterbrook 2018) p. 203, italics in original

12 Guthrie, George H., *2 Corinthians*, Baker Exegetical Commentary On The New Testament (Baker Academic 2015) 2 Corinthians 12:9, p. 594

Because that is so, Paul's weakness provided the perfect opportunity for his witness.[13] In his second letter to the church at Corinth Paul shared these words which God had spoken to him, "My grace is sufficient for you, for power is perfected in weakness."[14] Of course, the word "power" is our now familiar word *dunamis*. The original Greek could be understood as God saying, "My *dunamis* comes to full strength[15] when you need strength."[16] Paul knew he was a prototype, one among the first fruits and that God was no respecter of persons – God does not play favorites.[17] Paul was confident that what God had done for him He would do for *every talmid*.

When God told Paul that "power" is made perfect in weakness it was in response to a "thorn in the flesh" which Paul had earnestly prayed for God to remove. Instead of removing the *thorn* God told Paul His grace would be "*completely* adequate"[18] to meet his need. "Thus God told Paul in effect, 'You do not really need the thorn removed. All you need is my grace to deal with it.'"[19] Paul knew God was saying that He had placed within Paul the *dunamis* power to satisfy every need. That promise was calculated to give Paul hope, the source of confident expectation, that he already had the divinely given resource that would meet his need every time the *thorn* resulted in torment.

---

13 I credit Kelly Russell with this thought. In our group study of this particular lesson the Lord provided her with revelation such that she understood that her weakness *is* her witness.

14 2 Corinthians 12:9

15 *NET Bible Notes*, translator's note 13, 2 Corinthians 12:9

16 The word "weakness" as used in 2 Corinthians 12:9 is *astheneia* {as-then'-i-ah} which means want of strength, weakness, infirmity.

17 Romans 2:11; Colossians 3:25

18 The Greek word *charis,* translated as "grace" in 2 Corinthians 12:9, is placed at the beginning of God's answer to Paul thus placing emphasis on His grace as being "completely adequate" to meet Paul's need. Guthrie, George H., *2 Corinthians*, Baker Exegetical Commentary On The New Testament (Baker Academic 2015) 2 Corinthians 12:9, p. 593, italics in original

19 Guthrie, George H., *2 Corinthians*, Baker Exegetical Commentary On The New Testament (Baker Academic 2015) 2 Corinthians 12:9, p. 593

We have said that *energeia* is the exertion or the working of that promised power. That means *dunamis* becomes power to meet the need because of the "law of use." For purposes of illustration, let's assume (as many scholars do) that Paul's *thorn* was the human opposition he was experiencing in Corinth.[20] Every time the *thorn* caused torment, Paul would have two choices. Only one of them would permit God's power to work. Paul could respond with his flesh and fight back in his own way using his own strength. Or he could choose to overrule his flesh and allow the Holy Spirit to *energize* (activate) the *dunamis* power already in Paul. When that dynamic power (*dunamis*) was activated by Holy Spirit the result was sufficient God-glorifying power for Paul's need.

This is more than a mere splitting of hairs. What I want us to see is that God's promised grace was indeed *completely adequate* to meet Paul's need at every turn. However, God's available grace required Paul's cooperation to hit the target and demolish the scheme of the enemy. As Christ-followers it is easy for us to fall into the trap of believing *all* the work belongs to God when in reality He has planned for us to partner with Him. The *law of use* is our part. God is willing to supply all the power we need. However, we must activate and put into practice the resources He provides for them to become the "grace that is sufficient" as solutions for our needs.

The only way the law of use is implemented in the life of a Spirit-filled Christ-follower is that we refrain from turning down the volume knob when Holy Spirit is speaking and we refuse to turn down the power knob when He is acting! Let me explain what I mean. The promise of the Holy Spirit is an assurance of God's presence in us as effective power. But did you know we each

---

20 Matera, Frank J., *II Corinthians: A Commentary* (Westminster John Knox Press 2003) 2 Corinthians 12:7-9a, p. 283 indicating that *many* scholars follow, at least partially, the viewpoint originally posited by Chrysostom (Homily 26:2) that Paul's opponents were his "thorn in the flesh." God had referred to Israel's enemies as "thorns" in Numbers 33:55 and Ezekiel 28:24. *ESV Study Bible* (Crossway Books 2008) study note 2 Corinthians 12:7, p. 2238

control the degree to which the Holy Spirit is empowered to operate in our lives and do the very things God sent Him to do? As a Christ-follower you have all of the Holy Spirit, but that does not *automatically* mean Holy Spirit has all of you![21] The choice is ours as to whether we will be *closed* to the Holy Spirit, *partially open* to Him, or *wide open* to Him. In the words of scholar Scot McKnight, "*being wide open to the Spirit* .... means offering ourselves to God all day long and with every globule [drop] of our being."[22] For God to be fully enabled to do all that He desires, demands that we allow His Spirit to be fully in charge! Paul refers to this as being led by the Spirit (Romans 8:1-17).

Think of it like this: you know how you can turn a knob on a gas stove from *low* to *high*? The position of that knob regulates the amount of gas flame you have available on the stovetop. The Holy Spirit inside of us responds similarly to how the gas responds to the stove knob. As a result, even though Holy Spirit indwells us, we control the degree to which He is able to work in our life. We also control the volume at which He is permitted to speak to us to instruct, remind, guide and convict.

In Paul's case, even though the *dunamis* resided in him, if he had chosen to fight the opposition in his own power – according to the dictates of his natural flesh reactions – he would have turned down the power knob to Holy Spirit. Absent Holy Spirit power, Paul would have missed the opportunity to experience God's grace in action. The *dunamis* power in him would have been available, but it would be devoid of application. If that was the case, the scoreboard for the kingdom of darkness would display "1" for the enemy and the scoreboard for the Kingdom of Light would display "0" for God. On the other hand, every time Paul chose to die to his flesh and allow the Holy Spirit to activate (*energeia*) that *dunamis* power resident in him, the result would be a victory for

---

21 Shirer, Priscilla, *Discerning the Voice of God: How to Recognize When God Speaks* (LifeWay Press 2006) DVD Session 2, The Holy Spirit
22 McKnight, Scot, *Open To The Spirit: God In Us, God with Us, God Transforming Us* (Waterbrook 2018) p. 203, italics in original

the Kingdom of God. Scoreboard "1" for God and "0" for the enemy! In the midst of Paul's weakness, the grace of God worked to enable Paul to light up the Kingdom scoreboard with repeated victories. God's activated *dunamis* power enabled Paul to be more-than-a-conqueror.[23]

Before we conclude our lesson let's briefly consider three other key ways that activated power worked in Paul's ministry: 1) power that accredited him as God's messenger, 2) other miracles and 3) a sustaining power to endure suffering and hardships.

Demonstrations of power as God's messenger

Luke noted the increasing power released to Paul permitting him to prove that Jesus was the promised Messiah. In Acts 9:22 Luke wrote, "But [Paul] kept increasing in strength [*endunamoo*] and confounding the Jews who lived at Damascus by proving that this *Jesus* is the Christ." As I have noted, the word "strength" is the Greek verb *endunamoo* {en-doo-nam-o'-o} which is a compound word. It combines the preposition *en* (meaning in) and you guessed it, the noun *dunamis*. *Endunamoo* literally means "in-strengthened, inwardly strengthened."[24]

The use of *dunamis* in the Greek version of the Old Testament provides us with an interesting word picture Luke might have had in mind. In the Old Testament, *dunamis* was employed primarily to picture "the combined forces of a complete military."[25] Luke could have been telling his readers to imagine Paul being indwelt with the unstoppable power of an army that was ever increasing in strength!

At issue in Corinth was Paul's qualifications to be an apostle. Part of the defense he gave for his legitimate apostleship was that God's power attended and accredited his preaching and teaching.

---

23 Romans 8:37
24 Wenstrom, William E., Jr., *Greek Word Studies* (Wenstrom.org ©2016) entry for *Endunamoo*. Retrieved from http://wenstrom.org/downloads/written/word_studies/greek/endunamoo.pdf (last accessed December 27, 2021)
25 Renner, Rick, *Sparkling Gems from the Greek Volume II* (Harrison House Publishers 2016) July 12, p. 640, italics omitted

Paul contended, his "message and . . . preaching were not in persuasive words of wisdom, but in *demonstration* of the Spirit and of power [*dunamis*], so that [their] faith would not rest on the wisdom of men, but on the power [*dunamis*] of God."[26] In the first century, when orators came to town they would typically *demonstrate* their point with "wise and persuasive words."[27] When Paul speaks of *demonstrating* the Spirit and power, he used a term from the realm of public speaking. To demonstrate a point meant the orator used "a method of proving what is not certain by means of what is certain."[28] What Paul told the Corinthians was that the method he used to prove the truth of what he was preaching/teaching (that which did not seem certain to them) was through the activated power of Holy Spirit (what is certain).

Paul was highly educated with impeccable Jewish credentials.[29] Even so, he did not rely on those hard-earned credentials, he relied on Holy Spirit's power to demonstrate and persuade. He knew the growth of the church was *not* due to his cleverness, resourcefulness, or oratory skill. The church of Jesus Christ grew and matured through the convincing power of God's Spirit. Paul continuously testified to the working of God's power in his ministry.

---

26 1 Corinthians 2:4-5, italics added
27 Gill, David W., J., "1 Corinthians," in *Zondervan Illustrated Bible Backgrounds Commentary*, Vol. 3, edited by Clinton E. Arnold (Zondervan 2002) 1 Corinthians 2:4, pp. 116-117
28 Gill, David W., J., "1 Corinthians," in *Zondervan Illustrated Bible Backgrounds Commentary*, Vol. 3, edited by Clinton E. Arnold (Zondervan 2002) 1 Corinthians 2:4, p. 117, quoting Quintilian, 4.10.7
29 In Philippians 3:4-6 Paul testified of himself, "although I myself might have confidence even in the flesh. If anyone else has a mind to put confidence in the flesh, I far more: circumcised the eighth day, of the nation of Israel, of the tribe of Benjamin, a Hebrew of Hebrews; as to the Law, a Pharisee; as to zeal, a persecutor of the church; as to the righteousness which is in the Law, found blameless." But he then went on to proclaim in the very next verse, "But whatever things were gain to me, those things I have counted as loss for the sake of Christ (Philippians 3:7)."

> When I was with you [Corinthians], I certainly gave you proof that I am an apostle. For I patiently did many signs [*semeion*] and wonders [*teras*], and miracles [*dunamis*] among you. 2 Corinthians 12:12 NLT

> Yet I dare not boast about anything except what Christ has done through me, bringing the Gentiles to God by my message and by the way I worked among them. They were convinced by the power [*dunamis*] of miraculous signs [*semeion*] and wonders [*teras*] and by the power [*dunamis*] of God's Spirit. In this way, I have fully presented the Good News of Christ from Jerusalem all the way to Illyricum. Romans 15:18-19 NLT

Notice Paul stacks up a few more words to describe God's supernatural power. *Semeion* {say-mi'-on} can denote "a miraculous event contrary to the usual course of nature and intended as a pointer or means of confirmation."[30] According to a leading Greek lexicon, the word was used to "refer to 'a sign or distinguishing mark whereby something is known' or 'to an event that is an indication or confirmation of intervention by [divine] powers.'"[31] In other words, Paul maintained that God supernaturally verified, endorsed and authenticated the gospel message he preached.[32] By using the word *teras* {ter'-as} Paul was pointing out that what God did caused people to be in awe or amazed.[33]

---

30 *Romans 15:19-26 Commentary*, Precept Austin. Retrieved from http://www.preceptaustin.org romans_15_notes_pt3 (last accessed December 28, 2021)

31 Matera, Frank J., *II Corinthians: A Commentary* (Westminster John Knox Press 2003) 2 Corinthians 12:11b-12, p. 289, quoting from *BDAG* (Bauer, Danker, Arndt, and Gingrich, *Greek-English Lexicon of the New Testament*)

32 Renner, Rick, *Sparkling Gems from the Greek* (Harrison House Publishers 2003) April 18, p. 252

33 Renner, Rick, *Sparkling Gems from the Greek* (Harrison House Publishers 2003) November 27, p. 908

In the first century, there was nothing unusual about traveling teachers who did miracles.[34] Therefore, the fact that Paul's teaching was accompanied by miracles, signs and wonders is not the point. Paul's emphasis is that the authentication of his message was the result of Christ working through Paul's weakness to put the power of God on glorious display![35]

Before we move on it is important to take note that, "No text of Scripture says that the authority of Scripture rests on miracles [or other signs and wonders]! In reality, it is just the opposite. Scripture tests miracles, but miracles are not a test for Scripture."[36] When God chooses to use His supernatural power to endorse His message and His messenger, He does so "on the basis of grace, not out of a divine necessity to make up for a deficiency in the gospel message."[37]

Power displayed through other miracles

The words "signs" and "wonders" may refer to healing miracles, but they could just as easily refer to other types of phenomena or supernatural occurrences that exceed the boundaries of nature. In fact, the biblical record contains several such types of power encounters involving Paul. Consider for example: 1) God's power at work through Paul such that a pagan magician who was interfering with Paul's ministry was struck blind and 2) Paul's confrontation with the demonic spirit of divination working through a slave girl.

> So, being sent out by the Holy Spirit, [Paul and Barnabas] went down to Seleucia and from there they sailed to Cyprus. . . When they had gone through the whole island as far as Paphos, they found a magician,

---

34 Keck, Leander E., *Romans*, Abingdon New Testament Commentaries (Abingdon Press 2005) Romans 15:14-21, p. 361
35 Keck, Leander E., *Romans*, Abingdon New Testament Commentaries (Abingdon Press 2005) Romans 15:14-21, p. 361
36 Deere, Jack, *Surprised By The Power of The Spirit* (Zondervan 1993) p. 106
37 Deere, Jack, *Surprised By The Power of The Spirit* (Zondervan 1993) p. 110

a Jewish false prophet whose name was Bar-Jesus, who was with the proconsul, Sergius Paulus, a man of intelligence. This man summoned Barnabas and Saul and sought to hear the word of God. But Elymas the magician (for so his name is translated) was opposing them, seeking to turn the proconsul away from the faith. But Saul, who was also known as Paul, filled with the Holy Spirit, fixed his gaze on him, and said, "You who are full of all deceit and fraud, you son of the devil, you enemy of all righteousness, will you not cease to make crooked the straight ways of the Lord? Now, behold, the hand of the Lord is upon you, and you will be blind and not see the sun for a time." And immediately a mist and a darkness fell upon him, and he went about seeking those who would lead him by the hand. Acts 13:4,6-11

It happened that as we were going to the place of prayer, a slave-girl having a spirit of divination met us, who was bringing her masters much profit by fortune-telling. Following after Paul and us, she kept crying out, saying, "These men are bond-servants of the Most High God, who are proclaiming to you the way of salvation." She continued doing this for many days. But Paul was greatly annoyed, and turned and said to the spirit, "I command you in the name of Jesus Christ to come out of her!" And it came out at that very moment. Acts 16:16-18

In a more general sense, Luke attests to God's release of miracle-working power through Paul. In Acts 19:11-12, he wrote, "God was performing extraordinary miracles by the hands of Paul, so that handkerchiefs or aprons[38] were even carried from his

---

38 The handkerchiefs and aprons referred to here would have been rags which were tied around Paul's head to catch sweat and his work aprons which would have been tied around his waist. Scholar Craig Keener notes these articles of clothing might have been taken without Paul's knowledge. Keener, Craig

body to the sick, and the diseases left them and the evil spirits went out." In the first century, Ephesus was known as a center for magic (Acts 19:18-19). Luke's account of Paul's ministry in Ephesus highlights the fact that God did some "extraordinary miracles" (*dunamis* that hits the mark)[39] through Paul such that diseases and spirits left people by means of cloths that had been in contact with him. It seems most likely that God's miracles were extraordinary in order to demonstrate that the God Paul spoke of was the one true God. He is more powerful than the false gods behind the magical incantations the Ephesians were accustomed to.

Jesus had promised that those who followed Him would do the same works He had done and even greater works than those He did because He was going to His Father.[40] Paul is just one living example of exactly what Jesus promised! In the words of Jesus, He had come "to bring good news to the afflicted . . . bind up the brokenhearted, to proclaim liberty to captives and freedom to prisoners; to proclaim the favorable year of the Lord."[41] He intended His followers to continue the work He had begun. In fact, it is reasonable to conclude from Scripture that continuing the work of Jesus is the very reason why the Holy Spirit was sent from God.

Power to endure suffering and hardship

Paul's autobiography is not one many people would clamor to claim for themselves. He lists one distressing hardship after another: expended great labor, endured several imprisonments,

---

S., *The IVP Bible Background Commentary New Testament* (Intervarsity Press 1993) Acts 19:11-12, p. 378

39 The original Greek in essence says, "*Dunamis* and-together-with special *tygxánō* [which can denote hitting a mark with a weapon] God did by the hands of Paul." Translation from Hill, Gary, *The Discovery Bible*, HELPS Ministries, Inc., GK Critical Text (WH), Acts 19:11. Definition of *tygxánō* from Zodhiates, Spiros, *The Complete Word Study Dictionary: New Testament* (AMG Publishers 1992) word #5177, p. 1398

40 John 14:12

41 The text of Isaiah 61:1-2a which Jesus read in the Nazareth Synagogue as His mission statement

beaten times without number, often in danger of death, five different times he received thirty-nine lashes from the Jews, beaten with rods three times, once he was stoned, he spent a full night and a day floating in the sea and was shipwrecked three times.[42] How does one person not only survive such a litany of traumatic events let alone continue in faithfulness to the One who promised to never leave him nor forsake him? And even more, how does one such as Paul pen the words that "in any and every circumstance, I have learned the secret of contentment?"[43] There can be only one answer: the sustaining power of God's Spirit. In fact, Paul finishes his thought this way. "Not that I speak from want, for I have learned to be content in whatever circumstances I am .... [because] I can do all things through Him who strengthens [*endunamoo*] me (Philippians 4:11,13)." Then to the church at Corinth he wrote, "I am well content with weaknesses, with insults, with distresses, with persecutions, with difficulties, for Christ's sake; for when I am weak, then I am strong (2 Corinthians 12:10)."

As we noted earlier, *endunamoo* literally means in-strengthened, inwardly strengthened. Thus, Paul gives credit to the *dunamis* power of God's Spirit which strengthened him inwardly permitting him not only to endure extreme hardships, but to find contentment in his suffering. The supernatural power God faithfully supplied created a pathway for Paul's overcoming testimony. Paul was so convinced of the merit of God's power working through his weakness that he would "rather boast about [his] weaknesses, [so] that the power [*dunamis*] of Christ may dwell in [him]."[44]

What an amazing testimony of confident grace,[45] may that be our boast as well!

---

42 2 Corinthians 11:23-25
43 Philippians 4:12 NET
44 2 Corinthians 12:9b
45 I had never heard this phrase until I was journaling and God asked me to go to an upcoming ministry meeting in "confident grace." I understand the phrase to mean, I am to place my confidence in His all-sufficient grace. Personal Journal February 3, 2024

Hear What The Spirit is Saying to the Church: *My body is designed to operate in My power. Paul was indeed a prototype. Let's get back to the basics and watch the church of this day rise up in power.*

LESSON 7:

POWER TO SET THE CAPTIVE FREE

"But thank God that, although you used to be slaves of sin, you obeyed from the heart that pattern of teaching you were transferred to, and having been liberated from sin, you became enslaved to righteousness." Romans 6:17-18 HCSB

IN HIS TEACHING SERIES titled, *Not A Fan*, Pastor Kyle Idleman tells the story of a friend who heard the gospel one evening, believed what he heard and was *saved* that night.[1] The friend told Idelman that had been 10 years earlier and "looking back the only problem was that he did not die that night." Idelman's friend confessed he had spent about a decade of his life not understanding that he was also called to *follow* Jesus. The friend then said, "I wish that man [the one who had shared the gospel with him] would have told me that death starts now!" What he meant was that he *believed* the gospel message when he heard it, but he didn't apply its power to his life. We will use this lesson and the next one to look at the truth that it is the power of the cross that sets captives free and it is that same power that can keep them free! The paradox of this power is that living free comes at the expense of daily dying (Matthew 16:24).

We're going to jump right in to our Key Scripture for this lesson. Notice that Paul uses freedom and slavery in a figurative sense. This type of metaphor would resonate with his audience

---

1 Idleman, Kyle, *Not A Fan*, Video Segment #4, bury the dead (City On A Hill Studio 2016)

because many of those Paul was writing to would have had personal experience with slavery.[2] In Romans 8:2 Paul specifies the Holy Spirit as the source of freedom from sin's slavery.

> For the law of the Spirit of life has set you free in Christ Jesus from the law of sin and death. Romans 8:2 ESV

Let's add a few notes of clarification to this verse before we return to our Key Scripture. As an initial matter, when Paul refers to *the law of the Spirit* and *the law of sin and death* he likely employs the word "law" as a reference to "governing power," "rule" or "binding authority."[3] To be free to do those things a follower of Christ desires to do requires breaking the power of sin.[4] Paul says that's exactly what God has done through Christ's redeeming work! As Michael Green points out, "it is the Spirit who liberates Christ's risen power in us and enables us to share in his triumph."[5]

Calling the Holy Spirit "the Spirit of life" most likely highlights the fact that the "Spirit is the life-giving power which makes men and women anew."[6] That makes Him the perfect contrast

---

2 Martin and Wu, "Galatians," in *Zondervan Illustrated Bible Backgrounds Commentary*, Vol. 3, edited by Clinton E. Arnold (Zondervan 2002) Galatians 5:1, p. 288

3 Hoehner, Harold W., "Romans," in *The Bible Knowledge Word Study: Acts-Ephesians*, edited by Darrell L. Bock (Victor 2006) Romans 8:2 under *For the law of the Spirit of life*, p. 167, citing LN §33.333; Moo pp. 474-76. See also: Moo, Douglas J., "Romans," in *Zondervan Illustrated Bible Backgrounds Commentary*, Vol. 3, edited by Clinton E. Arnold (Zondervan 2002) Romans 8:2, p. 44; Schreiner, Thomas R., *Romans*, Baker Exegetical Commentary on the New Testament, 2nd edition (Baker Academic 1998, 2018) Romans 8:2, p. 396

4 Keck, Leander E., *Romans*, Abingdon New Testament Commentaries (Abingdon Press 2005) The Power of the Spirit ([Romans] 8:1-17) p. 198

5 Green, Michael, *I Believe in the Holy Spirit*, Revised edition (Eerdmans 2004) p. 109

6 Hill, David, *Greek Words and Hebrew Meanings: Studies in the Semantics of Soteriological Terms*, Society for New Testament Studies Monograph Series 5 (Wipf and Stock 2000, previously published Cambridge University Press 1967) p. 289 John's references to being born from above or being born from

The Power of My Spirit

to the spirit which leads to sin and death. In sum, Paul says that Christ's redemptive work is applied to a Christ-follower's life through the ruling authority (governing power) of the Holy Spirit in such a way that it breaks the dominion of their two archenemies: the ruling authority (governing powers) of sin and death.[7] Overruling the power of sin and death enables Christ-followers to enjoy a living relationship with God that is impossible for those who are not united with Christ.[8] As we will learn, the concepts of slavery (bondage, captivity) and freedom made the perfect metaphor for what was accomplished spiritually by the power of the cross.

When Paul speaks of being a slave to sin in our Key Scripture, he employs the Greek word *doulos* {doo'-los} which was a common word for a *slave*. The most accurate translation of *doulos* is "bondservant" denoting one who sells himself into slavery to another. According to the *Theological Dictionary of the New Testament* the term indicates compulsory service. A *doulos* conveys the idea of one closely bound with his master, belonging to him, obligated and desirous to do the master's will. It refers to one who is in a permanent relation of servitude and his own will is totally submitted to his master's will.[9] A bondservant could not resign from one master to go work for a different one.[10] "To be a slave [*doulos*]

---

the Spirit are similar "in substance" to Paul's concept of becoming a new creation. Ibid. pp. 289-290

7 Harrison and Hagner, "Romans," in *The Expositor's Bible Commentary: Romans - Galatians*, Vol. 11, Revised edition, edited by Longman III and Garland (Zondervan Academic 2008) Romans 8:1, p. 128; Romans 8:2, p. 129. "Sin, death, and the world are concrete enemies (Rom 8:37-39; 1 Cor 15:5ff; 1 John 5:4)." Zodhiates, Spiros, *The Complete Word Study Dictionary: New Testament* (AMG Publishers 1992) word #1657, p. 566

8 Hoehner, Harold W., "Romans," in *The Bible Knowledge Word Study: Acts-Ephesians*, edited by Darrell L. Bock (Victor 2006) Romans 8:2 under *Has set you free*, p. 167

9 Zodhiates, Spiros, *The Complete Word Study Dictionary: New Testament* (AMG Publishers 1992) word #1401, p. 483

10 *Spirit Filled Life Bible* (Thomas Nelson 1991) Romans 1:1 under *Bondservant*, p. 1686

of sin means that one is under its lordship and dominion and thus unable to extricate oneself from its tyranny."[11] In other words, without the power of the cross we were held captive to sin as if we were a *doulos* to sin. As such sin was our master and we were unable to free ourselves from compulsively obeying sin.[12]

Paul assures every Christ-follower that their bondage to sin was a thing of the past because God had rescued them from the dominion of sin. A Word Study will be helpful so that we can better understand the freedom/liberty word Paul employed.

---

11 Schreiner, Thomas R., *Romans*, Baker Exegetical Commentary on the New Testament, 2nd edition (Baker Academic 1998, 2018) Romans 6:17-18, p. 333

12 As we will see more fully in Lesson 7, there are two Greek words used in the New Testament which go hand-in-hand with this idea of captivity. The first is *skandalon* {skan'-dal-on} and the other is *pagis* {pag-ece'}. "The Son of Man will send out His angels, and they will gather from His kingdom everything that causes sin [*skandalon*] and those guilty of lawlessness. They will throw them into the blazing furnace where there will be weeping and gnashing of teeth. (Matthew 13:41-42 HCSB)." The Greek noun *skandalon* is an ancient word used originally to describe the bait stick in an animal trap. The hunter would place the bait on the stick to attract the prey. The bait stick is what triggered the trapping mechanism to capture the animal. The Bible also uses *pagis* in reference to Satan's ability to ensnare / trap / capture people. "The Lord's bond-servant must not be quarrelsome, but be kind to all, able to teach, patient when wronged, with gentleness correcting those who are in opposition, if perhaps God may grant them . . . [to] come to their senses and escape from the snare [*pagis*] of the devil, having been held captive by him to do his will. (2 Timothy 2:24-26)." *Pagis* comes from *pēgnymi* which means to "set a trap." The term *pagis* is the Greek word used for things that hold fast like net, a snare or a mousetrap. Sources: *Spirit Filled Life Bible* (Thomas Nelson 1991) *Word Wealth [Matthew] 11:6 offended, skandalizo*, p. 1424; Bromiley, Geoffrey W., *Theological Dictionary of the New Testament*, Abridged in One Volume (Eerdmans 1985) entry for *pagis* under *pagis*, p. 752; Hill, Gary, *The Discovery Bible*, HELPS Ministries, Inc., [G]3803 *pagis*

WORD STUDY

*The Greek word translated as **liberated** in our Key Scripture is eleutheroo {el-yoo-ther-o'-o} which refers to liberation that results from being redeemed. The picture is that of being emancipated from slavery.[13] The oo ending on the word eleutheroo "means not only will [we] be set free but [we] will be seen as set free."[14]*

The related noun eleutheria {el-yoo-ther-ee'-ah} describes the state of being free and stands in contrast to slavery or bondage.[15] In a concrete sense, its New Testament use refers to freedom from the enslaving power of sin and death.[16]

As noted in our Word Study, this concept of freedom from bondage that results from being redeemed is biblically applied to being set free from the power of sin that had previously enslaved

---

13 Zodhiates, Spiros, *The Complete Word Study Dictionary: New Testament* (AMG Publishers 1992) word #1659, p. 567; SermonIndex.net, *Text Sermons: Greek Word Studies: Free (1659) eleutheroo*. Retrieved from https://www.sermonindex.net/modules/articles/index.php?view=article&aid=34112 (last accessed May 6, 2024)

14 SermonIndex.net, *Text Sermons: Greek Word Studies: Free (1659) eleutheroo*. Retrieved from https://www.sermonindex.net/modules/articles/index.php?view=article&aid=34112 (last accessed May 6, 2024)

15 Zodhiates, Spiros, *The Complete Word Study Dictionary: New Testament* (AMG Publishers 1992) word #1657, pp. 565-566

16 Bromiley, Geoffrey W., *Theological Dictionary of the New Testament*, Abridged in One Volume (Eerdmans 1985) entry for *eleutheros* under *C. The Concept of Freedom in the NT*, p. 225; Grassmick, John D., "Galatians," in *The Bible Knowledge Word Study: Acts-Ephesians*, edited by Darrell L. Bock (Victor 2002) Galatians 5:1 under *Freedom… set free*, p. 402

us. But what does that mean as a practical matter? We can find the answer in 1 John 3.

> ⁶ No one who abides in Him **sins**; no one who **sins** has seen Him or knows Him. ⁷ Little children, make sure no one deceives you; the one who **practices** righteousness is righteous, just as He is righteous; ⁸ the one who **practices** sin is of the devil; for the devil has **sinned** from the beginning. The Son of God appeared for this purpose, to destroy the works of the devil. ⁹ No one who is born of God **practices** sin, because His seed abides in him; and he cannot sin, because he is born of God. 1 John 3:6-9, bold added

According to scholar Harold Berry, it is impossible to understand these verses without understanding the Greek tense which the Apostle John repeatedly employs.[17] Berry identifies the verb translated as "sin" twice in verse 6, the term translated as "practices" in verses 7, 8 and 9, the word "sinned" in verse 8 and the verb "abides" in verse 9 as all being in the Greek present tense. I have highlighted each of these words in bold. The fact that their verb tense is the Greek present tense means each of these words emphasizes ongoing, continuous, habitual action in the present. That said, we could rewrite these verses as follows:

> ⁶ No one who abides in God **habitually sins in the present time**; no one who **sins continually in the present time** has seen Him or knows Him. ⁷ Little children, make sure no one deceives you; the one who **continually practices righteousness in the present time** is righteous, just as He is righteous; ⁸ the one who **continually practices sin in the present time** is of the devil; for the devil has **sinned continually** from the beginning. The Son of God appeared for this purpose, to destroy the works of the devil. ⁹ No one who is born of God **habitu-**

---
17 Berry, Harold J., *Treasures from the Original* (Moody Press 1972, 1985) p. 7

ally practices sin in the present time, because His seed **continually abides** in him; and he cannot sin, because he is born of God. 1 John 3:6-9, my paraphrase

Once we properly understand the verb tense John used we are able to see very clearly that he is not saying Christ-followers never sin. Rather his point is that the one who habitually practices righteousness (doing what is right in his covenant relationship with God) does not sin continually.

"Righteousness is a dynamic term describing God or humans in relationship with people. The righteous *do* what is right [what is obligated in covenant relationship]; [that is to say] they live in accordance with God's expectations (see [Psalm] 4:1)."[18] Earlier in his epistle John had given assurance that when we do sin and we confess and repent of that sin, God is "faithful and righteous to forgive us our sins and to cleanse us from all unrighteousness (1 John 1:9)."

Now let's return to our discussion of our Key Scripture. After Paul recognizes that the Christ-followers in Rome were no longer obeying sin as their master, he acknowledges that they "obeyed from the heart that pattern of teaching [they] were transferred to." Obeying from the heart points to the fact that they made a choice to obey voluntarily, their obedience was not forced and it was authentic, not fabricated.[19]

Translating the verb *paradidomi* {par-ad-id'-o-mee} with the phrase "transferred to" falls short of conveying the full meaning of that Greek word. *Paradidomi* "denotes being delivered over to another power, as a slave is handed over from one master to another."[20] The idea is that once they became followers of Christ

---

18 Longman III and Garland, general editors, *The Expositor's Bible Commentary: Psalms*, Vol. 5, Revised edition (Zondervan 2008) Psalm 15:2, p. 183, italics in original
19 Gundry, Robert H., *Commentary on the New Testament* (Hendrickson Publishers 2010) Romans 6:15-18, p. 592
20 Schreiner, Thomas R., *Romans*, Baker Exegetical Commentary on the New Testament, 2nd edition (Baker Academic 1998, 2018) Romans 6:17-18,

and were delivered from the power of sin, they were delivered over to the power of a new master. "Grace has its norms"[21] and those norms are implanted as they obey the teaching of Christ who is their new master. In fact, "having been liberated from sin, [they] became enslaved to righteousness." When Paul refers to Christ-followers as becoming "enslaved to righteousness" he used the Greek word *douloo* {doo-lo'-o} which refers to making someone a *doulos*.[22] One who is set from being a *doulos* to sin immediately becomes a *doulos* of righteousness.

Paul knows full well that "life cannot be lived in a vacuum."[23] "In using the language of slavery and emancipation this way, Paul expresses the conviction that 'freedom from' always entails an obligatory 'freedom for.' He never envisages total absence of obligation .... As Paul sees it, one is always 'under' some structure of obligation, beholden to some power and authority."[24] Said differently, there is no middle ground here. Paul knows there is no such status of "nonenslavement."[25] There is only enslavement to sin or enslavement to righteousness.[26] Sin and righteousness both entail "a master so rigorous, so exacting, that it consumes the whole of

---

pp. 334-335
21 Harrison and Hagner, "Romans," in *The Expositor's Bible Commentary: Romans - Galatians*, Vol. 11, Revised edition, edited by Longman III and Garland (Zondervan Academic 2008) Romans 6:17, p. 111
22 Hoehner, Harold W., "Romans," in *The Bible Knowledge Word Study: Acts-Ephesians*, edited by Darrell L. Bock (Victor 2006) Romans 6:18 under *You were enslaved to righteousness*, p. 161
23 Harrison and Hagner, "Romans," in *The Expositor's Bible Commentary: Romans - Galatians*, Vol. 11, Revised edition, edited by Longman III and Garland (Zondervan Academic 2008) Romans 6:18, p. 111
24 Keck, Leander E., *Romans*, Abingdon New Testament Commentaries (Abingdon Press 2005) Freed from Sin, Enslaved to Rectitude ([Romans] 6:15-23) p. 172
25 Gundry, Robert H., *Commentary on the New Testament* (Hendrickson Publishers 2010) Romans 6:15-18, p. 592
26 Gundry, Robert H., Commentary on the New Testament (Hendrickson Publishers 2010) Romans 6:15-18, p. 592; Schreiner, Thomas R., *Romans*, Baker Exegetical Commentary on the New Testament, 2nd edition (Baker Academic 1998, 2018) Romans 6:20, p. 337

The Power of My Spirit

one's attention."[27] However, "[t]here is a difference as wide as the heavens between the two forms of bond service spoken of. The service of sin is *an actual bondage* and the service of righteousness and of God is *an actual freedom.*"[28]

Today, the world persistently strives to pursue freedom which is basically understood as doing *whatever* you want to do, *whenever* and *however* you want to do it – never having to deny any desire. The motto, "*If it feels good do it*" provides a false liberty. Paul found it "intolerable" for someone to have received the Spirit and yet live as though they had not![29] Gratifying the desires of the flesh is antagonistic to the freedom of life in the Spirit Paul wrote about. As a Jew, Paul's belief lined up with the common Jewish belief that a person can be free only as the obey God.[30]

> For you have been called to live in freedom, my brothers and sisters. But don't use your freedom to satisfy your sinful nature. Instead, use your freedom to serve one another in love. Galatians 5:13 NLT

> So I say, let the Holy Spirit guide your lives. Then you won't be doing what your sinful nature craves. The sinful nature wants to do evil, which is just the opposite of what the Spirit wants. And the Spirit gives us desires that are the opposite of what the sinful nature desires.

---

27 Harrison and Hagner, "Romans," in *The Expositor's Bible Commentary: Romans - Galatians*, Vol. 11, Revised edition, edited by Longman III and Garland (Zondervan Academic 2008) Romans 6:20, p. 112
28 Harrison and Hagner, "Romans," in *The Expositor's Bible Commentary: Romans - Galatians*, Vol. 11, Revised edition, edited by Longman III and Garland (Zondervan Academic 2008) Romans 6:19, p. 111, italics in the original, quoting Nygren, Anders, *Commentary on Romans*, translated by C. C. Rasmussen (Muhlenberg 1949) p. 257
29 Fee, Gordon D., *The First Epistle To The Corinthians*, New International Commentary on the New Testament (Eerdmans 1987) 1 Corinthians 3:2b-3, p. 127
30 McCartney, Dan G., *James*, Baker Exegetical Commentary on the New Testament (Baker Academic 2009) James 1:22-25, p. 123, citations omitted

These two forces are constantly fighting each other, so you are not free to carry out your good intentions. Galatians 5:16-17 NLT

When you follow the desires of your sinful nature, the results are very clear: sexual immorality, impurity, lustful pleasures, idolatry, sorcery, hostility, quarreling, jealousy, outbursts of anger, selfish ambition, dissension, division, envy, drunkenness, wild parties, and other sins like these. Let me tell you again, as I have before, that anyone living that sort of life will not inherit the Kingdom of God. But the Holy Spirit produces this kind of fruit in our lives: love, joy, peace, patience, kindness, goodness, faithfulness, gentleness, and self-control. There is no law against these things! Those who belong to Christ Jesus have nailed the passions and desires of their sinful nature to his cross and crucified them there. Since we are living by the Spirit, let us follow the Spirit's leading in every part of our lives. Galatians 5:19-25 NLT

Paul was simply repeating what Jesus taught when He said, "Everyone who commits sin is the slave of sin (John 8:34)." Scholar Craig Keener suggests John 8:34 reflects the basic idea that no one can serve two masters. Each person will either serve God or serve something else.[31] As has already been pointed out, *every* person will either be enslaved to sin or enslaved to righteousness.

In his letter to the Galatians Paul once again borrowed the slavery metaphor to make his point about true freedom.

It was for freedom [*eleutheria*] that Christ set us free [*eleuthero*]; therefore keep standing firm and do not be subject again to a yoke of slavery. Galatians 5:1

---

31 Keener, Craig S., *The Gospel Of John: A Commentary*, Volume One (Hendrickson Publishers 2003) John 8:31-36, p. 751, citing Matthew 6:24

The Power of My Spirit   137

    Here Paul combines the noun *eleutheria* with the verb *eleutheroo* to stress the complete and comprehensive nature of being set free and to indicate its momentary yet all-inclusive character. His argument rests on the truth that no one who had been redeemed and set free from the bondage of being a slave would ever tolerate returning to slavery again. Paul was writing to people whose lifestyle prior to Christ enslaved them to the worship of pagan gods (which according to Galatians 4:8-9 were by nature not gods).[32] In Galatians 5:1, Paul was specifically warning about the return to slavery which would result if they agreed it was necessary to obey the Jewish law in order to obtain right standing before God.[33] We are not using Galatians 5:1 in that precise context, but Paul would have argued strenuously that *any* requirement added to the cross would result in taking up the yoke of slavery again. In fact, scholar John D. Grassmick expands Paul's meaning of freedom in Galatians 5:1 to include not only liberation from improper enslavement to the Mosaic Law but also freedom from the bondage of sin or even liberation from hostile spiritual forces.[34]

---

32   Rapa, Robert K., "Galatians," in *The Expositor's Bible Commentary: Romans - Galatians*, Vol. 11, Revised edition, edited by Longman III and Garland (Zondervan Academic 2008) Galatians 4:8, p. 608; Gundry, Robert H., *Commentary on the New Testament* (Hendrickson Publishers 2010) Galatians 5:1, p. 748. Gundry points out that Paul's use of the word "again" in Galatians 5:1 refers to the fact that the Galatians were formerly enslaved to pagan rules and regulations of worship, which he refers to as "the weak and bankrupt elements of the world . . . elements that in principle don't differ from the [Jewish] Law, so that submitting to enslavement under the Law wouldn't differ essentially from prior enslavement to pagan rules and regulations...." Ibid., p. 748

33   When the arguments in Paul's epistle involved the laws of Moses, he was generally arguing that the "law" was not a substitute for the work of the cross, nor should those regulations be "added to" the work of the cross to accomplish redemption. Paul always argued from the truth that the cross was enough!

34   Grassmick, John D., "Galatians," in *The Bible Knowledge Word Study: Acts-Ephesians*, edited by Darrell L. Bock (Victor 2002) Galatians 5:1 under Freedom ... *set free*, p. 402, citing Galatians 5:13; *BDAG*, 316-317; *BAGD*, 250 and *TDNT* 2:496-502

In Galatian 5:1 Paul employed the metaphor of an oxen yoke "whose purpose is to hold in control its bearer" as a contrast to standing firm in new-found freedom.[35] Rather than submit themselves to a yoke of slavery of any sort, Paul exhorts the Galatians to live in the freedom that Christ's blood purchased for them. By understanding salvation how Paul understood it, we will be able to see just how perfectly descriptive his figurative (metaphoric) argument is.

As we learned in Lesson 1, the first occurrence of a word in the Bible will generally provide the natural foundation for the subsequent uses of that word. This interpretive principle is known as the "Law of First Mention" which simply maintains that the very first biblical use of a word is often very important as it establishes the primary or most significant meaning for all later uses.[36] That means that the best place to start our discussion of the meaning of salvation is back in the book of Exodus, the first time the word "saved" is used in the Bible. The foundational definition of biblical salvation comes from the exodus story as recorded in Exodus 2:16-17. We will look at these verses in two different translations.

> Now the priest of Midian had seven daughters. They came to draw water and filled the troughs to water their father's flock. Then some shepherds arrived and drove them away, but Moses came to their **rescue** [root word *yasha'*] and watered their flock. Exodus 2:16-17 HCSB, bold added

> Now the priest of Midian had seven daughters, and they came and drew water and filled the troughs to water

---

35 Gundry, Robert H., *Commentary on the New Testament* (Hendrickson Publishers 2010) Galatians 5:1, p. 748

36 Cooper, David L., *Rules of Interpretation, the Law of First Mention*, Biblical Research Monthly 1947, 1949, Biblical Research Studies Group. Retrieved from http://www.biblicalresearch.info/page56.html (last accessed February 4, 2022). It is important to refrain from being too rigid in the application of this interpretative rule. It is possible for language to change over time and for words to take on new meanings.

their father's flock. The shepherds came and drove them away, but Moses stood up and **saved** [root word *yasha'*] them, and watered their flock. Exodus 2:16-17 ESV, bold added

The English Standard Version (ESV) translation of Exodus 2:17 makes it easy to see the idea of "saved/salvation" in this text. Although the *Holman Christian Standard Bible* (HCSB) is also an accurate translation of the Hebrew verb used in this text, the word "rescue" makes the connection with biblical salvation less obvious to our Western mindset. A Word Study will be helpful.

WORD STUDY

The Hebrew word in Exodus 2:17 that is translated **rescue** *in the HCSB and* **saved** *in the ESV is the verb vayyoshi'an. Although it is often translated in this verse as "help" or "rescue," it is best translated "and he saved them" meaning he rescued (freed or liberated) and delivered them.*[37] *The Hebrew expression "hôšîa' min" translated as "to save from" "normally denotes rescue from trouble, especially deliverance from a person or power*[38] *in whose hands one is held captive or under whose authority one is oppressed."*[39]

---

37 *NET Bible Notes*, study note 70, Exodus 2:17
38 In Ezekiel 36:29-30 Israel is figuratively being held captive not by human enemies but by their own uncleanness. Block, Daniel I., *The Book of Ezekiel: Chapters 25-48*, The New International Commentary on the Old Testament (Eerdmans 1998) Ezekiel 36:29-30, p. 357
39 Block, Daniel I., *The Book of Ezekiel: Chapters 25-48*, The New International Commentary on the Old Testament (Eerdmans 1998) Ezekiel 36:28, p. 357. See for example: Judges 2:16; 8:22; 12:2; 13:12; 1 Samuel 9:16; Nehemiah 9:27

> *The verb yasha' {yaw-shah'} is a root word which is most frequently translated as "save" in its biblical uses.*[40] *It can mean to deliver, defend, help, liberate, rescue, give victory.*[41]
>
> *The concrete picture of yasha' is that of bringing one to safety.*[42] *It pictures being led from (delivered from) a narrow strait (symbolizing distress and danger) to a broad pasture (indicative of a wide-open place of provision and safety).*[43]

Since Exodus 2:16-17 provides us with the first biblical example of someone being saved, it is worth our while to explore this story. The daughters of the priest of Midian had come to the well to water their flock, but Moses witnessed other shepherds forcefully pushing the women and their sheep aside in order to water their own flocks. Moses comes to the women's defense and in that sense, he is said to "save" them. He stands up against those shepherds permitting the women rightful access to the well water. The

---

40 The *Theological Wordbook of the Old Testament* states that *yasha'* and its derivatives are used 353 times. Harris, Archer, and Waltke, editors, *Theological Wordbook of the Old Testament* (Moody Press 1999) word #929, p. 414; BibleWorks 9.0 identifies out of 205 uses of *yasha'* it is translated as "save" 149 times and another 3 times it is translated as "salvation."

41 Baker and Carpenter, *The Complete WordStudy Dictionary of the Old Testament* (AMG Publishers 2003) word #3467, p. 484; Harris, Archer, and Waltke, editors, *Theological Wordbook of the Old Testament* (Moody Press 1999) word #929, p. 414

42 Baker and Carpenter, *The Complete WordStudy Dictionary of the Old Testament* (AMG Publishers 2003) word #3467, p. 484; Harris, Archer, and Waltke, editors, *Theological Wordbook of the Old Testament* (Moody Press 1999) word #929, p. 414

43 Baker and Carpenter, *The Complete WordStudy Dictionary of the Old Testament* (AMG Publishers 2003) word #3467, p. 484; Harris, Archer, and Waltke, editors, *Theological Wordbook of the Old Testament* (Moody Press 1999) word #929, p. 414

actions of Moses results in the gratitude of the women and their father which we will consider before we conclude our discussion.

Even though we don't usually credit Moses with the first act of biblical salvation, his actions in context certainly help us understand what salvation meant to the Jews. In that first instance of someone being saved, we learn the core meaning of salvation which contains four interconnected elements, two of which involve actions of the *savior*:[44]

- a situation or circumstance presenting a need for physical rescue
- a literal rescue from danger by one called a "savior"
- followed by the disabling or destroying of what caused the danger
- resulting in gratefulness and praise from the one "saved"

A standard dictionary definition of "save/salvation" from its Old Testament usage typically includes the first three of these elements (see for example *Theological Wordbook of the Old Testament*).[45] However, I'd like to suggest there is more than sufficient evidence to establish that the core definition of salvation always includes the fourth element of gratitude. Biblical gratitude can be defined as "a grateful attitude ... expressed in thanksgiving ... demonstrated by specifically suitable responsive actions of service."[46] In other words, it is a heartfelt attitude of thankfulness that evidences our appreciation for salvation through our actions. Scholar Jon Levenson concludes that gratitude arises naturally and

---

[44] Elements identified in Exodus 2:16-17, 20-22. All elements, except gratitude, are confirmed by entry for *yasha'* in Harris, Archer, and Waltke, editors, *Theological Wordbook of the Old Testament* (Moody Press 1999) word #929, p. 414

[45] Harris, Archer, and Waltke, editors, *Theological Wordbook of the Old Testament* (Moody Press 1999) word #929, p. 414

[46] Goulet, Henri Louis, *The Love of God*, Messianic Studies Institute Anytime Online Course Workbook, p. 71

serves an important function in the relationship between the "savior" and the one "saved."[47]

> [O]ne who properly experiences **gratitude** for favors received has in the process incurred a moral debt to his benefactor. His failure to discharge that debt would not be a defensible option: it would indicate a moral defect. If, moreover, the benefactor wishes the best for his beneficiary, he will discourage him from persisting in the ungrateful behavior that has disrupted the relationship.

Naturally, we find this type of "moral debt" in the story of Moses. It is the precise response we see articulated without delay by the father of the "saved" Midianite women in the Exodus narrative.

> When [the women Moses had rescued] came to Reuel their father, he said, "Why have you come back so soon today?" So they said, "[A man] delivered us from the hand of the shepherds, and what is more, he even drew the water for us and watered the flock." He said to his daughters, "Where is he then? Why is it that you have left the man behind? Invite him to have something to eat." Moses was willing to dwell with the man, and he gave his daughter Zipporah to Moses. Exodus 2:18-21

When Reuel learns what Moses has done to benefit his daughters he looks to communicate his gratefulness to him. We are told he first extends a dinner invitation, then invites Moses to remain with them and finally, he offers his daughter's hand in marriage. We can see in these actions that one who has benefited from saving acts can't help but express heartfelt gratitude to the "savior" for his salvation.

---

47 Levenson, Jon D., *The Love of God: Divine Gift, Human Gratitude, and Mutual Faithfulness in Judaism* (Princeton University Press 2016) p. 52, bold added

The Power of My Spirit

As we move from the Old Testament to New Testament text it is very important to note that the ancient understanding of salvation did not change. After surveying all of the New Testament uses of salvation, Dr. Meier, whose formal education includes training in Hebrew and ancient Semitic languages, has concluded that in *every case* the New Testament use is consistent with both the Old Testament meaning as well as customary usage in the first-century world.[48]

New Testament scholar Craig Keener calls the first-century salvation word group "natural language for physical deliverances or safety, including in childbirth, military situations, or at sea."[49] To the authors of the New Testament, being saved meant "deliverance from physical calamity that is associated with present life."[50] This was not a new understanding. Even before Christ, Israel had an expectation of the sufficiency of God's saving acts which would ultimately rescue/deliver/preserve the righteous forever.[51] That belief, according to Keener, carried over and is found frequently in early Christian writings. However, as the following quote from

---

48 Meier, Sam, *Misunderstood Terms in the Bible 2020*, Messianic Studies Institute, Term 4 2020, Lesson 1
49 Keener, Craig S., *1 Peter: A Commentary* (Baker Academic 2021) 1 Peter 1:5, p. 71, cites contained in footnotes 71-75 omitted
50 Meier, Sam, *Misunderstood Terms in the Bible 2020*, Lesson 1, Messianic Studies Institute, Term 4 2020. For example, in his letter to the Philippians Paul expressed his confidence that God would redeem his current imprisonment literally saying that it will result in his *salvation* (Philippians 1:19). In one way or another Paul was expecting God to release him from prison which would be a saving act according to Paul's understanding of salvation. Garland, David E., "Philippians," in *The Expositor's Bible Commentary: Ephesians – Philemon*, Vol. 12, Revised Edition, edited by Longman III and Garland (Zondervan Academic 2006) Philippians 1:18b-20, p. 203
51 Keener, Craig S., *1 Peter: A Commentary* (Baker Academic 2021) 1 Peter 1:5, p. 71, citing Isaiah 43:3; 45:17; 46:13; 49:6; 52:7,10; 60:16; Ezekiel 34:22. See also: 1 Enoch 99:10; 4 Ezra 6:25; 7:60,131; 8:3,39; 9:8,13,15; 2 Baruch 23:7; 51:7,14

The Expositor's Bible Commentary: Psalms highlights for us, this biblical understanding of being saved has been lost in transition.[52]

> Regrettably, the phrase, "I have been saved" has become synonymous with "I have become a Christian." The Hebraic concept is much richer than our modern usage, but not richer than the [New Testament's] for there we come face-to-face with our great Redeemer, Jesus Christ. But we have robbed the NT of its rich OT background. From the usage of "deliver" and "deliverance," we have learned that Yahweh will completely redeem his people from all adversity, remove their troubles and wipe away their tears, vindicate them, honor them, and bestow a new quality of life on his beloved. This involves forgiveness of sin, reconciliation, covenantal fellowship, and divine compassion in the present, but also the expectation of God's holistic care for his people (in body and spirit, individuals and community, Jews and Gentiles, present and future).

To Paul salvation was not an abstract religious concept. It was very concrete and certain. Salvation meant being saved or rescued from the hand of a very real and present enemy in a situation or circumstance when it was not possible to save yourself. In fact, let's park here for a moment to look at a few word meanings that will clearly illustrate this point. To begin with, the New Testament employs terms for sin that vividly depict captivity. Let's look at two examples.

> The Son of Man will send his angels, and they will gather out of his kingdom all causes of **sin** [*skandalon*] and all law-breakers. Matthew 13:41 ESV, bold added

---

52 Longman III and Garland, general editors, *The Expositor's Bible Commentary: Psalms*, Vol. 5, Revised edition (Zondervan 2008) *Reflections: Yahweh Is My Redeemer under Conclusions*, p. 547

As noted, the word *sin* is a translation of the Greek term *skandalon {skan'-dal-on}*. Very simply it was an ancient word used to describe the bait stick (trigger stick) on a trap.[53] Of course, when the animal took the bait, it triggered the trap which was lowered to capture the animal and that was the whole point. Our second example employs a different, but equally picturesque word.

> The Lord's bond-servant must . . . with gentleness [correct] those who are in opposition, if perhaps God may grant them . . . [to] come to their senses *and escape from the* **snare** [*pagis*] *of the devil*, having been held captive by him to do his will. 2 Timothy 2:24-26, italics in original, bold added

Here Paul employs the Greek word *pagis* {pag-ece'} which is translated as "snare." *Pagis* is the word for things that hold fast like net, a snare or a mousetrap.[54] In fact in Paul's Hebrew mindset, the biblical idea of redemption emphasizes captives being delivered from sin like slaves who are set free from their captivity.[55]

Now let's go one step further. John informs us that Jesus came to *destroy* the works of Satan (1 John 3:8). In a manner of speaking, the Greek word *lyo* {loo'-o} translated as *destroy* is the very picture of salvation. *Lyo* was a common Greek word that could denote redemption which was granted by a deity.[56] It has two primary meanings when used in the New Testament: 1) set free what is bound (being held captive) and 2) to destroy (break

---

53 *Spirit Filled Life Bible* (Thomas Nelson 1991) *Word Wealth [Matthew] 11:6 offended, skandalizo*, p. 1424
54 Bromiley, Geoffrey W., *Theological Dictionary of the New Testament*, Abridged in One Volume (Eerdmans 1985) entry for *pagis* under *pagis*, p. 752
55 Fee, Gordon D., *The First Epistle To The Corinthians*, New International Commentary on the New Testament (Eerdmans 1987) 1 Corinthians 1:30-31, pp. 86-87
56 Bromiley, Geoffrey W., *Theological Dictionary of the New Testament*, Abridged in One Volume (Eerdmans 1985) entry for *lyo* under *lyo*, p. 544

up, dissolve, demolish, overthrow).⁵⁷ To make the connection even more clear, I'll restate the two actions of the savior as listed in the biblical meaning of salvation:

- a literal rescue from danger by one called a "savior" [compare to the first meaning of *lyo*: set free what is bound]
- followed by the disabling or destroying of what caused the danger [compare to the second meaning of *lyo*: to destroy (break up, dissolve, demolish, overthrow)]

Before our salvation, we were in the bondage of sin and held captive by the kingdom of darkness. We were slaves to our sin nature meaning we were "under its lordship and dominion and thus unable to extricate [ourselves] from its tyranny."⁵⁸ Because we were unable to save ourselves, we needed a savior. The work of the cross transferred us from the dominion of sin to the dominion of righteousness (Romans 6:17-18). Our freedom as Christ-followers is found in the truth that we are no longer in bondage to our sin nature. Sin no longer rules over us. Much of Paul's language about freedom is calling Christ-followers to become what we already are – to fully appropriate our new identity in Christ.⁵⁹ Paul takes the position that we have died to sin and we are obligated to display our freedom by presenting ourselves as slaves of righteousness.⁶⁰ We learned earlier in this lesson that those who

---

57   Bromiley, Geoffrey W., *Theological Dictionary of the New Testament*, Abridged in One Volume (Eerdmans 1985) entry for *lyo* under *lyo*, p. 544; *Thayer's Greek Lexicon*, entry for *Strongs NT 3089*. Retrieved from https://biblehub.com/greek/3089.htm (last accessed March 5, 2024)
58   Schreiner, Thomas R., *Romans*, Baker Exegetical Commentary on the New Testament, 2nd edition (Baker Academic 1998, 2018) Romans 6:17-18, p. 333
59   Keck, Leander E., *Romans*, Abingdon New Testament Commentaries (Abingdon Press 2005) Freed from Sin and Death ([Romans] 6:1-14) p. 167
60   Keck, Leander E., *Romans*, Abingdon New Testament Commentaries (Abingdon Press 2005) Freed from Sin and Death [Romans] 6:1-14) pp. 164-165; Schreiner, Thomas R., *Romans*, Baker Exegetical Commentary on the New Testament, 2nd edition (Baker Academic 1998, 2018) Romans 6:19, p. 336

are "righteous *do* what is right; they live in accordance with God's expectations."[61]

The concrete picture of salvation is one that results in freedom.[62] Jesus rescued us from sin and death when we were powerless and still in our sin.[63] By the cross, He destroyed the enemy's power to keep captive any Christ-follower who chooses to be led by Holy Spirit.[64] The final step of salvation is gratitude which explains an important reason why Paul exhorts his readers to live in freedom! And how does he expect them to do that? Through the power of Holy Spirit, Paul urges every Christ-follower to dedicate their new life to the One who saved them. Gratitude and praise find their best expression in continually living in the freedom purchased by the shed blood of Christ.

The freedom Jesus offers is spiritual freedom from the captivity of sin. We are called to continually live in this biblical pattern of freedom empowered by God's Spirit. In his first epistle to the Corinthians Paul had harsh words for those who had the Spirit but behaved as if they did not![65] In Galatians 5:1, Paul commands

---

61 Longman III and Garland, general editors, *The Expositor's Bible Commentary: Psalms*, Vol. 5, Revised edition (Zondervan 2008) Psalm 15:2, p. 183
62 *Yasha`* concretely pictures being led from a narrow strait (indicating distress and danger) to a broad pasture (a wide-open place of provision and safety). Baker and Carpenter, *The Complete WordStudy Dictionary of the Old Testament* (AMG Publishers 2003) word #3467, p. 484; Harris, Archer, and Waltke, editors, *Theological Wordbook of the Old Testament* (Moody Press 1999) word #929, p. 414
63 Habitually sinning makes you a bondservant to sin. John 8:34. "But God demonstrates His own love toward us, in that while we were yet sinners, Christ died for us." Romans 5:8
64 1 John 3:8. A true *talmid* will live in the freedom Christ provides by daily dying to self, asking Holy Spirit to lead and increasingly applying the truth of His Word to their life.
65 In 1 Corinthians 3 Paul accused the Corinthians of "living like unbelievers (1 Corinthians 3:3c HCSB)." The original Greek could be properly translated as, "You are *walking according to man*." The phrase "according to man" was a frequently used idiom to denote "living like a slave." In this case, Paul was writing to those who possessed the Holy Spirit. What he found inexcusable is that they were acting like they were still enslaved to sin! *Holman Christian*

Christ-followers to "stand fast." This command to stand is akin to a General who commands his army to stand firm in the midst of battle so that those soldiers are not captured and forced into slavery by their enemy.[66] Paul's exhortation alerts the Galatians, and us, to the reality that it takes focused effort to remain in this place of liberty. Maintaining our freedom is the subject matter of our next lesson.

Hear What The Spirit is Saying to the Church: *It is indeed true that I came to set the captives free and sent My Spirit so that my disciples could remain free. So few people understand that I've already provided the freedom they long for. All they need to do is appropriate it for themselves. Such power would flow through them if only they would believe and do what I said to do. Then would the world come to know me. It is the day I long for. I am faithful and so it will be.*

Standard Bible, Study Bible edition (Holman Bible Publishers 2010) study note 1 Corinthians 3:3c-4 under *living like unbelievers*, p. 1962; Verbrugge, Verlyn D., "1 Corinthians," *The Expositor's Bible Commentary: Romans - Galatians,* Vol. 11, Revised edition, edited by Longman III and Garland (Zondervan Academic 2006) 1 Corinthians 3:1-2, p. 282; Fee, Gordon D., *The First Epistle To The Corinthians*, New International Commentary on the New Testament (Eerdmans 1987) 1 Corinthians 3:2b-3, pp. 126-127

66 Gundry, Robert H., *Commentary on the New Testament* (Hendrickson Publishers 2010) Galatians 5:1, p. 749

LESSON 8:

POWER TO MAINTAIN FREEDOM

 "Submit therefore to God. Resist the devil and he will flee from you." James 4:7

WE HAVE PREVIOUSLY learned that the very idea of redemption implies that the recipient was in bondage. Prior to his salvation, every follower of Christ was being held captive to the power of sin and death by the kingdom of darkness. Once set free, Christ-followers are admonished to continually *walk in the Spirit* as we live out our faith in the power of Holy Spirit (Galatians 5:16-25). "'[T]o walk according to [Holy] Spirit' means that the Spirit, or impact of Christ's life, is determinative of all conduct."[1] The truth is, every "spiritual reality" for the follower of Christ is at the same time a "spiritual responsibility."[2] This is

---

1   Hill, David, *Greek Words and Hebrew Meanings: Studies in the Semantics of Soteriological Terms*, Society for New Testament Studies Monograph Series 5 (Wipf and Stock 2000, previously published Cambridge University Press 1967) p. 275
2   MacArthur, John, *Commentary on Romans 1-8* (Moody Press 1991) p. 412 as quoted in Ekstrand, D. W., *Living Life In The Spirit, (As taught by the apostle Paul in Romans 8)*, the transformedsoul.com. Retrieved from http://www.thetransformedsoul.com/additional-studies/spiritual-life-studies/living-life-in-the-spirit#:~:text=As%20John%20MacArthur%20says%20in%20his%20Commentary%20on,to%20%E2%80%9C%20be%20holy%20%E2%80%9D%20%281%20Pet%201%3A15-16%29 (webpage not accessible May, 2024). Donald W. Ekstrand is an adjunct professor of Christian Studies at Grand Canyon University, Phoenix, and Religious Studies in the Maricopa Community College District in Arizona.

"[o]ne of the [great] paradoxes of the Christian life ... God's gifts often require labor on our part."[3]

In our last lesson, we learned that Christ was able to save us because His obedience to His Father's will led Him to do all the work necessary to gain our freedom. Following our salvation, it is our responsibility to fully appropriate our new identity in Christ in order to maintain our freedom. Jesus, "[t]he one in whom the Spirit had a permanent dwelling[,] amazed men by the sinlessness of his life. Such was the character produced in human life by the Spirit of Yahweh once he was given full control. Such, therefore, should be the character in the followers of Jesus...."[4] In sum, the freedom Paul advocates is the freedom to put Christ's character on display in our lives.[5]

After He ascended back to the Father, Jesus gave His disciples the gift of the same Holy Spirit that had empowered Him. In fact, "The Holy Spirit is 'another Jesus.'"[6] He thereby supplied His disciples with all they needed to maintain the freedom He had purchased for them. The presence of Holy Spirit not only equips, enables and empowers *every* follower of Christ to live in accord with their new freedom, His presence *"obligates"* them to do it![7] Retaining our freedom from sin's rule over us is the subject of this lesson.

When Paul wrote to the Galatians he made very clear that the Holy Spirit is our vital link to maintaining our freedom.

---

[3] Blackaby and Blackaby, *Experiencing God Day-By-Day Devotional* (B & H 1998) May 7, p. 128

[4] Green, Michael, *I Believe in the Holy Spirit*, Revised edition (Eerdmans 2004) p. 35

[5] Green, Michael, *I Believe in the Holy Spirit*, Revised edition (Eerdmans 2004) p. 110

[6] Green, Michael, *I Believe in the Holy Spirit*, revised edition (Eerdmans 2004) p. 54

[7] Keck, Leander E., *Romans*, Abingdon New Testament Commentaries (Abingdon Press 2005) Expecting Redemption ([Romans] 8:18-30) p. 218, italics added

How foolish can you be? After starting your new lives in the Spirit, why are you now trying to become perfect by your own human effort? Galatians 3:3 NLT

For it is by the power of the Spirit, who works in us because we trust and are faithful, that we confidently expect our hope of attaining righteousness to be fulfilled. Galatians 5:5 CJB

Righteousness in Galatians 5:5 is the Greek word *dikaiosune* {dik-ah-yos-oo'-nay} (divine approval) which is credited to us when we choose Jesus Christ as Savior and Lord. At that moment our status with God is changed "from '*condemned*' to '*divinely-approved*.'"[8] This righteousness we receive from God is not something we have earned, it is a grace gift that is the result of God imputing Christ's righteousness to us. I'll call this *positional* righteousness to distinguish it from our *obedient* righteousness. God expects our initial *positional* righteousness to grow through our *obedience* as we maintain our freedom from the power of sin. (*Important note*: the terms *positional* and *obedient* righteousness are not used in the Bible. I am using them simply for the sake of clarity between these two aspects of biblical righteousness.)[9]

---

[8] Hill, Gary, *The Discovery Bible*, HELPS Ministries, Inc., [G]1343 *dikaiosýnē*

[9] David Stern refers to "(1) behavioral righteousness, actually doing what is right, and (2) 'forensic righteousness,' being regarded as righteous in the senses (a) that God has cleared [a person] of guilt for past sins, and (b) that God has given him a new nature inclined to obey God rather than rebel against him as before." Stern teaches, "The task of becoming behaviorally righteous begins with appropriating forensic righteousness by trusting in Yeshua [Jesus]; and it occupies the rest of a believer's life, being completed only at his own death, when he goes to be with Yehsua." Stern, David, H., *Jewish New Testament Commentary* (Jewish New Testament Publications, Inc. 1992) Galatians 2:16a, p. 535, citation omitted; Teresa Morgan refers to "propositional" trust which moves to "relational" trust. Morgan, Teresa, *Roman Faith and Christian Faith Pistis and Fides in the Early Roman Empire and Early Churches* (Oxford 2015) p. 230; Steven R. Cook refers to "positional" and "experiential" types of righteousness. "Positionally, every believer resides in a state of righteousness which is based solely on

Our freedom is maintained decision by decision. In our Key Verse for this lesson, James draws on military terms to refer to the "cosmological battle between Satan and his minions [followers] and God and his people happening in the world."[10]

Submit therefore to God. **Resist** the **devil** and he will **flee** from you. James 4:7, bold added

What James writes provides a straightforward road map to preserve our freedom and prevent further captivity. We are going to zoom in on the four words I have highlighted in bold text in this short verse: submit, resist, devil and flee. In any battle it is vitally important to know your enemy, therefore I'm choosing to begin a little out of order by looking at the word "devil" first. After that, we'll proceed in an orderly fashion to consider the other three words in the sequence in which they appear in our Key Scripture.

WORD STUDY

The Greek word translated as **devil** *is diabolos {dee-ab'-ol-os} which means prone to slander, slanderous, falsely accusing. It is a derivative of diaballo that denotes "to*

---

the imputation of God's righteousness as a gift at the moment of faith in Christ (Phil. 3:9). Experientially, the obedient-to-the-word believer learns to practice righteousness as he/she walks in conformity to God's commands (Rom. 6:13). The former necessarily precedes the latter." Cook, Steven R., *Biblical Righteousness: A Word Study*, Thinking On Scripture, posted August 11, 2017. Retrieved from https://thinkingonscripture.com/2017/08/11/the-righteousness-of-god-part-2/ (last accessed December 30, 2021). John MacArthur refers to "imputed righteousness" (Philippians 3:8,9) and "personal righteousness" (Philippians 3:12-14). MacArthur, John, *The MacArthur Study Bible* (Thomas Nelson 2006) study note John 13:10, p. 1577

10 McKnight, Scot, *The Letter of James*, New International Commentary on the New Testament (Eerdmans 2011) 6.3.3.2. Resistance ([James] 4:7b) p. 347

separate from,' 'to be set in opposition,' 'to be hated,' 'to accuse,' 'to repudiate,' 'to give false information.'"[11]

The Hebrew equivalent for diabolos is satan *{sawtawn}* from which we get the term Satan. The noun satan generally denotes one who is an adversary or one who impedes or opposes.[12] However, ancient Jewish sources also identified his role as an accuser, a tempter (who would then accuse the one he had successfully tempted) and a deceiver.[13]

We have made a number of references to the work of Satan in our study. It is worth our time in this lesson to slow down the pace and take a closer look at this one who is our adversary. The Old Testament and ancient Jewish literature are consistent in their conceptual references to the adversarial nature of *satan*.[14] Many believe, just as I have been taught, that Satan was created as a beautiful angel but he rebelled against God. He desired to be greater than God and because of that rebellion, God cast him out of heaven. To quote from the *Dictionary of Biblical Imagery*:[15]

---

11 Bromiley, Geoffrey W., *Theological Dictionary of the New Testament* (Eerdmans Publishing Co. 1985) entry for *diaballo* under *diaballo*, p. 150

12 Baker and Carpenter, *The Complete WordStudy Dictionary of the Old Testament* (AMG Publishers 2003) #7854, p. 1127

13 Keener, Craig S., *1 Peter: A Commentary* (Baker Academic 2021) *A Closer Look: Satan/the Devil in Early Jewish Understanding*, pp. 383-384

14 Korner, Ralph J., *Reading Revelation After Supersessionism: An Apocalyptic Journey of Socially Identifying John's Multi-Ethnic Ekklesiai with the Ekklesia of Israel, The New Testament after Supersessionism* (Cascade Books 2020) p. 81. Dr. Korner credits scholar Thomas Farrar for his conclusion that the ancient Jewish literature contains *"conceptual* consistency in the functions and attributes assigned to the Satan." Ibid., citing Farrar and Williams, *Talk of the Devil*, 80-82, especially Table 1, italics in original

15 Ryken, Wilhoit, and Longman III, editors, *Dictionary of Biblical Imagery* (Intervarsity Press 1998) entry for *Satan Cast Down*, pp. 761-762

It has ... been common to believe in a fall of Satan from heaven before human history began. [This belief] rests on two OT passages, which may or may not be adequate for the belief. In Isaiah's taunt against the king of Babylon, the prophet exclaims, "How art thou fallen from heaven, O Lucifer, son of the morning!" (Is 14:12 KJV) .... Ezekiel's oracle against Tyre elaborates the picture further, portraying a being who once resided in Eden, placed "with an anointed guardian cherub" on "the holy mount of God (Ezek 28:14 RSV)." This being was "blameless ... from the day you were created, till iniquity was found in you" (Ezekiel 28:15 RSV). Thereupon he was "cast ... as a profane thing from the mountain of God, and the guardian cherub drove [him] out from the midst of the stones of fire" (Ezek 28:16 RSV). Again, he was "cast ... to the ground" (Ezek 28:17).

Scholar Ralph Korner completed a thorough review of ancient literature and concluded that neither the Old Testament nor ancient Jewish literature develop the thought of Satan in any detail.[16] Notably "the demonic appears most profusely when Jesus is present."[17] Accordingly, it is in the biblical account of Jesus' earthly ministry we find the most fully developed understanding of Satan. For example, Jesus affirms there is a ruler of demons who is known by the name Beelzebul.[18] In the wilderness temptations of Jesus, Satan is acknowledged as the one who tempts people to disobey God. Jesus contrasts Himself as "the Truth" and Satan as

---

16 Korner, Ralph J., *Reading Revelation After Supersessionism, An Apocalyptic Journey of Socially Identifying John's Multi-Ethnic Ekklesai with the Ekklesia of Israel* (Cascade Books 2020) pp. 77–82
17 Harris, Archer, and Waltke, editors, *Theological Wordbook of the Old Testament* (Moody Press 1999) word #2330, p. 906, citing Kinlaw, p. 8
18 Matthew 12:24

"a liar and the father of lies."[19] Jesus makes clear that individual people can functionally do the work of Satan.[20]

Luke and John both inform us that "Satan entered into Judas" so that he betrayed Jesus.[21] The fact that Satan could spiritually enter someone to empower them to do evil would not have been unheard of in the first century. Scholar Craig Keener points out that the idea of spirits entering into people to empower them for either a good or evil task was a familiar concept in the Mediterranean world of that day.[22]

In that we are focused here on the nature of our adversary, Satan, I want to summarize two quotes from the *Jamieson-Fausset-Brown Bible Commentary*. These two quotes work together to provide us with a picture of how scholar David Brown envisions Satan's unfolding influence as he tempted Judas. Let's look at each in turn, using Brown's comments which I will summarize. Regarding Luke 22:3, he suggests a sequence of progressive steps:[23]

1. Jesus entrusted Judas with the money bag for the group
2. Judas broke that trust by stealing from the money bag

---

19 John 8:44
20 For example, when Peter strongly objects to the plans the Father has for His Son, Jesus rebukes Peter saying, "Get behind me, Satan (Matthew 16:23)!" Jesus was not saying Peter had actually become Satan but that Peter was aligning his thoughts and actions with the thoughts and actions of Satan and therefore Satan was able to use Peter to accomplish his objectives.
21 "And Satan entered into Judas who was called Iscariot, belonging to the number of the twelve (Luke 22:3)." "After the morsel, Satan then entered into him. Therefore Jesus *said to him, 'What you do, do quickly' (John 13:27)."
22 Keener, Craig S., *The Gospel Of John: A Commentary*, Volume Two (Hendrickson Publishers 2003) Interpreting the Washing in Light of the Cross ([John] 13:21-38) under *1. The Betrayal Announced ([John] 13:21-30)* p. 919, citing Homer, *Iliad* 17.210-211; Philostratus, *Heroikos* 27.2
23 Brown, David, *Jamieson, Fausset & Brown Commentary*, Luke 22:3. Retrieved from https://biblehub.com/commentaries/luke/22-3.htm (last accessed February 29, 2024)

3. Satan saw that open door to Judas' heart and determined to enter his heart by suggesting the thought that he betray Jesus
4. The thought was probably "converted into settled purpose" by the events that took place in Simon's house at Bethany (Judas objected when the woman anointed Jesus with the expensive perfume, he protested that the perfume should have been sold and the money given to the poor – hinting at the fact that Judas wanted access to that money for his own use)
5. Even though the thought of betrayal was offered earlier, it was not consummated until the last supper when Satan entered Judas

In his discussion of John 13:27 Brown outlines what he sees as the successive steps by which Satan worked to influence Judas:[24]

1. Satan had put it in Judas' heart to betray Jesus
2. Judas probably wrestled with that thought
3. When Jesus washed his feet at the last supper, Judas may even have had second thoughts
4. However, when Jesus announced that one who was reclining at the table with him would betray him, Judas may have thought: "I've been found out, it is too late now to back out of the plan."

The point is there was likely a methodical process behind the statement that Satan entered Judas.

Through Judas, Satan is credited as having a pivotal role in the death of Jesus, but only because God permits it.[25] The cross is identified as the place where Jesus decisively defeated Satan and the power of death. Throughout the gospel narratives, Jesus iden-

---

24 Brown, David, *Jamieson, Fausset & Brown Commentary*, John 13 under *27-30. after the sop Satan entered into him*, citing JF & B for Mt 12:43. Retrieved from https://www.blueletterbible.org/Comm/jfb/Jhn/Jhn_013.cfm (last accessed February 29, 2024)
25 John 19:11

tified Himself as having come to set people free from the work of Satan who had held them captive. John informs us that the purpose for which Jesus came was to destroy the works of Satan.[26]

The New Testament uses "Satan" to designate "a personal being."[27] Paul brings this *real being* to life for us when he makes clear that our daily battle is "not against flesh and blood, but against the rulers, against the powers, against the world forces of this darkness, against the spiritual *forces* of wickedness in the heavenly places."[28] Paul's understanding of Satan was informed by the Jewish thought of his day. His use of the Greek word *Belial* (also spelled *Beliar*) to refer to Satan in his second letter to the Corinthians is instructive.[29] Although that name for Satan was not known in the Old Testament, it does come from the Hebrew word *beliya`al* {bel-e-yah'-al} meaning "worthlessness" and was found frequently in Jewish writing to "stress Satan's activity as an opponent of God."[30]

---

26 1 John 3:8
27 Korner, Ralph J., *Reading Revelation After Supersessionism: An Apocalyptic Journey of Socially Identifying John's Multi-Ethnic Ekklesiai with the Ekklesia of Israel, The New Testament after Supersessionism* (Cascade Books 2020) p. 81. Dr. Korner quotes scholar David Aune's conclusion that the various aliases "ruler of this world," "Satan," and "Devil" are designations for a personal being. Ibid., citing Aune, *Dualism in the Fourth Gospel*, p. 135
28 Ephesians 6:12, italics in original
29 2 Corinthians 6:15
30 *ESV Study Bible* (Crossway Books 2008) study note 2 Corinthians 6:15, p. 2231. The Hebrew term *Belial* "is a very strong derogatory term" which became a word associated with Satan because he was viewed as being "worthless" or "treacherous." Ibid.; see also: Berlin and Brettler, editors, *The Jewish Study Bible: Featuring The Jewish Publication Society Tanakh Translation* (Oxford University Press 2004) study note Deuteronomy 13:14, p. 396 According to scholar Bruce Waltke, *beliya`al* "is used of troublemakers of all sorts, revolutionaries against God and his godly people ... his anointed king ... justice ... community solidarity ...social propriety... and even life itself...." Waltke, Bruce K., *The Book of Proverbs: Chapters 1-15*, The New International Commentary on the Old Testament (Eerdmans 2004) Proverbs 6:12, p. 342, citations omitted

As blood-bought disciples, the objective of the kingdom of darkness is to separate us from God's will and to thwart or impede our goal to become like Christ. In customary Hebraic fashion, Peter draws from a concrete image known to his readers in order to provide a comparison for Satan's activity. He wrote, "Be of sober *spirit*, be on the alert. Your adversary, the devil, prowls around like a roaring lion, seeking someone to devour."[31] In the Old Testament lion is used to symbolize "brute strength and a ferocious appetite."[32] The Greek word translated as *devour* is *katapino* {kat-ap-ee'-no}. In its absolute sense it denotes the extinction of human wisdom. Figuratively it can mean 'to assimilate,' 'to overwhelm,' or to 'to consume,' 'to use up.'"[33] This definition of *katapino* (devour) gives us a clear picture of the enemy's goals. He wants to assimilate us into the world and its ways thereby extinguishing any wisdom contrary to his. He does not give up easily and attempts to accomplish his objectives by overwhelming or overpowering the one he tempts.

Now that we have insight into our enemy, let's turn our attention to the remaining three words we want to define: submit, resist and flee. Those three terms succinctly lay out the strategy for maintaining our freedom. The first instruction James gives us in our fight against the adversary is to "submit" to God.

WORD STUDY

The Greek word translated as **submit** *is hupotasso {hoop-ot-as'-so} from hupó meaning under + tasso mean-*

---

31 1 Peter 5:8, italics in original
32 Longman III and Garland, general editors, *The Expositor's Bible Commentary: Psalms*, Vol. 5, Revised edition (Zondervan 2008) Psalm 17:10-12, p. 198
33 Bromiley, Geoffrey W., *Theological Dictionary of the New Testament*, Abridged in One Volume (Eerdmans 1985) entry for *pino* under *katapino*, p. 845

> *ing to arrange in an orderly manner.*[34] *It is a military term that speaks of soldiers being under the authority of a commanding officer.*[35]
>
> *Hupotasso involves surrendering your independent will to the leadership of another and conveys a strong indication of obeying the authority to which you have submitted yourself.*[36]

The first directive is to intentionally and purposefully place ourselves under God's faithful headship. "Before we can stand before Satan, we must bow before God. [When] Peter resisted the Lord [he] ended up submitting to Satan!"[37] Paul speaks in terms of presenting yourself or "your members to God as instruments for righteousness."[38] By that he means "to make [yourself] available, to become accessible to a governing reality [of God's advancing Kingdom]."[39] When Christ-followers want to defeat Satan they don't try harder, they submit more!

What we need most when facing the enemy is God's all sufficient grace. However, God places a condition on receiving His grace. Twice in the New Testament we read that He opposes the proud, but He gives grace to those who are humble.[40] In other words, humility is a condition to receive God's grace. So, what is

---

34 Zodhiates, Spiros, *The Complete Word Study Dictionary: New Testament* (AMG Publishers 1992) word #5293, p. 1427
35 Renner, Rick, *Sparkling Gems from the Greek* (Harrison House Publishers 2003) May 14, p. 332
36 Renner, Rick, *Sparkling Gems from the Greek Volume II* (Harrison House Publishers 2016) April 20, p. 387
37 Wiersbe, Warren W., *The Bible Exposition Commentary*, New Testament Vol 2 (Victor 2001) p. 433; see warning in Luke 22:31-34
38 Romans 6:13 ESV
39 Keck, Leander E., *Romans*, Abingdon New Testament Commentaries (Abingdon Press 2005) Freed from Sin and Death ([Romans] 6:1-14) p. 166
40 See: James 4:6; 1 Peter 5:5

humility? This quote is one of the best I've seen to explain humility in practical terms.[41]

> Humility is a profound distrust in our humanity. It distrusts our own ability, but overwhelmingly trusts in God's ability. Humility realizes our own strength, skill, intelligence, or even our luck, isn't enough to secure success. Our successes come through God's grace, mercy and power and that should humble us.
>
> Humility depends on the power of the Holy Spirit to intervene in our circumstances, not our own ability to maneuver.
>
> Humility depends on the Spirit's ability to speak, not our capacity to hear.
>
> Humility depends on the Spirit's proficiency to lead, not our skill to follow.

Submission requires putting to death our proud, independent spirit so we can firmly place ourselves under the authority of God.[42] Submitting is a voluntary act of the will, but it is not natural. We won't submit unless we first resolve in our hearts to submit. James instructs his readers to humble themselves by making a conscious, free-will choice to submit their will to God. This is not a once-in-a-lifetime action. Living the Kingdom life requires total and complete submission *every* day and in *all* things. In

---

41   Robert D. Pace, originally PulpitToday.org; now RevelationCentral.com. Original retrieval site https://robertdpace.com/how-to-hear-gods-voice. The original source site no longer exists on the internet. As of May 23, 2021, the Sermon titled: *How To Hear God's Voice* from which this quote was taken can be found at https://revelationcentral.com/how-to-hear-gods-voice. Pace received his degree in Biblical Historical Studies from Lee University in 1977 and is an international speaker.

42   Nicoll, William Robertson, editor, *The Expositor's Greek Testament* (G. H. Doran Company) James 4:7. Retrieved from https://biblehub.com/commentaries/james/4-7.htm (last accessed May 13, 2024)

short, as we learned in Lesson 6, this means "offering ourselves to God all day long and with every globule [drop] of our being."[43] Moreover, this submission involves our whole being, our minds, our thoughts *and* our actions. Mere intellectual submission to God's authoritative rule in our lives is of no benefit whatsoever if we fail to follow through with our actions. The sober warning of the Apostle Paul is that any mindset of the flesh which is not submitted to God is hostile to God.[44]

The next instruction James provides is to "resist" the devil.

> ### Word Study
>
> *The Greek word translated as* **resist** *is anthistemi {anth-is'-tay-mee} from anti meaning against + histemi meaning to cause to stand. It literally means to stand or be set against, to resist by our words and/or our actions.*[45]

James continues his use of a military metaphor. *Anthistemi* depicts a face-to-face confrontation and pictures an army arranging itself in a battle against the enemy.[46] This word "demonstrates the attitude of one who is fiercely opposed to something and therefore determines that he will do everything within his power to resist it, to stand against it, and to defy its operation."[47]

We would like to think there is a myriad of choices for us to make. However, James gives us the bottom line. He makes

---

43 McKnight, Scot, *Open To The Spirit: God In Us, God with Us, God Transforming Us* (Waterbrook 2018) p. 203

44 Romans 8:7

45 Zodhiates, Spiros, *The Complete Word Study Dictionary: New Testament* (AMG Publishers 1992) word #436, p. 178

46 *Ephesians 6:13 Commentary*, Precept Austin. Retrieved from http://www.preceptaustin.org/ephesians_613 (last accessed December 30, 2021)

47 Renner, Rick, *Sparkling Gems from the Greek* (Harrison House Publishers 2003) December 10, p. 942, italics omitted

crystal clear there are only two choices: we either resist the devil or be taken captive by him. This is a battle against a real enemy and James urges us to firmly and decisively take our stand against him.

James is not alone in his thinking. In his letter to the Romans, the apostle Paul warned that parts of our body can be used as weapons (Greek word *hoplon* {hop'-lon} referring to arms used in war) of *adikia* {ad-ee-kee'-ah} meaning wickedness, unrighteousness.[48] He was making it clear that resisting sin's desire to "'exercise dominion' in (or by) the mortal body is a real battle...."[49] Paul calls for ongoing active resistance to prevent sin from having control in the life of the Christ-follower.[50] The temptation to sin is too powerful for our flesh nature, however every temptation is easily defeated by the power of God's Spirit when we submit to Him and align ourselves with His will.

In the Greek text of our Key Scripture, the commands "submit and resist" convey a sense of urgency and demand immediate obedience. Just as submitting to God entails volitional choice, the Greek text is clear that resisting Satan likewise requires a choice of our will.[51] As a practical matter resisting the devil results in "prayerful obedience."[52] Unless we obey God, we will never resist the devil and cause him to flee.[53] In fact, when we choose to obey our own desires rather than God, those desires unwittingly "become weapons in the hands of wickedness."[54] On the other hand, when we resist Satan and walk in the freedom from sin's

---

48 Romans 6:13
49 Keck, Leander E., *Romans*, Abingdon New Testament Commentaries (Abingdon Press 2005) Freed from Sin and Death ([Romans] 6:1-14) p. 166
50 Keck, Leander E., *Romans*, Abingdon New Testament Commentaries (Abingdon Press 2005) Freed from Sin and Death ([Romans] 6:1-14) p. 167
51 *James 4:7 Commentary Precept Austin*. Retrieved from http://www.preceptaustin.org/james_47_commentary (last accessed January 7, 2022)
52 McKnight, Scot, *The Letter of James*, New International Commentary on the New Testament (Eerdmans 2011) James 4:7b, p. 349
53 McKnight, Scot, *The Letter of James*, New International Commentary on the New Testament (Eerdmans 2011) James 4:7b, p. 349
54 Keck, Leander E., *Romans*, Abingdon New Testament Commentaries (Abingdon Press 2005) Freed from Sin and Death ([Romans] 6:1-14) p. 166

The Power of My Spirit

dominion that Christ gave us, we thwart the enemy's plan. The result is that we are used by God as a weapon to destroy the works of the devil! A very practical strategy in resisting Satan is to ask God what thought or thought process we need to reject (take captive and make obedient to Christ) in order to be aligned with His will.

Resisting the devil means we cannot live in the *grey* area. We are either in the Kingdom of God with both feet planted solidly in the soil of His will and His authority or we are being tossed to and fro because of our double-mindedness. You might think a little tossing here and there isn't such a bad thing. However, listen to the warning James reveals in his epistle to those who just might have been walking in that half in/half out mindset.

> For that man ought not to expect that he will receive anything from the Lord, being a double-minded [of two minds, wavering, divided in interest] man, unstable [restless] in **all** his ways. James 1:7-8, bold added

On the other hand, the Bible is full of Covenant promises for those who habitually abide under God's authority. The Psalmist records clear and concise promises of spiritual protection to the man "who dwells in the shelter of the Most High [abides] in the shadow of the Almighty [and says] to the Lord, 'My refuge and my fortress, My God, in whom I trust!' (Psalm 91:1-2)" Jesus spoke of retaining a proper relationship with Him using the analogy of a vine and branches. He warned that apart from Him (the vine) we (the branches) can do nothing (John 15:1-8)! Psalm 91 and the promises of Jesus in John 15 for those who continually, persistently abide in the counsel of the Lord are among the plethora of additional assurances of spiritual safety, protection, well-being and Kingdom fruitfulness we find throughout the Bible.

James exhorts us to strongly resist Satan. What is Satan trying to get us to do? The record of his temptations, most notably those of Eve (Genesis 3) and Jesus (Matthew 4), indicates that he wants to make us doubt, deny, disregard and disobey God's instruction. In short, he wants us to choose another way, *any other way*, except the one God has chosen for us. This can mean a temptation toward a completely different and opposite action. But it can also mean working to convince us to choose a different timing than God's perfect timing – lagging behind or rushing ahead. We resist Satan by refusing to walk in the path he offers. When we do, he will give up and flee from us.

It is important to read carefully the instruction James is giving. James does not indicate that our ability to stand against Satan is based solely on our *intention* to submit to God. He gives us two separate and distinct actions that we must take. The first is yielding our will to God. In other words, our first step is submission, but then we need to *vote with our feet* by actively resisting what the enemy offers – actually walking on God's path rather than Satan's. These are two separate but inter-related actions. Each one requires us to take the initiative and then follow through. Each step begins with a freewill choice we must make, but then requires us to take the action to back up those choices.

James then provides a promise. By following the two exhortations he gives his readers the devil *will* flee! In other words, we are assured victory over our enemy. The word "flee" provides us with an interesting word picture. It is a translation of the Greek term *pheugo* {fyoo'-go} which means to seek safety by running or moving hastily away, escape danger or punishment, retreating out of fear.[55] There is no such thing as, "The devil made me do it." In fact, when we submit and resist him, he not only retreats – he hastily runs away as if he is in fear!

As Spirit-filled Christ-followers, a life lived on God's terms always produces a predictably consistent result. First, come under God's authority by aligning with His will. Then stand against what the enemy offers as an attractive alternative. As you do, you will likely watch him leave until some more "opportune time" just as

---

55 Zodhiates, Spiros, *The Complete Word Study Dictionary: New Testament* (AMG Publishers 1992) word #5343, p. 1440

he did after he tempted Jesus in the wilderness.[56] When that *kairos* opportunity rolls around again you repeat the same steps. You do this over and over again until this becomes your consistent pattern for daily living! In short, we habitually (as our lifestyle) need to add action to our choice to submit and that action needs to be entirely consistent with our God honoring submission.

What makes this strategy so successful against Satan's schemes is that the baseline of every temptation he offers is to engage in thoughts or actions that are outside of God's perfect will for us. Temptation is common to all of us, however, God has promised that He would provide us with the *way to escape* every temptation (1 Corinthians 10:13). The term translated as "way to escape" in that promise is the Greek word *ekbasis* {ek'-bas-is}. It essentially means "to walk out, as to walk out of a difficult place; to walk out of a trap; or to walk out of a place that isn't good for you."[57] As we see, *way out* does not mean we can avoid being tempted! *Way out* refers to the fact that God knows exactly how to defeat the tempter. The witness of the Bible is that every temptation can be defeated by choosing to think, speak and act like Christ. The essence of our battle against Satan is to stand against acting the way he wants us to act! That means, the way to win every battle is to imitate Christ.

In *Sparkling Gems From The Greek*, Rick Renner highlights the connection between Paul's choices and his ability to endure trials and suffering. Renner points out there is good reason we never read about Paul's defeat despite all he endured. Paul had the resolute determination he would not resign from his God-given assignment until he had crossed the finish line God had set.[58] For Holy Spirit to do His job, we must be wide open to His work in us and through us. His power works in those who resolve to stay

---

56 Luke 4:13
57 Renner, Rick, *Sparkling Gems from the Greek* (Harrison House Publishers 2003) August 22, p. 617, italics omitted
58 Renner, Rick, *Sparkling Gems from the Greek* (Harrison House Publishers 2003) August 17, pp. 601; see: Philippians 3:12

the course no matter what so that He can finish the work He was sent to do.

> . . . the power of the Holy Spirit ... works proficiently through people who have decided they will never turn back until the assignment is finished. God delights in using people who are steadfast and unmoving in their conviction, tenacious and diehard in their commitment. He takes pleasure in those who have stamina, spunk, and a dogged determination to hold on to the vision He put in their hearts .... *Satan can't make us quit. That choice lies in our hands alone.*[59]

When we have the same unyielding determination that Paul had, we will be able to withstand all of Satan's attacks and not quit until we have successfully completed the Kingdom assignment we have been given. Holy Spirit has a central role in each step of the battle strategy outlined by James in our Key Scripture.

> The power of the Holy Spirit was not designed solely for the first-century church. Rather, all Christians are indwelt by the Spirit and thus have His power available (1 Corinthians 6:19). However, living the Christian life under the Spirit's power must not be thought of as simply allowing the Spirit to take control while the believer does nothing. Believers still must live the Christian life, though they do it through the Spirit's power .... Christians who struggle in their own strength to live the Christian life will fail. They must by faith appropriate daily the power of the Holy Spirit (Romans 8:4,5). Described practically, this means that believers trust the Spirit to empower them in specific instances such as sharing their faith with others, resisting temptation, being faithful, and so on. There is no secret formula that

---

[59] Renner, Rick, *Sparkling Gems from the Greek* (Harrison House Publishers 2003) August 17, pp. 601-602, italics in original

makes the Spirit's power available. It is simply a reliance on the Spirit to help.[60]

In Lesson 6 we noted that "Paul saw the [Holy] Spirit as the key to everything in the Christian life."[61] On the other hand, scholar Gordon Fee observes that our modern-day version of Christianity lacks the reality and practicality of Paul's conviction that Holy Spirit is absolutely essential to every aspect of a Christ-follower's life. Fee then concludes, "It seems mandatory that such [conviction] prevail again if there is to be effective Christianity in our day."[62]

As individual Christ-followers throughout the world (collectively the body of Christ, the church) daily walk out their Spirit-empowered lives of freedom, they truthfully and effectively represent and RE•present Christ to a lost and dying world. They not only retain their own freedom, but they also become ambassadors for Christ to set other captives free.

Hear What The Spirit is Saying to the Church: *So I ask you, are you relying on Me and My Power? I died not only to give you salvation eternally but to give you power daily. I can offer it but only you can receive it and apply it in your life. If you are not already doing so, will you begin today? I will be faithful to do what I have promised to do as you faithfully do what I ask you to do.*

---

60 SermonIndex.net, *Text Sermons: Greek Word Studies: Power (Miracles) (1411) dunamis* quoting from *The Open Bible: New King James Version* (Thomas Nelson Publisher 2012). Retrieved from https://www.sermonindex.net/modules/articles/index.php?view=article&aid=34624 (last accessed December 29, 2021)

61 Fee, Gordon D., *The First Epistle To The Corinthians*, New International Commentary on the New Testament (Eerdmans 1987) 1 Corinthians 12:14, p. 607

62 Fee, Gordon D., *The First Epistle To The Corinthians*, New International Commentary on the New Testament (Eerdmans 1987) 1 Corinthians 12:14, p. 607

LESSON 9:

THE POWERFUL FRUIT OF THE HOLY SPIRIT

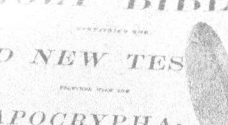

"But the fruit of the Spirit is love, joy, peace, patience, kindness, goodness, faithfulness, gentleness, self-control ...." Galatians 5:22-23a

IT IS NOT difficult in our day and age to acknowledge that there are "Christians" who have "just enough Jesus to be *informed*, but not enough to be *transformed!*"[1] In fact, the growing number of informed but not transformed "Christians" has led to two labels which would have been unheard of in the early church. Those who call themselves "Christians" can now be described as either a "convictional Christian" or a "nominal Christian."[2] The distinction between the two is implied by the labels themselves. A

---

1 Batterson, Mark, *All In* (Zondervan 2013) p. 25, italics mine
2 I question whether biblically speaking there is such a thing as a "nominal Christian," but for the use of the terms "convictional Christian" and "nominal Christianity" see for example: Stetzer, Ed, *Nominal Christians are becoming more secular, and that's creating a startling change for the U.S.,* The Washington Post, November 4, 2015. Retrieved from https://www.washingtonpost.com/news/acts-of-faith/wp/2015/11/04/nominal-christians-becoming-more-secular-and-thats-creating-a-startling-change-for-the-u-s/ (last accessed August 8, 2021); see also: *4 Trends in Christianity That Could Scare You, According to Ed Stetzer*, CharismaNews, June 4, 2014. Retrieved from https://www.charismanews.com/culture/44114-4-trends-in-christianity-that-could-scare-you-according-to-ed-stetzer (last accessed August 8, 2021); *Nominal vs. Convictional Christians*, blog by Servetus on May 27, 2016. Retrieved from https://approachingjustice.net/2016/05/27/nominal-vs-convictional-christians/ (last accessed August 8, 2021)

convictional Christian is one who ethically lives his life by putting Christ on display. On the other hand, a *nominal Christian* refers to someone who proclaims to be a follower of Christ but their life lacks supporting evidence.

It is inherently inconsistent to claim to be redeemed and yet display "no evidence of practical transformation."[3] According to the Bible, a "saving faith is one that has an effect on behavior."[4] In Ephesians 4:13 Paul set the discipleship goal for our transformed character as attaining nothing less than "the measure of the stature of the fullness of Christ."[5] Christ is the standard for maturity and reaching "*full Christlikeness*"[6] is an impossible goal unless we yield ourselves to what only the Holy Spirit can do.

Receiving Christ's Spirit in our hearts does not automatically assure us we will yield our lives fully to Holy Spirit. As we will see in this lesson, Paul points to the fact that being led by the Spirit involves intentional choice. It requires us to deny the desires of our flesh and submit to the leading of the Holy Spirit. In previous lessons we have referred to this choice as being *wide open* to the work of Holy Spirit. This means that we ask the Holy Spirit to lead us at the point of every need. However, "[i]t is much easier for

---

3   *ESV Study Bible* (Crossway Books 2008) study note Titus 2:14 under *zealous for good works*, p. 2350
4   McCartney, Dan G., *James*, Baker Exegetical Commentary on the New Testament (Baker Academic 2009) *Introduction to James*, p. 1
5   I recognize that scholars like Lynn Cohick and William Klein believe Paul was applying this goal to the corporate body of Christ-followers rather than individuals. However, my thinking in using this verse as an individual goal is that for the entire body to be mature, the individual members of that body must attain maturity. For more information on the opinion of these scholars see: Cohick, Linn H., *The Letter To The Ephesians*, The New International Commentary on the New Testament (Eerdmans 2020) Ephesians 4:13, p. 272; Klein, William W., "Ephesians," in *The Expositor's Bible Commentary: Ephesians - Philemon*, Vol. 12, Revised edition, edited by Longman III and Garland (Zondervan Academic 2006) Ephesians 4:13, p. 120
6   Klein, William W., "Ephesians," in *The Expositor's Bible Commentary: Ephesians - Philemon*, Vol. 12, Revised edition, edited by Longman III and Garland (Zondervan Academic 2006) Ephesians 4:13, p. 120, italics in original

The Power of My Spirit

people to observe the forms of religion than it is to bring the heart under [Holy Spirit's] controlling influence."[7]

In his Bible study, *Experiencing God: Knowing and Doing The Will of God*, Henry Blackaby shares a sad story of a man who had served in his church in a variety of leadership roles. However, he did so without an unawareness that every Christ-follower has been called into a personal relationship with Christ.[8]

> I [Henry Blackaby] was preaching in a church one Sunday about the way Christ's presence dramatically affects daily living. At the close of the service, a man came forward weeping. The pastor had him share with the congregation the commitment he had just made. The man confessed that a decade earlier his wife had urged him to come with her to church. When he attended, he liked the people, enjoyed worship, and decided to join the church. Later, he heard that the church needed teachers in the Children's Sunday School Department, so he volunteered. Over the years he served in numerous capacities in the church, including being a deacon and a Sunday School teacher. Yet as I preached that morning, the Holy Spirit awakened him to the fact that he did not have a personal relationship with Jesus. This good man had been practicing religion without genuine, life-changing relationship with Christ.

If he missed the fact of relationship with Christ then he also presumably missed the fact of relationship with the Holy Spirit. Christianity was never intended to be a set of beliefs. It is designed to be an active lifestyle fully connected to Christ and submitted

---

7 Barnes, Albert, *Barnes' Notes on the Whole Bible*, 2 Timothy 3:5. Retrieved from Hill, Gary, *The Discovery Bible*, HELPS Ministries, Inc. (last accessed December 9, 2023)

8 Blackaby, Blackaby and King, *Experiencing God: Knowing and Doing The Will of God (Lifeway Press 2007, reprinted 2015)* Participant Workbook, p. 249

to the leading of the Holy Spirit. Paul firmly believed that, "[w]hat gives power to [the Christian faith], is the life that is lived."[9] He taught that the only way to live the life God intended us to live is to be consistently led by the Holy Spirit.[10] But that's not necessarily easy, nor is it automatic!

In Romans 8 Paul addressed the very real struggle we have between two different powers or authorities that can govern our life – our flesh or the Holy Spirit that indwells us.[11]

> For those who live according to the flesh set their minds on the things of the flesh, but those who live according to the Spirit set their minds on the things of the Spirit. For to set the mind on the flesh is death, but to set the mind on the Spirit is life and peace. For the mind that is set on the flesh is hostile to God, for it does not submit to God's law; indeed, it cannot. Those who are in the flesh cannot please God. You, however, are not in the flesh but in the Spirit, if in fact the Spirit of God dwells in you. Anyone who does not have the Spirit of Christ does not belong to him. Romans 8:5-9 ESV

He addressed the same issue in his letter to the Galatians.

> But I say, walk by the Spirit, and you will not gratify the desires of the flesh. For the desires of the flesh are against the Spirit, and the desires of the Spirit are against the flesh, for these are opposed to each other, to keep you from doing the things you want to do. But if you are led by the Spirit, you are not under the law. Now the works

---

9 Gann, Windell, *Gann's Commentary on the Bible*, 2 Timothy 3:5 under *The Power*. Retrieved from https://www.studylight.org/commentaries/gbc/2-timothy-3.html. 2021 (last accessed December 9, 2023)

10 See for example: Romans 8:14. It is by faith in Jesus that we are saved "and being led by God's Spirit is the hallmark of this relationship." *NIV Study Bible* (Zondervan Publishing 1995) study note Romans 8:14

11 Keck, Leander E., *Romans*, Abingdon New Testament Commentaries (Abingdon Press 2005) The Power of the Spirit ([Romans] 8:1-17) pp. 201,202

of the flesh are evident: sexual immorality, impurity, sensuality, idolatry, sorcery, enmity, strife, jealousy, fits of anger, rivalries, dissensions, divisions, envy, drunkenness, orgies, and things like these. I warn you, as I warned you before, that those who do such things will not inherit the kingdom of God. But the fruit of the Spirit is love, joy, peace, patience, kindness, goodness, faithfulness, gentleness, self-control; against such things there is no law. And those who belong to Christ Jesus have crucified the flesh with its passions and desires. If we live by the Spirit, let us also keep in step with the Spirit. Let us not become conceited, provoking one another, envying one another. Galatians 5:13-26 ESV

Neither Romans 8 nor Galatians 5 describes two conflicting parts or aspects of a person.[12] The contrast Paul makes between the Spirit and the flesh is best understood as the conflict between two spiritual powers.[13] He is alerting those who follow Christ that there are two different powerful spiritual agents which vie for control over their life: the Holy Spirit and their flesh. In Galatians 5 Paul lists a number of ways in which fleshly desires express themselves. In verse 21 when he says "and things like these," he signals the fact that he has not listed all of the fleshly behaviors known to man, rather he is simply providing examples and then leaving the list open-ended.[14]

Paul counsels that every Christ-follower is to live life permitting Holy Spirit to be "the norm and guide" for all of life.[15] As

---

12　Keck, Leander E., *Romans*, Abingdon New Testament Commentaries (Abingdon Press 2005) The Power of the Spirit ([Romans] 8:1-17) p. 201

13　Keck, Leander E., *Romans*, Abingdon New Testament Commentaries (Abingdon Press 2005) The Power of the Spirit ([Romans] 8:1-17) p. 201

14　Gundry, Robert H., *Commentary on the New Testament* (Hendrickson Publishers 2010) Galatians 5:19-21, p. 752

15　Hill, David, *Greek Words and Hebrew Meanings: Studies in the Semantics of Soteriological Terms*, Society for New Testament Studies Monograph Series 5 (Wipf and Stock 2000, previously published Cambridge University Press 1967) p. 275

Paul makes clear, every time we allow Holy Spirit to have His way in us He prevents us from gratifying the desires of our flesh and we can be assured that we are fully aligned with God's perfect will. Whenever we make the choice to die to the flesh and allow Holy Spirit to lead us in our relationships with others, the naturally supernatural result will be the fruit that only Holy Spirit can produce. Notably this is not a one-time decision. It is more realistically a moment-by-moment decision.

In Galatians 5:22-23 Paul lists nine Spirit-produced virtues or character traits which will flow effortlessly in a fully yielded Christ-follower's life. "The Greeks defined a virtue as the mean between two extremes. On either hand there was an extreme into which a man might fall; in between there was the right way."[16] Paul identifies the character traits which are *the right way* for every Christ-follower as: love, joy, peace, patience, kindness, goodness, faithfulness, gentleness and self-control. Paul employs the term fruit in its figurative use to denote "the result of an action."[17] Fruit is a commonly used metaphor in both the Old Testament and the New Testament. Robert Gundry suggests Paul used the term fruit because as a "standard figure of speech" it connotes *evidence*.[18] Biblically speaking, fruit is how you recognize who people really are in an ethical sense. The fruit-bearing metaphor assumes that those who are truly devoted to God and align themselves with His ways will demonstrate what they believe by what they do.

In the natural (as well as figuratively), a tree's fruit benefits others, not itself. When we permit the Holy Spirit to act, the result will be Christ-like character in our life that is recognizable through at least nine distinct, yet inter-related, expressions. As it is expressed, each characteristic will benefit our relationships with

---

16 Barclay, William, *William Barclay's Daily Study Bible*, Hebrews 5:1-10. Retrieved from https://www.studylight.org/commentaries/dsb/hebrews-5.html (last accessed February 12, 2024)

17 Ryken, Wilhoit, and Longman III, editors, *Dictionary of Biblical Imagery* (Intervarsity Press 1998) entry for *Fruit, Fruitfulness*, p. 310

18 Gundry, Robert H., *Commentary on the New Testament* (Hendrickson Publishers 2010) Galatians 5:22-24, p. 752

others as well as give credibility to our witness. We'll spend the remainder of our lesson considering each one of these Christ-like qualities.

The fruit of Love

The word "love" is the Greek noun *agape* {ag-ah'-pay}. Jesus was asked by a scribe, a Jewish expert on the law, "What commandment is the foremost of all?" to which He replied:

> ... "The foremost is, 'HEAR, O ISRAEL! THE LORD OUR GOD IS ONE LORD; AND YOU SHALL LOVE [*agapao*] THE LORD YOUR GOD WITH ALL YOUR HEART, AND WITH ALL YOUR SOUL, AND WITH ALL YOUR MIND, AND WITH ALL YOUR STRENGTH.'..." Mark 12:29-30, uppercase text in original

When Jesus gave this answer He quoted Deuteronomy 6:5. By doing so, He revealed that this foundational requirement under the New Covenant is the very same obligation God had already established for His people under the Old Covenant. In fact, the *Shema*[19] (which the Jewish people said twice every day) narrows "Israel's obedient response to a single command to 'love.'"[20] This love is more about evidence of Covenant commitment than it is about emotion. To love God is to be totally loyal, faithful, trustworthy and obedient to Him in every respect.[21]

Of the various Greek words meaning love Jesus chose *agapao* – the one that best matches the concept of Covenantal love in Deuteronomy 6.[22] *Agape* is the very nature of God (1 John 4:8). He simply asks us to give back to Him what He gives to us (1 John 4:7)! Jesus said, "Those who accept my commandments

---

19 The *Shema* is a twice daily (morning and evening) recitation of Deuteronomy 6:4–9, Deuteronomy 11:13–21 and Numbers 15:37–41.
20 Nelson, Richard D., *Deuteronomy*, The Old Testament Library (Westminster John Knox Press 2002) Deuteronomy 6:4-5, p. 90
21 *NET Bible Notes*, translator's note 8, Deuteronomy 6:5
22 In New Testament times, there were at least four different Greek words that properly translate as the English word love: *agape, phileo, eros* and *stergo*

and obey them are the ones who love me.... Anyone who doesn't love me will not obey me."[23] After specifying the foremost commandment, Jesus added that there was a second commandment which was like it.

> "...The second [greatest commandment] is this, 'YOU SHALL LOVE YOUR NEIGHBOR AS YOURSELF.' There is no other commandment greater than these." Mark 12:31, uppercase text in original

Whenever the Holy Spirit leads us to respond to a neighbor's need, the standard for our response is always the same. It is our self-love which sets the bar. Treat the person you are called to love in the same way in which you would treat yourself under similar circumstances. That's the loving response that Jesus intends even when the "neighbor" is one we consider to be our enemy.[24] Jesus commands a loving response that is a matter of self-will, not a matter of our feelings or emotions.[25] *Agape* love does not derive its motivation from the desirability of the one in need but gives unconditionally with no expectation of return. That means that when *agape* is given and not returned you don't stop extending love. Christ-followers are called to be a unique kind of community – one that is "lubricated with love."[26] The type of love commanded

---

23 John 14:21a, 24a NLT
24 Jesus commands His followers to love even their enemies. Matthew 5:44-47
25 "... *agape* is not a word that denotes feeling or sentiment. Rather, it focuses on the will. So the fundamental nature of the command to love our neighbor is a matter of will, not feeling. Jesus was a realist who knew that we cannot command our feelings to be warm when they are cold or positive when they are negative. But we *can* exercise our will to act in another person's best interest no matter how we happen to feel about that person." Tarrants, Thomas A., *Loving God And Neighbor,* Knowing & Doing 2014 Fall, September 4, 2014 under *Loving Our Neighbor,* italics in original. Retrieved from https://www.cslewisinstitute.org/resources/loving-god-and-neighbor/?gad_source=1 (last accessed March 18, 2024)
26 I give credit to George Mallone for the phrase "lubricated with love." Mallone, George, *Those Controversial Gifts: Prophecy Dreams Visions Tongues Interpretation Healing* (InterVarsity Press 1983) p. 27

"always seeks the highest good of the other person, even though that person may despise the one who loves him."[27]

We love because we make an intentional choice to love like Jesus. He understood perfectly well the absolute impossibility of what He was commanding. He knew the command to love our neighbors ranks in second position because it is entirely dependent on our obedience to the commandment that is our first priority. Only when we love God with our all our heart, soul, mind and strength can we truly love our neighbors. That wholly-devoted love for God provides the fuel for our obedience to *agapao* our neighbors.[28]

The Bible makes clear that "we can't genuinely love until we are loving others the way God loves."[29] Whatever God commands, He empowers and enables Christ-followers to accomplish through the power of the Holy Spirit. God's love for us is constant. It never changes, it never leaves, it never weakens, it never fails! Because of God's unfailing love we will always have the resource we need to respond to every person and every situation/circumstance with love! It is in God's love that we find the ability to love those who are otherwise unlovely and unlovable. His love supplies all the fuel we need and His Spirit supplies the power all the power we need. "The Spirit is the One who can transform us from people who love only the people we like and the people who are like us, into people who love the people we don't like, the people who are different from us, and yes, even our enemies."[30] In short, "living in the power of God's Spirit enables [us] to live a life of love …."[31]

---

27   Berry, Harold J., *Gems From The Original Vol. II: Studies in II Timothy* (Back To The Bible 1978) 2 Timothy 1:7, p. 23
28   1 John 4:8,16
29   McKnight, Scot, *Open To The Spirit: God In Us, God with Us, God Transforming Us* (Waterbrook 2018) p. 126
30   McKnight, Scot, *Open To The Spirit: God In Us, God with Us, God Transforming Us* (Waterbrook 2018) p. 128
31   Rapa, Robert K., "Galatians," in *The Expositor's Bible Commentary: Romans - Galatians*, Vol. 11, Revised edition, edited by Longman III and Garland

The question may arise, how can *agape* be a commandment if it is a "fruit" which the Holy Spirit produces? The commandments to love are not directives to *produce* the love, but to become a willing vessel through which God can express His love. This type of love is not human affection. *Agape* love is a divine love produced by the Holy Spirit as fruit in the heart of an obedient Christ-follower.[32] It is fully within our discretion to be wide open to the Holy Spirit and when we are He will empower *agape* love in our lives sufficient to meet God's commands. When we are wide open to the Holy Spirit we never need to fear that we will face a crisis where we are not equipped to love our way through it! That's amazing grace!

As we look at the remainder of Paul's list we will see that each one involves our personal relationships with others and they are in fact "the embodiment of the command to love your neighbor as yourself."[33] This leads a number of scholars, such as Robert Gundry, to conclude that Paul lists *love* first because where love is expressed all the other virtues are found.[34] In the words of Scot McKnight, the nine virtues listed as fruit of the Spirit "can be read as a description of one big virtue, captured in the word *love*, along with eight smaller ones."[35]

The fruit of Joy

The *Dictionary of Biblical Imagery* points out that "With nearly four hundred instances of the specific vocabulary of joy

---

(Zondervan Academic 2008) 1. Life in the Spirit ([Galatians] 5:13-18) under *Overview*, p. 624

32 ". . .the love of God has been poured out within our hearts through the Holy Spirit who was given to us." Romans 5:5

33 Harmon and Sloat, *Galatians: A Commentary By Matthew Harmon and John Sloat*, Galatians 5:16-26, citing Galatians 5:14. Retrieved from https://www.thegospelcoalition.org/commentary/galatians/#section-32 (last accessed December 8, 2023)

34 Gundry, Robert H., *Commentary on the New Testament* (Hendrickson Publishers 2010) Galatians 5:22-24, p. 752

35 McKnight, Scot, *Open To The Spirit: God In Us, God with Us, God Transforming Us* (Waterbrook 2018) p. 123, italics in original

and rejoicing, joy is a major motif in the Bible."[36] In the world in which Paul lived (as in our world today), joy was related to personal happiness and could be expected only when circumstances were favorable.[37] The joy (Greek term *chara* {khar-ah'}) produced by Holy Spirit is not at all dependent upon circumstances nor is it the same as happiness. Biblical joy "is a deep sense of contentment and pleasure in God and his ways."[38]

"Paradoxically, Christ-followers experience joy in the midst of great persecution and personal suffering."[39] That's because the crux of this joy is found in contentment with God's plan and confidence that He will bring salvation. It is acceptance/belief/trust that all is well no matter what I see. It is rooted in absolute certainty of who God is and flows from a depth of acceptance and confidence that is fully satisfied with God and His ways. "Only [unconditional] trust in God motivates confident obedience in times of crisis."[40] When I choose to accept God's plan and His ways without reservation or qualification then I have positioned my heart to be supernaturally filled with joy.[41] That joy will flow upward in my relationship with God, but also outward in my relationships with others.

---

36 Ryken, Wilhoit, and Longman III, editors, *Dictionary of Biblical Imagery* (Intervarsity Press 1998) entry for *Joy*, p. 465
37 Grassmick, John D., "Galatians," in *The Bible Knowledge Word Study: Acts-Ephesians*, edited by Darrell L. Bock (Victor 2002) Galatians 5:22 under *Joy*, p. 409
38 Harmon and Sloat, *Galatians: A Commentary By Matthew Harmon and John Sloat*, Galatians 5:16-26. Retrieved from https://www.thegospelcoalition.org/commentary/galatians/#section-32 (last accessed December 8, 2023)
39 Garland, David E., "Philippians," in *The Expositor's Bible Commentary: Ephesians - Philemon*, Vol. 12, Revised edition, edited by Longman III and Garland (Zondervan Academic 2006) Philippians 1:4, p. 192, citing Matthew 5:10-12; Acts 5:41; James 1:2; 1 Peter 1:6-7
40 *ESV Study Bible* (Crossway Books 2008) study note Jeremiah 17:7 under *whose trust is the* LORD, p. 1405
41 Personal Journal November 14, 2022

The fruit of Peace

When the world talks of "peace" the reference is generally speaking about an absence of conflict and trouble. The Greek word Paul used is *eirene* {i-ray'-nay}. It denotes not only the absence of turmoil or conflict, but also the idea of blessing, most notably the blessing of a right relationship with God which enables confidence that "all is well" in life.[42] It is the equivalent of the Hebrew word *shalom*, which expresses the idea of "wholeness, completeness, or tranquility in the soul that is unaffected by outward circumstances or pressures. The word *eirene* strongly suggests the rule of order in place of chaos."[43]

Eirene can prevail internally even in the midst of violent war. This peace is a "state of being that lacks nothing and has no fear of being troubled in its tranquility; it is euphoria coupled with security."[44] God Himself is the sole author of this type of peace and He is therefore the only one who can give it as a grace gift.[45]

Having *eirene with* God permits us to experience the peace *of* God in our hearts.[46] God desires for everyone to walk in the peace He alone can provide. However, only those who accept His

---

42 *ESV Study Bible* (Crossway Books 2008) study note John 14:27, p. 2053
43 Renner, Rick, *Sparkling Gems from the Greek* (Harrison House Publishers 2003) July 24, p. 529, italics omitted. "The description [of God's covenant of peace in Ezekiel 37:26 and Isaiah 54:10] offers one of the fullest explications of the Hebrew notion of *šālôm*. The term obviously signifies much more than the absence of hostility or tension. It speaks of wholeness, harmony, fulfillment, humans at peace with their environment and with God." Block, Daniel I., *The Book of Ezekiel: Chapters 25-48*, The New International Commentary on the Old Testament (Eerdmans 1998) Ezekiel 34:25-29, p. 303
44 Mounce, William D., editor, *Complete Expository Dictionary of Old & New Testament Words* (Zondervan 2006) entry for *peace* under *New Testament*, p. 503
45 Zodhiates, Spiros, *The Complete Word Study Dictionary: New Testament* (AMG Publishers 1992) word #1515, p. 519. "Shalom is the fullness of God's grace and goodness directed at a person." Personal Journal May 7, 2021
46 Detzler, Wayne A., *New Testament Words In Today's Language* (Victor Books 1986) entry for *peace* under *Bible Usage*, p. 302, italics in original

gracious gift of salvation put themselves in the position to receive His gift which gives us peace *with* God. Salvation is an individual gift of grace, but it is walked out in community. It involves not only our individual reconciliation (peace) with God but it is also intended to include our reconciliation (being at peace) with other people.[47] When our relationship with God is right, then because of the presence of Holy Spirit we can experience wholeness in every other relationship.[48] This is the biblical essence of the fruit of *eirene* which is to guard our minds (Philippians 4:7) and be the "chief relational dynamic in the home (1 Cor 7:15) and in the church (1 Cor 14:33)."[49]

The fruit of Patience

The Greek word translated as "patience" is *makrothumia* {mak-roth-oo-mee'-ah}. It is a compound word from *makros* meaning long, distant, of long duration + *thumos* meaning temper, passion, emotion (or *thumoomai* meaning to be furious or burn with intense anger). When compounded into one word the resulting word means long-temper, patiently restraining anger.[50] *Makrothumia* always has to do with our reaction to other people. It refers to a combination of remaining calm in waiting seasons and endurance.[51] A person who is benefitting from the fruit of patience has

---

47 Garland, David E., "Philippians," in *The Expositor's Bible Commentary: Ephesians – Philemon*, Vol. 12, Revised edition, edited by Longman III and Garland (Zondervan Academic 2006) Philippians 2:12, p. 225
48 Rapa, Robert K., "Galatians," in *The Expositor's Bible Commentary: Romans – Galatians*, Vol. 11, Revised edition, edited by Longman III and Garland (Zondervan Academic 2008) Galatians 5:22-23, p. 631
49 Rapa, Robert K., "Galatians," in *The Expositor's Bible Commentary: Romans – Galatians*, Vol. 11, Revised edition, edited by Longman III and Garland (Zondervan Academic 2008) Galatians 5:22-23, p. 631
50 Renner, Rick, *Sparkling Gems from the Greek* (Harrison House Publishers 2003) July 25, p. 533, italics omitted; Zodhiates, Spiros, *The Complete Word Study Dictionary: New Testament* (AMG Publishers 1992) word #3115, p. 938
51 Harmon and Sloat, *Galatians: A Commentary By Matthew Harmon and John Sloat*, Galatians 5:16-26. Retrieved from https://www.thegospelcoalition.

a long fuse which enables "enduring hardship or wrong without complaint or thought of vengeance."[52]

This word is commonly used in the New Testament in reference to God's attitude towards men.[53] In other words, the fruit of patience is Holy Spirit's enablement for a Christ-follower to express the very attitude of God's own patience toward men.

The fruit of Kindness

The Greek word is *chrestotes* {khray-stot'-ace} which is "more volitional than emotional."[54] It describes the Holy Spirit produced "ability to act for the welfare of those [who are] taxing your patience."[55] Scholars refer to it as "the grace which pervades the whole nature, mellowing all which would be harsh and austere."[56] In other words, when we allow the Holy Spirit to lead He is able to remove abrasive character traits which would otherwise be natural to express.[57] Robert Gundry suggests that the word "magnanimity" would be a good substitute for the word "kindness" because he believes it more fully captures Paul's instruction. The word mag-

---

org/commentary/galatians/#section-32 (last accessed December 8, 2023)
52 Rapa, Robert K., "Galatians," in *The Expositor's Bible Commentary: Romans – Galatians*, Vol. 11, Revised edition, edited by Longman III and Garland (Zondervan Academic 2008) Galatians 5:22-23, p. 631, citations omitted
53 See for example: Romans 2:4; 9:22; 1 Timothy 1:16; 1 Peter 3:20; 2 Peter 3:15
54 *Titus 3:4 Commentary*, Precept Austin, quoting *The Tyndale Bible Dictionary*. Retrieved from www.preceptaustin.org /titus_34 (last accessed December 9, 2023)
55 *Spirit Filled Life Bible* (Thomas Nelson 1991) *Word Wealth Galatians 5:22 kindness*, p. 1780
56 Zodhiates, Spiros, *The Complete Word Study Dictionary: New Testament* (AMG Publishers 1992) word #5544, p. 1482; see also *Titus 3:4 Commentary*, Precept Austin, quoting Trench, R. C., *Synonyms of the New Testament* (Hendrickson Publishers 2000). Retrieved from www.preceptaustin.org / titus_34 (last accessed December 9, 2023)
57 *Spirit Filled Life Bible* (Thomas Nelson 1991) *Word Wealth Galatians 5:22 kindness*, p. 1780

nanimity includes high-mindedness unselfishness which enables a person to rise above being petty and mean-spirited.[58]

Christ-followers are to reflect God's kindness in their relationship with others.[59] It is the supernatural work of the Holy Spirit which enables us to be adaptable in meeting the needs of other people around us with a genuine interest in their welfare.[60]

The fruit of Goodness

God's goodness "is a synonym of 'love,' 'forgiveness,' and 'fidelity.'"[61] In the Old Testament the goodness of God usually signifies benefits He bestowed on Israel.[62] Accordingly, the fruit of goodness basically "manifests itself in genuine interest in the welfare of others."[63]

In Ephesians 5:7-10 Paul exhorts Christ-followers to be like God and have "a vibrant, active concern for others so as to benefit them."[64] When Holy Spirit produces the fruit of goodness

---

58 Gundry, Robert H., *Commentary on the New Testament* (Hendrickson Publishers 2010) Galatians 5:22-24, p. 752
59 See for example: Ephesians 4:32. Rapa, Robert K., "Galatians," in *The Expositor's Bible Commentary: Romans - Galatians*, Vol. 11, Revised edition, edited by Longman III and Garland (Zondervan Academic 2008) Galatians 5:22-23, p. 631
60 Renner, Rick, *Sparkling Gems from the Greek* (Harrison House Publishers 2003) July 25, p. 534; Harmon and Sloat, *Galatians: A Commentary By Matthew Harmon and John Sloat*, Galatians 5:16-26. Retrieved from https://www.thegospelcoalition.org/commentary/galatians/#section-32 (last accessed December 8, 2023)
61 Longman III and Garland, general editors, *The Expositor's Bible Commentary: Psalms*, Vol. 5, Revised edition (Zondervan 2008) *Reflections: The Perfections of Yahweh* under *Good (tob)*, citations omitted, p. 272
62 Childs, Brevard S., *The Book of Exodus: A Critical, Theological Commentary*, The Old Testament Library (The Westminster Press 1974) Exodus 33:18-23, p. 596
63 Harmon and Sloat, *Galatians: A Commentary By Matthew Harmon and John Sloat*, Galatians 5:16-26. Retrieved from https://www.thegospelcoalition.org/commentary/galatians/#section-32 (last accessed December 8, 2023)
64 Cohick, Linn H., *The Letter To The Ephesians*, The New International Commentary on the New Testament (Eerdmans 2020) Ephesians 5:8-9, p. 328

in us we engage in "that which is always spiritually edifying and beneficial to everybody [we] come in contact with."[65] Scholar Harold Hoehner clarifies the difference between goodness and justice. "Justice gives only what is due or deserved whereas goodness goes beyond justice to give all that is beneficial for a person's well-being. It is generous, liberal, and open-handed...."[66] Hoehner points out that the opposite of goodness would be *ponēros* {pon-ay-ros'}.[67] That Greek word refers to someone who is evil or wicked in either a moral or a spiritual sense, including those who seek to corrupt others.[68]

The fruit of Faithfulness

The Greek noun here is *pistis* {pis'-tis} which in this context speaks to the issue of being dependable. It denotes a reliable, trustworthy person in whom someone else can be confident.[69] To be "faithful" is to be steadfast, consistent and unswerving in loyalty. In Galatians 5:22, *pistis* "refers to relying on the Spirit to remain faithful to Christ."[70]

---

65 *Ephesians 5:9-10 Commentary*, Precept Austin, quoting Wayne Barber. Retrieved from https://www.preceptaustin.org/ephesians_59-10 (last accessed March 19, 2024)

66 Hoehner, Harold W., "Romans," in *The Bible Knowledge Word Study: Acts-Ephesians*, edited by Darrell L. Bock (Victor 2006) Romans 15:14 under *Full of goodness*, p. 199

67 Hoehner, Harold W., "Romans," in *The Bible Knowledge Word Study: Acts-Ephesians*, edited by Darrell L. Bock (Victor 2006) Romans 15:14 under *Full of goodness*, p. 199

68 Zodhiates, Spiros, *The Complete Word Study Dictionary: New Testament* (AMG Publishers 1992) word #4190, p. 1198

69 Rapa, Robert K., "Galatians," in *The Expositor's Bible Commentary: Romans - Galatians*, Vol. 11, Revised edition, edited by Longman III and Garland (Zondervan Academic 2008) Galatians 5:22-23, p. 631; Grassmick, John D., "Galatians," in *The Bible Knowledge Word Study: Acts-Ephesians*, edited by Darrell L. Bock (Victor 2002) Galatians 5:22 under *faithfulness*, p. 410

70 Harmon and Sloat, *Galatians: A Commentary By Matthew Harmon and John Sloat*, Galatians 5:16-26. Retrieved from https://www.thegospelcoalition.org/commentary/galatians/#section-32 (last accessed December 8, 2023)

God is faithful and that means His Spirit is a Spirit of faithfulness. When we allow God's Spirit to freely work in our life He supernaturally supplies all the faithfulness we need which enables us to meet our covenantal demand of reliability and trustworthiness. As we are faithful to our Covenant obligations, we will consistently treat others in a Christ-like manner.

The fruit of Gentleness (Meekness)

Prautes {prah-oo'-tace} is the Greek word which is translated as "gentleness" or in some translation, "meekness." This particular fruit of the Spirit "combines humility, meekness, and consideration of others' needs."[71] It "indicates a mildness that is not easily provoked or angered … and includes the notion of showing consideration for others."[72]

For meekness to be demonstrated there must be a conflict of some sort in which we are unable to control or influence the circumstances.[73] Under those conditions, typical human responses include frustration, bitterness, or anger. On the other hand, when we are guided by Holy Spirit we accept God's ability to direct events and *that* is the epitome of meekness at work. *Prautes* realizes that everything comes from God. It accepts, without complaining or disputing, what He gives/allows even to the point of patiently submitting to any offense (and every type of offense) without a desire for revenge or retribution![74] Meekness is not the same thing

---

71 Harmon and Sloat, *Galatians: A Commentary By Matthew Harmon and John Sloat*, Galatians 5:16-26. Retrieved fromhttps://www.thegospelcoalition.org/commentary/galatians/#section-32 (last accessed December 8, 2023)

72 Rapa, Robert K., "Galatians," in *The Expositor's Bible Commentary: Romans – Galatians*, Vol. 11, Revised edition, edited by Longman III and Garland (Zondervan Academic 2008) Galatians 5:22-23, p. 631, citing Burton, p. 317, citations omitted

73 Elwell, Walter A., editor, *Baker's Evangelical Dictionary of Biblical Theology* (Baker Books 1996) entry for *meekness*. Retrieved from https://www.studylight.org/dictionaries/eng/bed/m/meekness.html (last accessed May 15, 2024)

74 *Galatians 5:23 Commentary*, Precept Austin. Retrieved from http://www.preceptaustin.org/galatians_523 (last accessed December 9, 2023)

as resigning yourself to fate. It is not a passive and reluctant submission to events. Meekness is an active and deliberate acceptance of undesirable circumstances because they are viewed through the lens of wisdom and seen as being part of God's bigger picture.

The fruit of Self-Control

The Greek term is *enkrateia* (also transliterated *egkrateia*) {eng-krat'-i-ah} which refers to having "'dominion over the self or something' with the nuances of 'steadfastness' and 'self-control.'"[75] *Enkrateia* could be translated as restraint, moderation, discipline, balance or temperance. It is the Holy Spirit produced "ability to restrain desires and emotions."[76] Because self-control amounts to "mastery over one's impulses and faculties [this virtue aids] in one's struggle in resisting temptation."[77]

The biblical teaching is that everyone in covenant relationship with God has the responsibility to reject Satan's plan and align with God's plan. In its most basic sense, Adam and Eve's sin resulted from lack of self-control. The Bible teaches us that we must *die* to the flesh to live (Romans 8:13). Galatians 5:16 says that when we walk by the Spirit we do not gratify the desires of our flesh. Dying to self, or the flesh, is an intentional decision we make. It is an act of obedience to God and this type of *dying* requires the power of Holy Spirit which manifests as the "fruit of self-control" He produces.

In his first letter to the Corinthians, Paul provides Christ-followers down through the centuries with the assurance that "[n]o temptation [regardless of its source] has overtaken *or* enticed [us] that is not common to human experience [nor is any temptation

---

75 Bromiley, Geoffrey W., *Theological Dictionary of the New Testament* (Eerdmans 1985) entry for *enkratei*a under *1.*, p. 196

76 Harmon and Sloat, *Galatians: A Commentary By Matthew Harmon and John Sloat*, Galatians 5:16-26. Retrieved from https://www.thegospelcoalition.org/commentary/galatians/#section-32 (last accessed December 8, 2023)

77 Rapa, Robert K., "Galatians," in *The Expositor's Bible Commentary: Romans - Galatians*, Vol. 11, Revised edition, edited by Longman III and Garland (Zondervan Academic 2008) Galatians 5:22-23, p. 631

unusual or beyond human resistance]."[78] Paul then supplies the good news that God comes to our aid in every temptation.

> ... but God is faithful [to His word—He is compassionate and trustworthy], and He will not let you be tempted beyond your ability [to resist], but along with the temptation He [has in the past and is now and] will [always] provide the **way out** as well, so that you will be able to endure it [without yielding, and will overcome temptation with joy]. 1 Corinthians 10:13 AMP, bold added

While we didn't quote this verse in Lesson 9, although we did discuss it. On the heels of the truth that temptation is common Paul is quick to point to God's faithfulness! The test may be long-lasting and require endurance, but God guarantees that His faithfulness will outlast the scope and duration of every test. The fact that He "does not allow us to be exposed to irresistible temptations is a reflection of his faithfulness to us."[79]

The second assurance Paul provides is that every temptation has an exit point. You may recall that we said, *way out* does not mean we escape the temptation altogether! *Way out* refers to the fact that God knows exactly how to defeat the tempter. He will show you how to avoid Satan's trap to sin in the midst of every difficult circumstance. Following God's counsel will allow you to bear up under the test/temptation leading to endurance until He brings the trial to an end. The temptation itself provides the means by which you can grow spiritual muscle! As you obediently stand up against the temptation, you are giving your spiritual muscles a workout that results in growth.

Let me illustrate this growth principle with a personal example. I had quickly recovered from a fairly minor viral infection, but the post-viral cough that remained was a source of great

---

78   1 Corinthians 10:13a AMP, italics in original
79   Beale and Carson, editors, *Commentary on the New Testament Use of the Old Testament* (Baker Academic 2007) 1 Corinthians 10:13, p. 727

annoyance. Eating, talking and sometimes just breathing triggered coughing spasms that disrupted life at almost every point and were sometimes physically challenging. I knew God had placed me in a testing season and that meant the cough would remain until it had accomplished the purpose for which He had permitted it. Over the course of several weeks I began to discern that my typical response of impatience, frustration, grumbling and complaining was not pleasing to the Lord. This was a trial and I knew I needed to choose joy. So, I began a habit of mentally "choosing joy" every time I coughed. I certainly wasn't feeling joyful but the benefit was that I was getting practice in getting my eyes off of my circumstances and putting them on God. The illustration I often use in teaching is that I was changing the focus of the magnifying glass in my hand. Rather than holding that magnifying glass over my unpleasant circumstances I was changing its position so that I could magnify the Lord! When the cough persisted beyond the date I believe God said He had released my healing, refraining from frustration and complaint became even more difficult. I pressed in to the Lord for a strategy that would lead to an overcoming victory and bring the trial to an end. God brought the exit strategy to me in prayer one morning. When I had a coughing spasm and felt the temptation to express my impatience, I needed in that very moment to die to my flesh and allow the Holy Spirit to lead. I employed a very simple strategy. Every time I coughed, I would simply say, "Holy Spirit I want you to lead me right now." I can't tell you how many times I had to employ that strategy, but I can tell you it worked! Not only was it the "way out" of the temptation, spiritual muscle to stand against temptation developed from repetitive use.

The only thing that stands between me and free flowing fruit of the Spirit is my self-will. When I say *yes* to God's invitation of salvation it should be the first of a lifelong continual flow of yes responses to God. Every yes I breathe keeps open the flow of the Holy Spirit in my life. When I assert my self-will over God's will however, I'm on my own. I've in effect said, "never mind God I've

The Power of My Spirit   189

got this one, I can do it all by myself." In that case He allows me to do it *my* way; but I can never ever accomplish *His* will *my* way. To accomplish His will requires a free flow of His Spirit in me and through me. Over time as I mature and grow into Christ-likeness I desire to only do what I see my Father doing.

It has been suggested the fruit of the Spirit can be employed as a "spiritual thermometer" to measure our spiritual health.[80] We might wonder why Paul chose to list these nine particular expressions of God's character. I think the answer may well be that the "fruit of the Spirit" was Paul's version of a common Old Testament formula for God's nature. The first biblical expression of that formula is found in Exodus 34:6-7a when God revealed His character to Moses (rather than His physical appearance): "Then the LORD passed by in front of him and proclaimed, "The LORD, the LORD God, compassionate and gracious, slow to anger, and abounding in lovingkindness and truth; who keeps lovingkindness for thousands, who forgives iniquity, transgression and sin." Those words became central to understanding God's person[81] and that formulation of His nature was repeated many times over in the Old Testament.[82] What Paul tells us is that when we submit to God's Spirit, He will reproduce God's character in us. If that is not happening in your life, it suggests something has hindered the Holy Spirit. There is a solution. Stop

---

80 Arnold, Clinton E., general editor, *Zondervan Illustrated Bible Backgrounds Commentary*, Vol. 3 (Zondervan 2002) *Reflections*, p. 293
81 "The frequent use through the rest of the Old Testament of the formula in [Exodus 34] v. 6 by which the nature of God is portrayed (Num. 14.18; Neh. 9.17; Ps. 86.15, etc.) is an eloquent testimony to the centrality of this understanding of God's person." Childs, Brevard S., *The Book of Exodus: A Critical, Theological Commentary*, The Old Testament Library (The Westminster Press 1974) Exodus 34:1-10, p. 612
82 "The confession that follows the double calling of Yahweh's name is clearly reflected in eight OT passages, three of them in the Psalms (86:15; 103:8; 145:8) and one each in Num 14:18; Joel 2:13; Nah 1:3; Neh 9:17; and Jonah 4:2. Possible allusions to it can be discovered at additional places in the OT, Exod 20:5 among them ...." Durham, John I., *Word Biblical Commentary: Exodus*, Volume 3 (Word Books 1987) Exodus 34:6-7, pp. 453-454

right now and pray. Ask God what is blocking the harvest in your life? Then confess, repent, realign with God's growth plan and watch fruit begin to form in you! As it does don't forget to praise God for His amazing grace.

Hear What The Spirit is Saying to the Church: *Too many people who say they know me live life on their own terms. They fail to understand the truth that every aspect of following me is accomplished by their submission to the Holy Spirit. The truth is that living life as a disciple entails submitting more not trying harder.*

LESSON 10:

THE POWER-FILLED GIFTS OF THE HOLY SPIRIT

"Now concerning spiritual gifts, brethren, I do not want you to be unaware.... [T]here are varieties of gifts, but the same Spirit. And there are varieties of ministries, and the same Lord. There are varieties of effects, but the same God who works all things in all persons. But to each one is given the manifestation of the Spirit for the common good.... But one and the same Spirit works all these things, distributing to each one individually just as He wills."
1 Corinthians 12:1-11

IN OUR LAST LESSON we unpacked the biblical subject of spiritual fruit and learned that "Holy Spirit removes abrasive qualities from the character of one under His control."[1] Scholar Scot McKnight refers to the fruit of the Spirit and the gifts of the Spirit as "*mates lost without each other.*"[2] That said, a study on the Holy Spirit would be incomplete without addressing the matter of what McKnight calls "Spirit-prompted gifts."[3] In his re-titling of what is commonly referred to as *spiritual gifts*, McKnight places the emphasis squarely on the fact that each of these gifts is the

---

1 *Spirit Filled Life Bible* (Thomas Nelson 1991) *Word Wealth Galatians 5:22 kindness,* p. 1780
2 McKnight, Scot, *Open To The Spirit: God In Us, God with Us, God Transforming Us* (Waterbrook 2018) p. 122, italics added. "For the Spirit-prompted gifts to work well, we need the Spirit-prompted fruit as well." Ibid.
3 McKnight, Scot, *Open To The Spirit: God In Us, God with Us, God Transforming Us* (Waterbrook 2018) p. 116

work of Holy Spirit. A spiritual gift can be broadly defined as "any ability that is empowered by the Holy Spirit and used in any ministry of the church."[4]

A good place to begin this lesson is by looking at the primary biblical references to this aspect of the Spirit's work. In addition to our Key Scripture, which I'm restating here more fully, there are two other relevant passages in the writings of the Apostle Paul as well as the lesser recognized verses which come from Peter's first epistle.

> For by the grace given to me I say to everyone among you not to think of himself more highly than he ought to think, but to think with sober judgment, each according to the measure of faith that God has assigned. For as in one body we have many members, and the members do not all have the same function, so we, though many, are one body in Christ, and individually members one of another. Having gifts [*charismata*] that differ according to the grace given to us, let us use them: if prophecy, in proportion to our faith; if service, in our serving; the one who teaches, in his teaching; the one who exhorts, in his exhortation; the one who contributes, in generosity; the one who leads, with zeal; the one who does acts of mercy, with cheerfulness. Romans 12:3-8 ESV

> To each is given the manifestation of the Spirit for the common good. For to one is given through the Spirit the utterance of wisdom, and to another the utterance of knowledge according to the same Spirit, to another faith by the same Spirit, to another gifts [*charismata*] of healing by the one Spirit, to another the working of miracles, to another prophecy, to another the ability to distinguish between spirits, to another various kinds of tongues, to another the interpretation of tongues. All these are

---

4   Grudem, Wayne, *Systematic Theology: An Introduction to Biblical Doctrine* (InterVarsity Press 1994) p. 1016, italics omitted

empowered by one and the same Spirit, who apportions to each one individually as he wills.... Now you are the body of Christ and individually members of it. And God has appointed in the church first apostles, second prophets, third teachers, then miracles, then gifts [*charismata*] of healing, helping, administrating, and various kinds of tongues. 1 Corinthians 12:7-11,27-28 ESV

There is one body and one Spirit—just as you were called to the one hope that belongs to your call—one Lord, one faith, one baptism, one God and Father of all, who is over all and through all and in all. But grace was given to each one of us according to the measure of Christ's gift [*dorea*].... And he gave the apostles, the prophets, the evangelists, the shepherds and teachers, to equip the saints for the work of ministry, for building up the body of Christ, until we all attain to the unity of the faith and of the knowledge of the Son of God, to mature manhood, to the measure of the stature of the fullness of Christ, so that we may no longer be children, tossed to and fro by the waves and carried about by every wind of doctrine, by human cunning, by craftiness in deceitful schemes. Rather, speaking the truth in love, we are to grow up in every way into him who is the head, into Christ, from whom the whole body, joined and held together by every joint with which it is equipped, when each part is working properly, makes the body grow so that it builds itself up in love. Ephesians 4:4-7,11-16 ESV

As each has received a gift [*charisma*], use it to serve one another, as good stewards of God's varied grace: whoever speaks, as one who speaks oracles of God; whoever serves, as one who serves by the strength that God supplies—in order that in everything God may be glorified through Jesus Christ. To him belong glory and dominion forever and ever. Amen. 1 Peter 4:10-11 ESV

I have pointed out that three of these Scripture quotes employ either the singular word *charisma*, which is commonly translated in the Bible as "gift," or its plural *charismata* (gifts). The one exception is found in Ephesians 4:7 which, as noted, uses the noun *dorea*, also commonly translated as "gift." We'll address both words in a Word Study.

> **WORD STUDY**
>
> *The Greek word translated as* **gifts** *in our Key Scripture (as well as in the 1 Corinthians quote) is the plural noun charismata (singular charisma {khar'-is-mah} is used in the 1 Peter 4 quote). It is one of several Greek nouns which can be properly translated as gift(s). Charisma is a verbal noun of charizomai, a Greek verb meaning to "give freely" or "show pleasure."*[5]
>
> *Charisma "means 'gift that is freely and graciously given.'"*[6] *By adding the suffix ma to the word cháris the focus of attention is on the end-result of the grace given.*[7] *Accordingly, charisma denotes "something that is given or imparted by grace."*[8] *In the Greek culture, charisma described "that moment when the gods graced or donated*

---

5   Bromiley, Geoffrey W., *Theological Dictionary of the New Testament*, Abridged in One Volume (Eerdmans 1985) entry for *chairo* under *charizomai*, p. 1298; see also under *charisma A. Usage*, p. 1306 and under *A. Secular Greek 1. Usage, b.* p. 1301

6   Hoehner, Harold W., "Romans," in *The Bible Knowledge Word Study: Acts-Ephesians*, edited by Darrell L. Bock (Victor 2006) Romans 12:6 under *Gifts*, p. 190

7   Hill, Gary, *The Discovery Bible*, HELPS Ministries, Inc., Cognate:5486 *xárisma*

8   Renner, Rick, *Sparkling Gems from the Greek Volume II* (Harrison House Publishers 2016) July 20, p. 662, italics omitted; Bromiley, Geoffrey W.,

supernatural ability, favor, or power to an individual."[9]
"[I]n the technical Pauline sense χαρίσματα [charismata] (... gifts) denote 'extraordinary powers, distinguishing certain Christians and enabling them to serve the church of Christ, the reception of which is due to the power of divine grace operating in their souls by the Holy Spirit.'"[10]

The Greek word translated as **gift** *in Ephesians 4:7 is dorea {do-reh-ah'} which generally places emphasis on the fact that what is received is gratuitous, unwarranted and unearned.*[11] *It derives from the word didomi which means "to give."*[12] *Vine's Expository Dictionary of New Testament Words points out that dorea is always used in the New Testament of a gift that is spiritual or supernatural.*[13] *The Bible employs the word dorea to refer to the "gift" of the Holy Spirit.*[14]

From our four Scripture quotes at the beginning of this lesson we can summarize the named gifts by placing them in a simple chart. As we do, it is easy to recognize that the lists somewhat overlap each other but we must also consider the fact that no two

---

Theological Dictionary of the New Testament, Abridged in One Volume (Eerdmans 1985) entry for *chairo* under *charisma A. Usage*, p. 1306

9 Renner, Rick, *Sparkling Gems from the Greek Volume II* (Harrison House Publishers 2016) July 20, p. 662, italics omitted

10 *Thayer's Greek Lexicon*, citing Cremer, *Herzog*, edition 2 vol. v. 10ff under the word *Geistesgaben*. Retrieved from https://www.blueletterbible.org/lexicon/g5486/kjv/tr/0-1/ (last accessed March 22, 2024)

11 Mounce, William D., editor, *Complete Expository Dictionary of Old & New Testament Words* (Zondervan 2006) entry for *Gift* under *New Testament Noun*: δωρεά *dorea*, p. 283

12 Bromiley, Geoffrey W., *Theological Dictionary of the New Testament*, Abridged in One Volume (Eerdmans 1985) entry for *didomi*, p. 166

13 *Vine's Expository Dictionary of New Testament Words*, entry for *Gift, Giving*, Scripture citations omitted. Retrieved from https://www.blueletterbible.org/lexicon/g1431/kjv/tr/0-1/ (last accessed February 13, 2024)

14 See for example: Acts 2:38; 10:45

lists are identical. Scholars conclude that none of these lists were intended to be an exhaustive catalogue of every possible gift.[15] Rather, the gifts enumerated in these four texts are merely illustrations of the types of gifts distributed to Christ-followers for the benefit of the Body of Christ. In other words, the gifts expressly mentioned in Scripture are merely representative examples. It is noteworthy that these examples are entirely consistent with the Old Testament understanding that God's Spirit is the source of special endowments or abilities.[16]

Romans 12:3-8	1 Corinthians 12:7-11,27-30[17]	Ephesians 4:11	1 Peter 4:10-11
prophesying	apostle (serve as a divinely commissioned emissary)	apostle	speaking
serving	prophesying (proclaim revelations from God in spontaneous utterance)[18]	prophet	serving/ministering

---

15 See for example: Fee, Gordon D., *The First Epistle To The Corinthians*, New International Commentary on the New Testament (Eerdmans 1987) 1 Corinthians 12:4-11, p. 585; McKnight, Scot, *Open To The Spirit: God In Us, God with Us, God Transforming Us* (Waterbrook 2018) p. 121; Schreiner, Thomas R., *Romans*, Baker Exegetical Commentary on the New Testament, 2nd edition (Baker Academic 1998, 2018) Romans 12:6, p. 637

16 Hill, David, *Greek Words and Hebrew Meanings: Studies in the Semantics of Soteriological Terms*, Society for New Testament Studies Monograph Series 5 (Wipf and Stock 2000, previously published Cambridge University Press 1967) p. 266

17 Unless otherwise noted, the definitions in this column are from Smith, Jay E., "1 Corinthians," in *The Bible Knowledge Word Study: Acts-Ephesians*, edited by Darrell L. Bock (Victor 2002) 1 Corinthians 12:8-10,28-30 Spiritual Gifts, see table under *Description [The special God-given ability to …]*, p. 289

18 Thomas Schreiner asserts that prophecy provides practical guidance and can be either spontaneous or revelation that follows prior reflection. Schreiner, Thomas R., *Romans*, Baker Exegetical Commentary on the New Testament, 2nd edition (Baker Academic 1998, 2018) Romans 12:6, p. 637

Romans 12:3-8	1 Corinthians 12:7-11,27-30[17]	Ephesians 4:11	1 Peter 4:10-11
teaching	teaching (teach the Scriptures with precision & clarity)	evangelist	
encouraging	miracles (perform supernatural acts of power)	pastor	
giving	healing (heal diseases miraculously)	teacher[19]	
leading	[gifts of] helping (serve others with insight & sensitivity)		
showing mercy	administration (organize & lead kingdom activities with efficiency)		
	various kinds of tongues (speak in unlearned language the speaker does not understand)[20]		

---

19 "While some people see one gift of 'pastor-teacher' here based on one Greek article in the original language it is probably better to see two separate gifts due to the fact that the words are plural and teaching is seen as a separate gift in Romans 12." Davis, James, *Study of the Holy Spirit, Spiritual Gifts*, Lesson Eight from the series: Core Faith: Understanding The Essentials Of The Christian Life, Bible.org. See: Wallace, Dan, *Greek Grammar Beyond the Basics: An Exegetical Syntax of the New Testament* (Zondervan 1996) p. 284. Retrieved from https://bible.org/seriespage/lesson-8-study-holy-spirit (last accessed February 13, 2024)

20 This definition is from Green, Michael, *I Believe in the Holy Spirit*, Revised edition (Eerdmans 2004) p. 210. "[I]t is probably best to give the fullest possible breadth to Paul's phrase 'different kinds of tongues' and to conclude that whereas some glossolalia may be speaking in a language unknown to the speaker but intelligible to somebody who knows the particular language employed, other 'tongues' may not be a particular language at all but will rather be the effusion of the deepest longings of the heart released by the Spirit of God in prayer, praise or song." Ibid., p. 211. "Those who were open to the Spirit at times were empowered with gifts to communicate in a manner that transcends their inabilities with language. Sometimes believers can speak in a language they do not know for the glory of God; others can pray privately in a way that edifies. Other people can speak in tongues in public, in a setting where the Spirit prompts an interpretation for the whole

Romans 12:3-8	1 Corinthians 12:7-11,27-30[17]	Ephesians 4:11	1 Peter 4:10-11
	word of wisdom (enablement to know God's purposes in Christ's victory at the cross)[21]		
	word of knowledge (exercise extraordinary theological insight, including the ability to apprehend the Sonship of Christ-followers)[22]		
	faith (allegiance to God)[23] / (revelation that finds its home in a heart)[24]		
	interpretation of tongues (interpret/translate tongues)		
	distinguishing of spirits (discern the origin of an inspired utterance)		

---

assembly. And yet others either in private or in public are empowered to sing ecstatically in a way that glorifies God." McKnight, Scot, *Open To The Spirit: God In Us, God with Us, God Transforming Us* (Waterbrook 2018) p. 178

21 Hill, David, *Greek Words and Hebrew Meanings: Studies in the Semantics of Soteriological Terms*, Society for New Testament Studies Monograph Series 5 (Wipf and Stock 2000, previously published Cambridge University Press 1967) p. 267 citing 1 Corinthians 2:7ff. Dr. Hill explains that Paul's statement to the Spirit searching "the deep things of God" in 1 Corinthians 2:10 refers "to the spiritual truths about the purpose of God in Christ." Those purposes are known by God's Spirit alone and He is the only one who can reveal those purposes to us. Ibid. p. 267, including footnote 4

22 Hill, David, *Greek Words and Hebrew Meanings: Studies in the Semantics of Soteriological Terms*, Society for New Testament Studies Monograph Series 5 (Wipf and Stock 2000, previously published Cambridge University Press 1967) p. 268

23 This definition is from McKnight, Scot, *Open To The Spirit: God In Us, God with Us, God Transforming Us* (Waterbrook 2018) p. 174, crediting Matthew Bates

24 This definition comes from my personal study.

Scholar Scot McKnight suggests a Christ-follower who does not know what gift(s) he has received should ask the question, "What is God doing through me for my local Body of Christ?" McKnight suggests that the answer points to your gift(s).[25] Some other ways to identify your giftedness is to ask someone who knows you what gift(s) they see operating in you, or take advantage of a spiritual gifts inventory which can be found on the internet.

Sadly, the issue of spiritual gifts has become a divisive issue for much of the western church. As a result, we are going to address this present reality with grace and love right up front. That will allow us to set it aside and devote the remainder of our lesson to a fruitful discussion of God's divine purpose for these gifts.

There are Christ-followers who contend that spiritual gifts have either entirely (or partially) ceased as well as those who believe all of these supernatural endowments are relevant and functioning gifts today. In general, those Christians who are called cessationists do not deny that *all* Spirit-empowered gifts have ceased. It is common for people with this viewpoint to "believe that gifts such as teaching, evangelism, mercy, service, and giving are designed by God to continue until the end of the age."[26] However, their understanding of Scripture is that the gifts which are "of a more overtly supernatural nature, ceased to be given by God to the church sometime late in the first century AD (or more gradually through the course of the next few centuries)."[27] On the other

---

25 McKnight, Scot, *Open To The Spirit: God In Us, God with Us, God Transforming Us* (Waterbrook 2018) p. 121

26 Storms, Sam, *Understanding Cessationism from a Continuationist Perspective*, Zondervan Academic Blog, December 10, 2021. Retrieved from https://zondervanacademic.com/blog/understanding-cessationism-from-a-continuationist-perspective (last accessed February 07, 2024)

27 "Cessationists do not deny that God can on occasion still perform miracles, such as physical healing. But they do not believe the spiritual gift of miracles or the gift of healing is given to believers today. Whereas 'healing' still exists in the life of the church, 'healers' do not. God's people may still experience miracles, but God no longer empowers 'miracle workers.'" Storms, Sam, *Understanding Cessationism from a Continuationist Perspective*, Zondervan Academic Blog, December 10, 2021. Retrieved from https://zondervanac-

hand, there are Christ-followers, called non-cessationists or continuationists, who contend "that all the gifts of the Spirit continue to be given by God and are therefore operative in the church today and should be prayed for and sought after."[28]

When addressing whether spiritual gifts legitimately exist in the Body of Christ today, it is important to recognize that there is no specific verse in the Bible that explicitly and unequivocally states spiritual gifts have ceased in whole, or even in part. What that means is that both the arguments for and the arguments against the continuation of Spirit-prompted gifts are based on how various Bible verses are interpreted. The good news is that some common ground can be found among many cessationists and non-cessationists. Both groups generally share a belief that at least some of the Spirit-empowered gifts identified in Scripture continue to be distributed to Christ-followers today. For example, as already noted, it is most likely that many, if not all, Christ-followers believe Holy Spirit led and empowered abilities to teach and evangelize will continue to exist until Christ returns. There may also be a somewhat common understanding that Spirit-endowed mercy, service to others and generous giving have not ceased,[29] nor has the role of the local pastor. A Venn diagram will help illustrate the point I'm making.

---

ademic.com/blog/understanding-cessationism-from-a-continuationist-perspective (last accessed February 07, 2024)

28 Storms, Sam, *Understanding Cessationism from a Continuationist Perspective*, Zondervan Academic Blog, December 10, 2021. Retrieved from https://zondervanacademic.com/blog/understanding-cessationism-from-a-continuationist-perspective (last accessed February 07, 2024)

29 Storms, Sam, *Understanding Cessationism from a Continuationist Perspective*, Zondervan Academic Blog, December 10, 2021. Retrieved from https://zondervanacademic.com/blog/understanding-cessationism-from-a-continuationist-perspective (last accessed February 07, 2024)

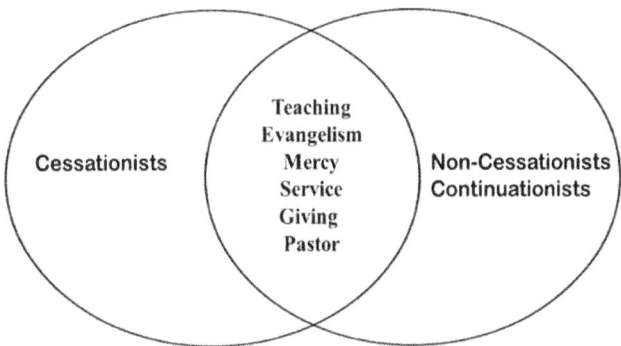

This common ground is important to acknowledge and celebrate. The witness of Scripture is that the Holy Spirit creates unity but then leaves it up to Christ-followers to maintain it. "Paradoxically, like so much in the Christian life, unity is a gift of God, and yet we have to work at it."[30]

Because common ground does exist in much of the Christian community, it is worth our while to explore *why* God has chosen to give such gifts in the first place. We'll return to the four Scripture quotes at the beginning of this lesson which will supply us with a workable outline to guide our discussion.

[Spiritual gifts are given] for the common good [of the Body] (1 Corinthians 12:7)

I am purposefully moving this phrase to the top of the list so that we can begin our discussion here. The reason I'm doing so is because it essential to a proper understanding of the entire subject of spiritual gifts. The phrase "common good" is a translation of the Greek word *sumphero* {soom-fer'-o} which means "to bring together, to benefit, to be advantageous."[31] *Sumphero* describes

---

30 Green, Michael, *I Believe in the Holy Spirit*, Revised edition (Eerdmans 2004) p. 131
31 *Spirit Filled Life Bible* (Thomas Nelson 1991) *Holy Spirit Gifts and Power* by Paul Walker under *The Gifts of the Godhead*, p. 2023

blending or combining of individual elements to form something better.[32] We have talked much in this study about our individual relationship with Holy Spirit. Here it is the corporate aspect of the Church which is being highlighted. As John MacArthur points out, "Spiritual gifts are special capacities bestowed on believers to equip them to minister supernaturally to others, especially to each other. Consequently, if those gifts are not being used, or not being used rightly, the body of Christ cannot be the corporate manifestation of its Head, the Lord Jesus Christ, and the work of God is hindered."[33]

Paul places primary emphasis on the Body of Christ and its individual members as secondary. In his mind, "the whole Church is the loser if it is not so constituted that all members get the chance to make their God-given contribution to its life and worship …. [In 1 Corinthians 12 he makes clear] that [the Christ-followers in Corinth] were not individually 'little Christs' with all the gifts, but rather members of Christ with some gifts."[34] Even those gifts were not given for their personal benefit but for building up the Body of Christ as a whole.[35] Paul was very critical of the Corinthians for playing the game of one-upmanship as they compared and contrasted their individual spiritual gifts with one another.

In the New Testament the Body of Christ is the instrument through which Christ continues His ministry on earth.[36] "To

---

32 Hill, Gary, *The Discovery Bible*, HELPS Ministries, Inc., [G]4851 *symphérō*
33 *1 Peter 4:10-13 Commentary*, Precept Austin, quoting John MacArthur, *1 Corinthians* (Moody Press). Retrieved from https://www.preceptaustin.org/1_peter_410-13#4:10 (last accessed February 17, 2024)
34 Green, Michael, *I Believe in the Holy Spirit*, Revised edition (Eerdmans 2004) p. 156
35 Fee, Gordon D., *The First Epistle To The Corinthians*, New International Commentary on the New Testament (Eerdmans 1987) 1 Corinthians 12:7, p. 589
36 Hill, David, *Greek Words and Hebrew Meanings: Studies in the Semantics of Soteriological Terms*, Society for New Testament Studies Monograph Series 5 (Wipf and Stock 2000, previously published Cambridge University Press 1967) p. 268

be part of the Body of Christ is to receive a new orientation, or spiritual gift. Each Christian is given something to do for the sake of others. Those orientations are called 'spiritual gifts.'"[37] In sum, Spirit-prompted gifts orient us toward others. God's divine purpose for these supernatural abilities serves to shift our natural self-focus to being supernaturally focused on others so that the Body can fulfill her God-given purpose.

I say to everyone among you not to think of himself more highly than he ought to think, but to think with sober judgment, each according to the measure of faith that God has assigned (Romans 12:3)

In the culture of that day, the pursuit for honor and status was the norm.[38] Paul cautions Christ-followers they are to be different because through the Holy Spirit their norm is to be "other-oriented."[39] He reminds them that God has given each one of them the gift of faith to serve others. Because none of those Spirit-prompted gifts results from their own virtue, there is no room for pride among them.

Scholars admit that the phrase *according to the measure of faith* is not entirely clear and therefore there is disagreement among them as to exactly what Paul means.[40] Leander Keck suggests

---

37 McKnight, Scot, *Open To The Spirit: God In Us, God with Us, God Transforming Us* (Waterbrook 2018) p. 116
38 Schreiner, Thomas R., *Romans*, Baker Exegetical Commentary on the New Testament, 2nd edition (Baker Academic 1998, 2018) Romans 12:3, p. 633
39 McKnight, Scot, *Open To The Spirit: God In Us, God with Us, God Transforming Us* (Waterbrook 2018) p. 117
40 Citing various other scholars, Thomas Schreiner concludes that "Paul is speaking of the quantity of faith or trust that each believer possesses." Schreiner, Thomas R., *Romans*, Baker Exegetical Commentary on the New Testament, 2nd edition (Baker Academic 1998, 2018) Romans 12:3, p. 634, citation of other scholars found in footnote 7. On the other hand, Harrison and Hagner understand the word "measure" in the sense of being a standard, "the divine qualification for a task." They conclude Paul means "that one's faith should provide the basis for a true estimation of oneself, since it reveals that one is dependent, along with other believers, on the

that Paul is not saying God gifts different people with differing amounts of faith which then becomes the standard by which they should view themselves. Keck concludes such a self-measurement would actually lead to the pride Paul wants to avoid![41] He believes Paul is saying that Christ-followers should think of themselves soberly because faith (the gospel message itself) levels the playing field. Every Christ-follower stands equal at the foot of the cross! On the other hand, Thomas Schreiner asserts that Paul *is* in fact speaking of the quantity of faith or trust each Christ-followers enjoys, pointing out that this would not be the first time Paul has referenced differing *amounts* of faith.[42] To Schreiner pride is mitigated by Paul's reminder that faith is God's grace gift; it is not based on the receiver's merit or moral excellence.[43] The common thread seems to be that whatever Paul intends, at a minimum, he aims to silence their pride.

For as in one body we have many members, and the members do not all have the same function, so we, though many, are one body in Christ, and individually members one of another (Romans 12:4-5)

As an initial matter, let's refresh our memory that we have learned the word "one" in the Bible often refers to something other than the numeric number one. If we go all the way back to Lesson 2, we find a Word Study on the Greek word *heis* {hice}. It is the word Paul uses here when he says "in *one* body we have many members" and "we, though many, are *one* body in Christ" and

---

saving mercy of God in Christ." Harrison and Hagner, "Romans," in *The Expositor's Bible Commentary: Romans – Galatians*, Vol. 11, Revised edition, edited by Longman III and Garland (Zondervan Academic 2008) Romans 12:3, p. 186

41 Keck, Leander E., *Romans*, Abingdon New Testament Commentaries (Abingdon Press 2005) Mandates for the New Ethos ([Romans] 12:3-21) p. 297

42 See for example: Romans 14:1

43 Schreiner, Thomas R., *Romans*, Baker Exegetical Commentary on the New Testament, 2nd edition (Baker Academic 1998, 2018) Romans 12:3, p. 635

"we, though many, are ... individually members *one* of another." In our Word Study we discovered that *heis* "describes that which is united as one in contrast to that which is divided or consisting of separate parts."[44] In other words, Paul employs *heis* to underscore their cohesive unity not the distinctiveness of individual parts.

Comparing a community to a human body which was made up of diverse organs was a common metaphor in the first century. It was particularly suitable when the goal was to urge unity in civic affairs.[45] The point is that the unity of the physical body "is by definition characterized by diversity."[46] Because the unity among Christ-followers stems from the fact that they are "in Christ" (spiritually incorporated into Christ), "this diversity is not something to be overcome but to be treasured and actualized rightly."[47] In fact, Paul views *being in Christ* to demand unity,[48] but again he is *not* speaking of unity in conformity or uniformity. Rather the Holy Spirit enables unity in diversity!

> [A] healthy church will have a great diversity of gifts, and this diversity should not lead to fragmentation but to greater unity among believers in the church. Paul's whole point in the analogy of the body with many members (1 Cor. 12:12-26) is to say that God has put

---

44 *Ephesians 4:4-6 Commentary*, Precept Austin. Retrieved from http://www.preceptaustin.org/ephesians_44-6.htm (last accessed December 18, 2021)

45 Keck, Leander E., *Romans*, Abingdon New Testament Commentaries (Abingdon Press 2005) Mandates for the New Ethos ([Romans] 12:3-21) pp. 297-298

46 Schreiner, Thomas R., *Romans*, Baker Exegetical Commentary on the New Testament, 2nd edition (Baker Academic 1998, 2018) Romans 12:4-5, p. 636

47 Keck, Leander E., *Romans*, Abingdon New Testament Commentaries (Abingdon Press 2005) Mandates for the New Ethos ([Romans] 12:3-21) p. 298. See also: Schreiner, Thomas R., *Romans*, Baker Exegetical Commentary on the New Testament, 2nd edition (Baker Academic 1998, 2018) Romans 12:4-5, p. 636

48 Mathis II, Donny Ray, *Romans: A Commentary By Donny Ray Mathis II*, Romans 12:1–2. Retrieved from https://www.thegospelcoalition.org/commentary/romans/#section-37 (last accessed February 13, 2024)

us in the body with these differences *so that we might depend on each other...* It runs counter to the world's way of thinking to say that we will enjoy greater unity when we join closely together with those who are different from us, but that is precisely the point that Paul makes in 1 Corinthians 12, demonstrating the glory of God's wisdom in not allowing anyone to have all the necessary gifts for the church, but in requiring us to depend upon each other for the proper functioning of the church.[49]

In other words, according to God's plan, diversity of gifts is absolutely essential to unity. As John MacArthur points out, "God gives His people varieties of gifts just as players on a [football] team have varieties of positions."[50] The same is true of any team sport and that illustrates perfectly the point of spiritual gifts. God's purpose can only be fulfilled when each member of the Body uses their gift(s), as diverse as they are, for the good of the whole Body.

Now there are varieties of gifts [charismata] but the same Spirit (1 Corinthians 12:4); To each is given the manifestation of the Spirit (1 Corinthians 12:7); All these are empowered by one and the same Spirit, who [distributes] to each one individually as he wills (1 Corinthians 12:11)

Very simply, after salvation Christ-followers each receive one or more spiritual gifts which are a "manifestation" (a disclosure) of Holy Spirit's activity at work among them.[51] Spirit-prompted

---

49 Grudem, Wayne, *Systematic Theology: An Introduction to Biblical Doctrine* (InterVarsity Press 1994) p. 1022, italics in original
50 *1 Peter 4:10-13 Commentary*, Precept Austin, quoting John MacArthur, *1 Corinthians* (Moody Press). Retrieved from https://www.preceptaustin.org/1_peter_410-13#4:10 (last accessed February 17, 2024)
51 Fee, Gordon D., *The First Epistle To The Corinthians,* New International Commentary on the New Testament (Eerdmans 1987) 1 Corinthians 12:7, p. 589, also 1 Corinthians 12:8-10, p. 590. John MacArthur points out that gifts are distributed only after a person's salvation. *1 Peter 4:10-13 Commentary*, Precept Austin, citing MacArthur, John, *1 Corinthians* (Moody

The Power of My Spirit 207

gifts "cannot be earned, pursued, or worked up."[52] The only way one obtains a spiritual gift is to receive it through the grace of God.

Notice that there is no qualification concerning how mature a Christ-follower must be before he receives a gift. Even immature followers receive Spirit-empowered gifts from God.[53] "It is the Spirit who chooses who does what in the Body of Christ. Our only responsibility is to receive [and put to use] the gifts that God gives."[54] Once again, we see the paradox of Christian life. God supplies the gift but He then requires labor on our part.

The word translated as "empower" in 1 Corinthians 12:11 is the Greek word *energeo* {en-erg-eh'-o}. When we discussed resurrection power at work in Christ-followers we learned that the Greek noun *energeia* {en-erg'-i-ah} is used exclusively in the New Testament to refer to supernatural power.[55] When referencing God, it is *"the supernatural ability to get something done."*[56] The related verb *energeo* {en-erg-eh'-o} denotes a force that is energizing (including divine or demonic force), power that is actively at work and produces an outcome.[57] In other words, Paul wants

---

Press). Retrieved from https://www.preceptaustin.org/1_peter_410-13#4:10 (last accessed February 17, 2024)

52 *1 Peter 4:10-13 Commentary*, Precept Austin. Retrieved from https://www.preceptaustin.org/1_peter_410-13#4:10 (last accessed February 17, 2024)

53 Grudem, Wayne, *Systematic Theology: An Introduction to Biblical Doctrine* (InterVarsity Press 1994) p. 1030

54 McKnight, Scot, *Open To The Spirit: God In Us, God with Us, God Transforming Us* (Waterbrook 2018) p. 147

55 *NET Bible Notes*, study note 54, Ephesians 1:19. In the New Testament, *energeo* almost always describes supernatural energizing activity which is attributed to God. *Philippians 2:13 Commentary*, Precept Austin. Retrieved from https://www.preceptaustin.org/philippians_213 (last accessed July 8, 2021)

56 Renner, Rick, *Sparkling Gems from the Greek Volume II* (Harrison House Publishers 2016) July 10, p. 634, italics in original

57 Bromiley, Geoffrey W., *Theological Dictionary of the New Testament*, Abridged in One Volume (Eerdmans 1985) entry for *ergon* under *energéō, enérgeia, enérgēma, energēs*, p. 254; Renner, Rick, *Sparkling Gems from the Greek*

there to be no misunderstanding about how spiritual gifts work. Gifts operate not by human strength, but by the supernatural power of the Holy Spirit.

As each has received a gift, use it to serve one another, as good stewards of God's varied grace (1 Peter 4:10)

The word *each* (ESV) (rendered *each one* in other translations like NASB 1995 and NKJV) is a translation of the Greek word *hekastos* {hek'-as-tos}. It means each and every one in the entire group. The idea here is to refer "to each one separately."[58] Peter, like Paul, is certain that every individual Christ-follower has received at least one specific gift from the Holy Spirit and that the purpose of that gift is to serve others, particularly those in the Body of Christ.

Peter would have been surrounded by people who were under compulsion to serve their masters because they were bondservants (*doulous*). Here he chooses a different word for "serve" (Greek verb *diakoneo* {dee-ak-on-eh'-o}). By doing so Peter places emphasis on the voluntary nature of this service to others. When the term *diakoneo* is employed it always denotes willingly helping someone else, generally by caring for their needs and thereby bringing them advantage of some kind.[59] In its figurative use, "*diakoneo* is used to refer to serving people in the interests of preserving and enhancing their spiritual life with God…. Christian ministry is fundamentally a practical activity, consisting of acts of service to others for the purpose of sustaining their life as a community of faith, promoting their maturity and growth in Christ-likeness, and enhancing their ability to carry on the mission of Christ. Ministry

---

(Harrison House Publishers 2003) January 31, p. 59; "The active operation or working of power and its effectual results." *Spirit Filled Life Bible* (Thomas Nelson 1991) *Word Wealth [1 Thessalonians] 2:13 effectively, energeo*, p. 1827

58   Zodhiates, Spiros, *The Complete Word Study Dictionary: New Testament* (AMG Publishers 1992) word #1538, p. 534

59   Zodhiates, Spiros, *The Complete Word Study Dictionary: New Testament* (AMG Publishers 1992) word #1247, p. 429

is obedient service done on behalf of the Master for the benefit of his people."[60]

The Greeks did not consider serving others (whether voluntarily or as a bondservant/slave) to be honorable. In fact, to serve someone else was downright humiliating! The Greek people saw their duty as being exclusively to themselves in order to achieve their greatest "potential for excellence."[61] Jesus did it differently. In fact, He inverted the social structure for His disciples. He not only dignified serving others, He made it the benchmark for all who would choose to follow Him.[62] "In Christ, serving is the highway to greatness. In Christ we achieve our full potential by giving, not by grasping."[63]

Peter, like Paul, highlights the fact that one of the ways Christ-followers serve each other is by employing the spiritual gifts they have received. Peter then proceeds to clarify that the recipients are stewards of those gifts, not owners. In the culture of Peter's day, a steward (*oikonomos* {oy-kon-om'-os}) was expected to manage the affairs of his employer as responsibly as the owner himself would handle them. The rabbis considered Moses to be

---

60 *2 Timothy 1:15-18 Commentary*, Precept Austin, quoting Hepner, Mark, *Waiting Table in God's Household: A Personal Theology of Ministry*, Ashland Theological Journal Volume 37. 2005, bold omitted. Retrieved from https://www.preceptaustin.org/2_timothy_115-18#serve (last accessed February 20, 2024)

61 *2 Timothy 1:15-18 Commentary*, Precept Austin, quoting Richards, L. O., *Expository Dictionary of Bible Words* (Regency). Retrieved from https://www.preceptaustin.org/2_timothy_115-18#serve (last accessed February 20, 2024)

62 "Christian service has been dignified by Deity." *2 Timothy 1:15-18 Commentary*, Precept Austin, quoting John Blanchard. Retrieved from https://www.preceptaustin.org/2_timothy_115-18#serve (last accessed February 20, 2024)

63 *2 Timothy 1:15-18 Commentary*, Precept Austin, quoting Richards, L. O., *Expository Dictionary of Bible Words* (Regency). Retrieved from https://www.preceptaustin.org/2_timothy_115-18#serve (last accessed February 20, 2024)

God's steward.⁶⁴ In similar fashion, Peter uses *oikonomos* metaphorically for every Christ-follower. They are each *entrusted* by God with one or more spiritual gifts (resources which belong to God) for which they will need to give an account.⁶⁵ Every steward was measured by his faithfulness. A steward must be "worthy of the master's confidence."⁶⁶ Grace can be wasted if "it only comes *to* us but doesn't move *through* us."⁶⁷ Even so, as scholar Thomas Schreiner asserts, the more important yardstick of our spirituality is our godliness, not our spiritual gifts.⁶⁸

It is important to address one remaining issue about being a good steward before we move on in our discussion. Every recipient of a spiritual gift is responsible for stewarding that gift in a manner which maintains decency and order in public gatherings. Paul makes this clear in 1 Corinthians 14 when he instructs that the operation of a spiritual gift (prophecy for example) is subject to the gift recipient (verse 33) and that "all things [including the manifestation of all gifts] must be done properly and in an orderly manner (verse 40)."

… to equip the saints for the work of ministry, for building up the body of Christ, until we all attain to the unity of the faith and of the knowledge of the Son of God, to mature manhood, to the measure of the stature of the fullness of Christ, so that we may no longer be children, tossed to and fro by the waves

---

64 Bromiley, Geoffrey W., *Theological Dictionary of the New Testament*, Abridged in One Volume (Eerdmans 1985) entry for *oikos* under *oikonomos*, p. 678

65 Hill, Gary, *The Discovery Bible*, HELPS Ministries, Inc., Cognate: 3623 *oikonómos*, italics omitted

66 Hill, Gary, *The Discovery Bible*, HELPS Ministries, Inc., Cognate: 3623 *oikonómos*, quoting C. Spicq (2, 569)

67 Guzik, David, *Study Guide for 1 Peter 4* under *(1 Peter 4:8-11) d. As each one has received a gift, minister it to one another*, italics in original. Retrieved from https://www.blueletterbible.org/comm/guzik_david/study-guide/1-peter/1-peter-4.cfm (last accessed February 17, 2024)

68 Schreiner, Thomas, *The Gifts of the Spirit: An Essay By Thomas Schreiner*, The Gospel Coalition https://www.thegospelcoalition.org/essay/the-gifts-of-the-spirit/ (last accessed February 10, 2024)

and carried about by every wind of doctrine, by human cunning, by craftiness in deceitful schemes (Ephesians 4:12-14)

These three verses in Ephesians 4 are part of the second half of a very long sentence that began at verse 11 and concludes at verse 16. In his commentary on Ephesians, Dr. S. M. Baugh cautions that, "It is easy to get overwhelmed in the surge of scholarly work on [the] issues [presented in this portion of Ephesians 4], but the details of what Paul says should not overshadow the big idea: Christ's gifting of the church in his triumph was to bring about unifying, truth-telling lives of edification and love among his people."[69] Dr. Baugh provides us with wise counsel which we will follow and thereby avoid getting bogged down in the details and the controversies.

Simply stated, in the first portion of this sentence Paul declares Christ distributes Spirit-empowered gifts that permit the recipients to perform functions necessary to the growth, strengthening and maturing of His Body. He identifies five different roles – apostles, prophets, evangelists, pastors and teachers – but in doing so his emphasis is on these individuals functioning as a team and on their responsibility to *equip* Christ-followers.[70] When Paul says these functions are given "to *equip* the saints for the work of ministry, for building up the body of Christ," the term *equip* is the Greek word *katartismos* {kat-ar-tis-mos'}. It means "to make someone completely adequate or sufficient for something."[71] When

---

69 Baugh, S. M., *Ephesians: A Commentary By S. M. Baugh*, Ephesians 4:7-16. Retrieved from https://www.thegospelcoalition.org/commentary/ephesians/#section-16 (last accessed February 14, 2025). Dr. Baugh is Professor Emeritus of New Testament at Westminster Seminary California. His areas of interest and research includes the book of Ephesians.

70 "The focus is not on how the Spirit gifts individuals for ministry, but on the duties of such roles [apostles, prophets, evangelists, pastors and teachers] in helping the church mature." Cohick, Linn H., *The Letter To The Ephesians*, The New International Commentary on the New Testament (Eerdmans 2020) Ephesians 4:11-16, p. 267

71 Klein, William W., "Ephesians," in *The Expositor's Bible Commentary: Ephesians - Philemon*, Vol. 12, Revised edition, edited by Longman III and Garland

these roles are properly undertaken, Christ-followers become completely adequate to attain two specific goals: to walk in unity and to become mature.[72]

Rather, speaking the truth in love, we are to grow up in every way into him who is the head, into Christ, from whom the whole body, joined and held together by every joint with which it is equipped, when each part is working properly, makes the body grow so that it builds itself up in love (Ephesians 4:15-16)

Paul speaks of the corporate growth of the church in Ephesians 4:15-16 and points out that every Christ-follower is to do their part in building up the Body. "... [S]ince everyone is called to contribute his own share to the servant work and growth of the church (4:12), each is also provided with a specific *charisma*.... Every saint is to make his own contribution to the mission and unity of the church."[73]

Whether you were a Gentile Christ-follower who converted from your former pagan lifestyle or of Jewish birth and began to follow Messiah, behavioral transformation would have been a normal part of your understanding of what discipleship required. Gentile Christ-followers understood culturally that when a person was persuaded by a particular philosophy or religious claim then the expectation was that they would become a member of the community that held those beliefs. As a member they would begin to follow that group's way of life.[74] In other words, identification with other Christ-followers meant that you automatically

---

(Zondervan Academic 2006) Ephesians 4:12, p. 116, quoting Louw and Nida (75.5)

72 Cohick, Linn H., *The Letter To The Ephesians*, The New International Commentary on the New Testament (Eerdmans 2020) Ephesians 4:13, p. 271

73 Barth, Markus, *Ephesians: Translation and Commentary on Chapters 4-6*, The Anchor Bible Vol. 34 (Doubleday 1974) Notes on Ephesians 4:16 under *according to the needs of each single part*, pp. 449-450

74 Cohick, Linn H., *The Letter To The Ephesians*, The New International Commentary of the New Testament (Eerdmans 2020) Ephesians 1:4-5, p. 98

assumed their behavioral commitments. For those who became Jewish Messiah followers they also understood that discipleship was "concretely behavioral."[75] From their Jewish background they already accepted the fact that genuine faith is not simply intellectually agreeing with the right concepts. Faith necessarily includes "fidelity, commitment, and truth"[76] which is demonstrated by "right living in accordance with those [truths]."[77]

Jesus gave His disciples one commandment that would shape and unambiguously define His community of followers: they are to love one another as He has loved them (John 13:34). Here Paul presents his own version of that commandment. Whatever Christ-followers say should be spoken in love. "This love, which can never be worked up by human effort, is the supreme gift of the Holy Spirit to his people."[78]

> This love has at least three dimensions: it is the love of God and Christ for man, man's reciprocal love of God and Christ, and the mutual love of the saints. A church in which this manifold love is at work will not occupy herself with the erection of a Tower of Babel and an empire vying for world dominion. Rather the structure erected will have the character of a building useful for rendering a service to many people. It will resemble, e.g., a pilgrim's inn or a halfway house. It will have gates that are open day and night for all who wish to enter (cf. Rev 21:25; 22:14).[79]

---

75 McKnight, Scot, *The Letter of James*, New International Commentary on the New Testament (Eerdmans 2011) James 1:4, p. 81

76 McCartney, Dan G., *James*, Baker Exegetical Commentary on the New Testament (Baker Academic 2009) James 1:3, p. 86

77 McCartney, Dan G., *James*, Baker Exegetical Commentary on the New Testament (Baker Academic 2009) Introduction to James under *Character*, p. 3

78 Green, Michael, *I Believe in the Holy Spirit*, Revised edition (Eerdmans 2004) p. 156

79 Barth, Markus, *Ephesians: Translation and Commentary on Chapters 4-6*, The Anchor Bible Vol. 34 (Doubleday 1974) Notes on Ephesians 4:16 under *so*

... in order that in everything God may be glorified through Jesus Christ (1 Peter 4:11)

"Ancient Mediterranean reciprocity and obligation ideals understood that recipients of 'grace' ([1 Peter] 4:10) were to respond by honoring the giver."[80] Peter encourages Christ-followers to use the spiritual gifts they have received to serve one another in the power and strength God provides *so that* God is the one who receives the glory.[81] Said another way, as God's grace moves through the recipient of the spiritual gift it must never be expressed in a way that glorifies the gift recipient.

When we rely on the Holy Spirit and then give credit to God for what He has accomplished through us it brings glory and honor to God.[82]

Hear What The Spirit is Saying to the Church: *My plan has always been to equip my Body to serve one another.*

---

that it builds itself up in love, p. 451

80 Keener, Craig S., *1 Peter: A Commentary* (Baker Academic 2021) 1 Peter 4:11, p. 333 citing DeSilva, *Honor, Patronage, Kinship, and Purity: Unlocking New Testament Culture* (InterVarsity 2000); also citing: Harrison, James R., *Paul's Language of Grace in Its Graeco-Roman* Context, WUNT 2/172 (Mohr Siebeck 2003); Barclay, John M. G., *Paul & the Gift* (Eerdmans 2015)

81 Storms, Sam, *1 Peter: A Commentary By Sam Storms*, Ephesians 4:9-11. Retrieved from https://www.thegospelcoalition.org/commentary/1-peter/#-section-18 (last accessed February 14, 2024)

82 Keener, Craig S., *1 Peter: A Commentary* (Baker Academic 2021) 1 Peter 4:11, p. 333

LESSON 11:

UNDERSTANDING THE PARACLETE AS OUR ADVOCATE

"I will ask the Father, and he will give you another Advocate to be with you forever." John 14:16 NET

THUS FAR IN our study we've considered the power of Holy Spirit operating in the cosmos and His *dunamis* power as He operates in and through Christ-followers who align their will with God. In this lesson, we'll shift gears once again and consider an entirely different role as He performs His legal function and works in the courts of heaven to the benefit of the *talmidim*.[1]

To appreciate the promise in our Key Scripture, two Word Studies will be instructive for us. First, we will focus on the word translated as "another" and then the term rendered "Advocate" both of which are found in John 14:16.

WORD STUDY

The Greek word translated as **another** *is allos {al'-los} and it means another numerically. It is a duplicate of exactly the same sort.*[2]

---

1 Recall *talmidim* is the Hebrew word for disciples. Refer back to the Preface for an explanation of its use in this study.
2 Zodhiates, Spiros, *The Complete Word Study Dictionary: New Testament* (AMG Publishers 1992) word #243, p. 125

> *This word is in contrast to heteros {het'-er-os} which denotes another one of a different kind, another that is qualitatively different.*[3]

The word "another" provides us with an important key to understand the nature of God's Spirit. Whatever Jesus was to His disciples during His earthly ministry, the Spirit whom the Father sends will be another of exactly the same qualitative sort. In other words, Jesus was assuring His disciples that the essential or distinctive characteristics and attributes of the Spirit sent by the Father will be identical to what they were in Jesus. We might use the term "carbon copy" to describe this sameness. That means the word *allos* gives us one of the clearest windows in all of Scripture through which to correctly view the nature of God's Spirit. The definition of *allos* permits us to look at the biblical record of Jesus' earthly ministry and when we make a carbon copy of His distinctiveness, we can be confident the end result will qualitatively be an accurate picture of Holy Spirit. When Jesus ascended, He sent a duplicate of Himself to remain on earth with His *talmidim* and to dwell *in* them. The world cannot see or know this Spirit.[4]

The next instructive word in our Key Scripture is "Advocate." The Greek word *parakletos* {par-ak'-lay-tos} is unique to John's explanation of Holy Spirit.[5] All five New Testament occurrences of *parakletos* are in John's writings.[6] I think, as we will see, this is a word whose original meaning has been largely lost in translation. In fact, some scholars have noted that finding an appropri-

---

3   Zodhiates, Spiros, *The Complete Word Study Dictionary: New Testament* (AMG Publishers 1992) word #243, p. 125
4   John 14:17
5   Keener, Craig S., *The Gospel Of John A Commentary*, Volume Two (Hendrickson Publishers 2003) John 14:1-31, p. 953; *NET Bible Notes*, translator's note 3, 1 John 2:1
6   John 14:16; 26; 15:26; 16:7; 1 John 2:1

ate English translation of *parakletos* is a very difficult task because no single English word has exactly the same range of meaning.[7] In fact, one way to resolve that concern is to simply transfer the Greek word *parakletos* into English which results in the more familiar word *paraclete*.[8] Placing this Greek word back into the context which any first-century listener in the Roman Empire would have known will perhaps provide us with a surprising role for this Advocate.

> ### WORD STUDY
>
> *As we have noted, the Greek word translated as **advocate** is the noun parakletos {par-ak'-lay-tos}. It's use in the New Testament is more closely linked to the Old Testament concept of advocate than it is to the idea of a heavenly helper found in other ancient Near Eastern literature.[9] The sense of advocacy is consistent with its use by early Christian writers.[10]*
>
> *Parakletos was regularly used in the first century for the person who gave evidence in a courtroom (known as the lawyer).[11]*

---

7   *NET Bible Notes*, translator's note 37, John 14:16
8   *International Standard Bible Encyclopedia* entry for *Paraclete* under *1. Where Used*. Retrieved from https://biblehub.com/topical/p/paraclete.htm (last accessed April 4, 2024)
9   Bromiley, Geoffrey W., *Theological Dictionary of the New Testament*, Abridged in One Volume (Eerdmans 1985) entry for *parakletos* under *B. The Religious Background, 2. The Advocate, d.*, p. 783
10 Bromiley, Geoffrey W., *Theological Dictionary of the New Testament*, Abridged in One Volume (Eerdmans 1985) entry for *parakletos* under *A. The Linguistic Problem, 2. The Meaning in the NT*, p. 783
11 Hill, Gary, *The Discovery Bible*, HELPS Ministries, Inc., [G]3875 *paráklētos*

> *The ancient idea of parakletos is a person who advocates or intercedes for someone else often in another's presence and often within a legal connotation.*[12]

Despite this well-established meaning of *parakletos*, the *King James Version* of our Key Scripture reads:

> And I will pray the Father, and he shall give you another *Comforter*, that he may abide with you for ever. John 14:16 KJV, italics added

Other translations have followed suit by rendering *parakletos* as "comforter."[13] In modern understanding, the word "comfort" pictures being reassured or encouraged by someone in time of grief or distress. Translating *parakletos* in this way did not begin until Wycliffe's translation was published in the 14th century.[14] In those days the word "comfort" (derived from the Latin root, *comfortare* "to strengthen") suggested "make strong" or fortify.[15] However, as scholar Craig Keener notes, to render *parakletos* as *comforter* "is simply **not** the standard use of the Greek noun."[16] In ordinary

---

12 SermonIndex.net, *Text Sermons: Greek Word Studies: Encourage (exhort, comfort, implore) (3870) parakaleo*. Retrieved from https://img.sermonindex.net/modules/articles/article_pdf.php?aid=33952 (last accessed May 17, 2024). See also: Keener, Craig S., *The Gospel Of John A Commentary*, Volume Two (Hendrickson Publishers 2003) Jesus' Coming and Presence by the Spirit ([John] 14:15-26) under *2. Background of the Paraclete Image, 2A. Senses Related to παρακαλέω*, p. 955 pointing out that the Greek noun *paraclete* "typically connotes an intercessory function."

13 See for example: John 14:16 American Standard Version, English Revised Version, Literal Standard Version, Webster's Bible Translation

14 Keener, Craig S., *The Gospel Of John A Commentary*, Volume Two (Hendrickson Publishers 2003) Jesus' Coming and Presence by the Spirit ([John] 14:15-26) under *2. Background of the Paraclete Image, 2A. Senses Related to παρακαλέω*, p. 955

15 Hill, Gary, *The Discovery Bible*, HELPS Ministries, Inc., [G]3875 *paráklētos*

16 Keener, Craig S., *The Gospel Of John A Commentary*, Volume Two (Hendrickson Publishers 2003) Jesus' Coming and Presence by the Spirit ([John]

secular Greek the vast majority of uses of the verb *parakaleo* and the noun *parakletos* is in the context of help that was being given in some kind of legal trial.[17] Greek writers used the word *parakletos* of a "legal advisor, pleader, proxy, or advocate, one who comes forward in behalf of and as the representative of another."[18]

Next, we need to add two contextual historical facts to further facilitate our understanding of the Advocate's role as described in John's Gospel.

1. In ancient Greek practice, an accused person would call in a friend to speak in support of his character. This person was called the *parakletos*. His primary role was to solicit the sympathy of the judges in favor of the accused.[19] For our purposes we can think of this role as being like that of a modern-day defense attorney.
2. There were no public prosecutors in Roman courts. The courts "depended on an interested party to bring charges."[20] Those who provided witness against another

---

14:15-26) under *2. Background of the Paraclete Image, 2A. Senses Related to παρακαλέω*, p. 955, italics and bold added. See also *Theological Dictionary of the New Testament*, "The meaning 'comforter,' although adopted in some renderings, does not fit any of the passages." Bromiley, Geoffrey W., *Theological Dictionary of the New Testament*, Abridged in One Volume (Eerdmans 1985) entry for *parakletos* under A. *The Linguistic Problem, 2. The Meaning in the NT*, p. 783

17 SermonIndex.net, *Text Sermons: Greek Word Studies: Encourage (exhort, comfort, implore) (3870) parakaleo*. Retrieved from https://img.sermonindex.net/modules/articles/article_pdf.php?aid=33952 (last accessed May 17, 2024)

18 Zodhiates, Spiros, *The Complete Word Study Dictionary: New Testament* (AMG Publishers 1992) word #3875, p. 1107

19 SermonIndex.net, *Text Sermons: Greek Word Studies: Encourage (exhort, comfort, implore) (3870) parakaleo*, citing William Barclay. Retrieved from https://img.sermonindex.net/modules/articles/article_pdf.php?aid=33952 (last accessed May 17, 2024)

20 Keener, Craig S., *The IVP Bible Background Commentary New Testament* (Intervarsity Press 1993) John 16:8-11, p. 303. Keener notes that while charges were brought by an interested party, trained orators were hired by

could fulfill the role of a prosecutor.[21] For our purposes we can think of this role as being like that of a modern-day prosecuting attorney.

These two facts provide critical background information for us to properly interpret the role of God's Spirit as portrayed by the Apostle John. Let's look at each one in order. As we do, we'll see that what appears to be opposite and mutually exclusive roles (that of defense attorney and prosecuting attorney) are actually two sides of the same coin. They are one and the same roles. Sadly, they are roles we don't usually ascribe to Holy Spirit because they have been generally lost in translation.

Parakletos as defense attorney

Parakletos was a very common word.[22] Although it is not found in the Greek translation of the Old Testament, ancient Jewish writings show that Jewish authors were familiar with the term. In fact, they used it in its typical meaning of advocacy, someone to plead one's cause. For example:[23]

---

those who could afford them and it was these trained speakers who then debated on their behalf.

21 Keener, Craig S., *The Gospel Of John: A Commentary*, Volume Two (Hendrickson Publishers 2003) John 16:8-11 under *1. Prosecuting the World*, p. 1031

22 William Barclay notes that this word was so common that in addition to the English New Testament, "the Syriac, Egyptian, Arabic, and Ethiopic versions all keep the word *parakletos* (G3875) just as it stands." Barclay, William, *William Barclay's Daily Study Bible* (John Knox Press 1976) 1 John 2:1-2 under *Jesus Christ, The Paraclete*. Retrieved from https://www.studylight.org/commentaries/dsb/1-john-2.html (last accessed January 4, 2022)

23 Barclay, William, *William Barclay's Daily Study Bible* (Westminster John Knox Press 1976) 1 John 2:1-2 under *Jesus Christ, The Paraclete*, Strong's number references omitted in quotes, William Barclay does not provide source citations for these quotations. Retrieved from https://www.studylight.org/commentaries/dsb/1-john-2.html (last accessed January 4, 2022)

"The man who keeps one commandment of the Law has gotten to himself one *parakletos* (G3875); the man who breaks one commandment of the Law has gotten to himself one accuser."[24]

They said, "If a man is summoned to court on a capital charge, he needs powerful *parakletoi* (G3875) (the plural of the word) to save him; repentance and good works are his *parakletoi* (G3975) in the judgment of God."

"All the righteousness and mercy which an Israelite does in this world are great peace and great *parakletoi* (G3875) between him and his father in heaven." They said that the sin-offering is a man's *parakletos* (G3875) before God.

As we might expect, *parakletos* and *parakletoi* are used by these authors in opposition to a real or imagined Accuser. Undoubtedly John's use of *parakletos* was informed by his Jewish roots. In other ancient Jewish writings, the archangel Michael, prince of Israel, is called "the advocate" who defends Israel in the heavenly court against Satan's accusations.[25] The book of Daniel highlights his advocacy role on behalf of the Jewish people.[26] John presents Jesus as standing before the Father acting as an intercessor and a defensive advocate for God's Covenant people.[27] John's view of Jesus is consistent with Paul (Romans 8:34) and the author of Hebrews (Hebrews 7:25). All speak of the fact that Jesus intercedes on behalf of His *talmidim*. As we have noted, John had heard Jesus say He was sending "another" like Him. He knew that meant that one of the roles of Holy Spirit would be to stand against the Accuser as our character reference and our defense attorney!

But why would Christ's followers need such a competent defense attorney? The answer is found in one of the notable job

---

24 A rabbinic saying about what would happen in the day of God's judgment.
25 Beale and Carson, editors, *Commentary on the New Testament Use of the Old Testament* (Baker Academic 2007) Revelation 12:9-10, p. 1126, citing *T. Levi* 5:6; *T. Dan.* 6:1-6; *Midr. Rab.* Exod. 18:5
26 Daniel 12:1
27 1 John 2:1, Brown, Raymond E., *The Epistles of John: A New Translation With Introduction and Commentary by Raymond E. Brown*, The Anchor Yale Bible (University Press 1982) 1 John 2:1d under *Notes*, p. 217

descriptions for Satan. Consistent with the courtroom imagery in the book of Revelation, John records hearing a voice in heaven refer to Satan as the "accuser of the brethren."

> Then I heard a loud voice in heaven, saying, 'Now the salvation, and the power, and the kingdom of our God and the authority of His Christ have come, for *the accuser of our brethren* has been thrown down, he who accuses them before our God day and night.' Revelation 12:10, italics added

The language of the original Greek text places the focus on the fact that the accusations referenced are habitual.[28] The imagery is consistent with early Jewish writings where Satan is regularly viewed as the accuser of Israel.[29] Satan is called the accuser "as if he were standing in a court of law"[30] where he is functioning in the role of a prosecuting attorney. The first question is what accusations are Satan bringing against Christ-followers? John's vision does not apparently address the issue. However, there are two other accusation scenes in Scripture that are specifically attributed to Satan. We find the first in Job and the second in Zechariah. These texts might provide us with a hint to better understand the reference to accusations in Revelation 12:10.

> Then Satan answered the Lord, "Does Job fear God for nothing? Have You not made a hedge about him and

---

28 Perowne, John, general editor, *The Cambridge Bible for Schools and Colleges*, Revelation 12:10 under *which accused*; Ellicott, Charles John, *Ellicott's Commentary for English Readers*, Revelation 12:10. Both commentaries retrieved from Hill, Gary, *The Discovery Bible*, HELPS Ministries, Inc.

29 Keener, Craig S., *The Gospel Of John: A Commentary, Volume Two* (Hendrickson Publishers 2003) John 16:8-11 under *2. Background in the Biblical Prophets*, p. 1032; Beale and Carson, editors, *Commentary on the New Testament Use of the Old Testament* (Baker Academic 2007) Revelation 12:9-10, p. 1126, citing *Jub.* 1:20; 17:15-16; 18-9-12; 48:15-18; *1 En.* 40:7; *T. Levi* 5:6; *T. Dan* 6:2

30 Zodhiates, Spiros, *The Complete Word Study Dictionary: New Testament* (AMG Publishers 1992) word #1228, pp. 418-419

> his house and all that he has, on every side? You have blessed the work of his hands, and his possessions have increased in the land. But put forth Your hand now and touch all that he has; he will surely curse You to Your face." Job 1:9-11

Here Satan's concern seems to center on Job's relationship with God and specifically the cause of Job's faithfulness. Satan suggests that if Job is forced to suffer loss he will turn his back on God. Of course, the outcome of Job's suffering test serves to prove Satan underestimated Job's faithfulness and his accusations against Job were without basis.

Our second example is found in Zechariah 3.

> Then the guiding angel showed me Joshua the high priest [representing disobedient, sinful Israel] standing before the Angel of the LORD, and Satan standing at Joshua's right hand to be his adversary *and* to accuse him. And the LORD said to Satan, "The LORD rebuke you, Satan! Even the LORD, who [now and ever] has chosen Jerusalem, rebuke you! Is this not a log snatched *and* rescued from the fire?" Zechariah 3:1-2 AMP, italics in original

In this text the specific charges Satan brings against Joshua and Israel's priesthood must be discerned from God's response. Keep in mind that Zechariah is one of the Old Testament books that was written after the Jewish people returned to the land of Israel following their exile to Babylon. Zechariah, like Haggai, is used by God to remind the Jewish people that He is the one who controls the resources they need to rebuild the temple as well as their new life in the land.[31] It seems Satan has charged God's Covenant people with sufficient disobedience so as to be permanently

---

31 Hoglund and Walton, "Zechariah," in *Zondervan Illustrated Bible Backgrounds Commentary*, Vol. 5, edited by John H. Walton (Zondervan 2009) under *Introduction*, p. 204

rejected by God. The punishment he advocated is that Jerusalem and its temple should never be rebuilt again. He additionally seems to advocate that 1) the priesthood should not be restored to Israel and/or 2) Joshua has been permanently defiled and is not qualified to be the priest.[32]

These Old Testament texts portray Satan as accusing God's Covenant people of sin and unfaithfulness to their Covenant. The natural result, according to his accusations, is that they should be rejected by God because they do not deserve His salvation or His blessing. Everything in Scripture seems to supply evidence that Satan's goals and methods have not changed!

The good news of the gospel is that God's Covenant people have their own Advocate. He points to the finished work of the cross and that settles the matter! We could select numerous places in the New Testament to make our case. We'll turn to Paul, who chooses a heavenly courtroom setting to sing out the praises of our security.

> If God *is* for us, who *is* against us? He who did not spare His own Son, but delivered Him over for us all, how will He not also with Him freely give us all things? Who will bring a charge against God's elect? God is the one who justifies; who is the one who condemns? Christ Jesus is He who died, yes, rather who was raised, who is at the right hand of God, who also intercedes for us. Romans 8:31b-34, italics in original

I love John MacArthur's characterization when he views Paul as singing "a [poetic] hymn of security."[33] In common rhetorical style, Paul first asked and then answered his own questions. Of course, as one who had suffered so much for the sake of the

---

32 Meyers and Meyers, *Haggai, Zechariah 1-8: A New Translation with Introduction and Commentary*, The Anchor Bible Vol 25B (Doubleday 1987) Notes Zechariah 3:1 under *high priest*, p. 185

33 MacArthur, John, *The MacArthur Study Bible* (Thomas Nelson 2006) study note Romans 8:31-39, p. 1676

gospel, Paul is *not* denying the fact that Christ-followers will face opposition as they live out the gospel. His point is that God will have the last word in the matter. *Every* enemy that opposes God's Covenant people *will* ultimately be defeated. Paul says our assurance is found in the fact that God sent His own Son to the cross and if He did that we can be certain He will not withhold the natural flow of benefits and blessings. Where does our confidence come from? Again, Paul answers the question. We know that Christ is now seated in a heavenly place of honor and authority interceding for us (Romans 8:34) and His Spirit also intercedes on our behalf according to the will of God (Romans 8:26-27). In his commentary on *Romans*, Leander Keck concludes that Holy Spirit is central to Paul's understanding of the power of the gospel. Holy Spirit "is essentially the name for *God's power experienced immediately* (without mediation). The presence of Holy Spirit … confirms what the gospel announces about God's act in Christ …."[34] *Because* Christ sent us the Holy Spirit we can be confident about our freedom from the bondage of sin and death! So, "Who will bring a [successful] charge against God's elect?"[35] The clear answer is, no one! In fact, "[w]hat God will do can be relied on to such an extent that it can be spoken of as already having happened."[36]

Parakletos as prosecuting attorney

Jesus not only defines the role of the *Parakletos* as the defense attorney for His *talmidim*, He likewise characterizes Him as the prosecuting attorney who stands against the kingdom of darkness on our behalf. Using courtroom language once again Jesus continues to describe the legal function of Holy Spirit.

---

34 Keck, Leander E., *Romans*, Abingdon New Testament Commentaries (Abingdon Press 2005) Expecting Redemption ([Romans] 8:18-30) p. 218, italics in original
35 Romans 8:33a
36 Harrison and Hagner, "Romans," in *The Expositor's Bible Commentary: Romans - Galatians*, Vol. 11, Revised edition, edited by Longman III and Garland (Zondervan Academic 2008) Romans 8:30, p. 142

And He, when He comes, will *convict the world concerning sin and righteousness and judgment*; concerning sin, because they do not believe in Me; and concerning righteousness, because I go to the Father and you no longer see Me; and concerning judgment, because the ruler of this world has been judged. John 16:8-11, italics added

The phrase "convict the world concerning sin and righteousness and judgment" sounds like courtroom language and that is exactly the context in which John uses it. The word translated as "convict" is the Greek word *elegcho* {el-eng'-kho}. *Vincent Word Studies in the New Testament* indicates that the definition of *elegcho* includes "to cross-examine or question, for the purpose of convincing, convicting, or refuting...."[37] In his commentary on the New Testament, Robert Gundry points out that the phrase "will convict" (*elegcho*) makes clear that Jesus is not referring to some type of psychologically convincing persuasion, He is revealing the Spirit's role in procuring a legal guilty verdict.[38]

In this sense we could say that Holy Spirit is God's prosecuting attorney.[39] In fact, that's exactly how *The Message* translates these verses.

---

37   SermonIndex.net, *Text Sermons: Greek Word Studies: Convict (expose) (1651) elegcho*, citing Vincent, M. R., *Word Studies in the New Testament*, Vol. 2, pp. 1-102. Retrieved from https://www.sermonindex.net/modules/articles/index.php?view=article&aid=33753 (last accessed January 4, 2022)

38   Gundry, Robert H., *Commentary on the New Testament* (Hendrickson Publishers 2010) John 16:4d-6, p. 438

39   Scholar Craig Keener describes this role of Holy Spirit as follows: "it appears clear that the Spirit's work in [John] 16:8-11 is through the disciples. Jesus sends the Spirit to the disciples (16:7), but through the disciples the Spirit-Paraclete continues Jesus' ministry to the world (16:8-11). Thus, as Jesus prosecuted the world [John] (3:20; cf. 8:46), the Paraclete continues to prosecute the world (16:8-11) through the apostolic preaching of Jesus (cf. 16:7)." Keener, Craig S., *The Gospel Of John A Commentary*, Volume Two (Hendrickson Publishers 2003) The World's Prosecutor ([John] 16:8-11) p. 1030

> When he comes, he'll expose the error of the godless world's view of sin, righteousness, and judgment: He'll show them that their refusal to believe in me is their basic sin; that righteousness comes from above, where I am with the Father, out of their sight and control; that judgment takes place as the ruler of this godless world is brought to trial and convicted. John 16:8-11 MSG

The Dictionary of Biblical Imagery characterizes the legal background in the Old Testament as a familiar and pervasive one. "[T]he broad outline of the biblical narrative could be summarized as an extended judicial proceeding, going from the sin and punishment ... of Genesis to the final sifting of the Last Judgment."[40] There is sound historical and contextual reasoning for such a legal background. In the ancient Near East when a vassal kingdom violated the terms of its covenant, the greater king would send messengers to warn them of his intentions to enforce the curse sanctions of their agreement. If faithfulness was not restored and the violations continued, a covenant lawsuit was initiated against that vassal.[41]

In the Old Testament, the Prophets acted as God's messengers intending to restore Israel's observance of her Covenant obligations. When the Prophet failed to bring Israel, as the vassal kingdom, back into obedient relationship with Yahweh (the greater King), he was commanded to announce Yahweh's *Covenant lawsuit* against Israel. For example, Isaiah and Hosea announced a Covenant lawsuit against the Northern Kingdom Israel. Jeremiah and Ezekiel announced Yahweh's Covenant lawsuit against the Southern Kingdom of Judea.

---

40   Ryken, Wilhoit, and Longman III, editors, *Dictionary of Biblical Imagery* (Intervarsity Press 1998) entry for *Legal Images*, p. 500

41   Huffmon, Herbert Bardwell, *Covenant Lawsuits in the Prophets*, Journal of Biblical Literature, 78 no 4 Dec 1959, pp. 285-295

The Apostle John appropriates the common Old Testament motif and presents his Gospel in a legal framework.[42] A wide variety of studies on the Gospel of John have recognized the trial and witness motifs that are prevalent in it.[43] John wants his readers to

---

42 Examples of biblical courtroom scenes involving God and Israel or God and other nations include: Isaiah 3:13-15, 43:8-13; Jeremiah 2:9, 25:31-32; Hosea 4:1

43 Bowman Robert M., Jr., *The Personhood of the Holy Spirit in John and Acts: A Narrative Approach*, Institute for Religious Research, posted August 21, 2014, Part Three: The Holy Spirit as the Paraclete in John, footnote 7, citing the following studies that have explored these legal motifs and demonstrated that they dominate the structure and presentation of the narrative and speeches in John. See Theo Preiss, "Justification in Johannine Thought," in *Life in Christ*, trans. Harold Knight, SBT 13 (Naperville, IL: Alec R. Allenson, 1952), 9-31; David E. Holwerda, *The Holy Spirit and Eschatology in the Gospel of John: A Critique of Rudolf Bultmann's Present Eschatology* (Kampen: J. H. Kok, 1959), 38-48; James Montgomery Boice, *Witness and Revelation in the Gospel of John* (Exeter: Paternoster, 1970); Severino Pancaro, *The Law in the Fourth Gospel: The Torah and the Gospel, Moses and Jesus, Judaism and Christianity according to John*, NovTSup 42 (Leiden: E. J. Brill, 1975), esp. 194-208; A. E. Harvey, *Jesus on Trial: A Study in the Fourth Gospel* (London: SPCK, 1976); Allison A. Trites, *The New Testament Concept of Witness*, SNTSMS 31 (Cambridge: Cambridge University Press, 1977), 78-124; Jerome H. Neyrey, "*Jesus the Judge: Forensic Process in John 8:21-59*," Bib 68 (1987): 509-41; J. Daryl Charles, "'Will the Court Please Call in the Prime Witness?': John 1:29-34 and the Witness-Motif," TrinJ 10 (1989): 71-83; Antony Billington, "*The Paraclete and Mission in the Fourth Gospel*," in Mission and Meaning: Essays Presented to Peter Cotterell, ed. Antony Billington, Tony Lane, and Max Turner (Carlisle: Paternoster Press, 1995), 95-102 (90-115); Robert Gordon Maccini, *Her Testimony Is True: Women as Witnesses according to John*, JSNTSup125 (Sheffield: Sheffield Academic Press, 1996); Jerome H. Neyrey, "*The Trials (Forensic) and Tribulations (Honor Challenges) of Jesus: John 7 in Social Scientific Perspective*," BTB 26 (1996): 107-124; Martin Asiedu-Peprah, *Johannine Sabbath Conflicts as Juridical Controversy: An Exegetical Study of John 5 and 9:1-10:21*, WUNT 2/132 (Tübingen: Mohr Siebeck, 2000); Andrew T. Lincoln, *Truth on Trial: The Lawsuit Motif in the Fourth Gospel* (Peabody, MA: Hendrickson, 2001); and George L. Parsenios, *Rhetoric and Drama in the Johannine Lawsuit Motif*, WUNT 258 (Tübingen: Mohr Siebeck, 2010)." Retrieved from https://bib.irr.org/part-three-holy-spirit-paraclete-in-john#_irr_end7 (last accessed January 3, 2022)

see that it is the ***world*** that is on trial.[44] Through His teaching and earthly ministry Jesus was prosecuting the world and its ways. The challenge for Jesus' disciples is that He had announced that He was returning to His Father. He knew their question would be, "What will happen then?" In His Farewell Discourse, Jesus explained the plan. The trial of the world will continue (see John 15:18-16:11). He assured them they were not being abandoned. Jesus promised to send the *Parakletos* (John 14:16) to them. When He comes, the Holy Spirit will aid them in the continuing battle between Jesus and the world.[45]

Jesus revealed that Holy Spirit comes to bring charges against the world before God's heavenly court. As we noted above, a person who "witnessed against" someone was functionally a prosecutor. The *Parakletos*, who advocates on behalf of Christ-followers, witnesses against the world's ways and therefore becomes a prosecutor of the world. In John 16:8-11 "the Spirit's coming works to the disciples' advantage by convicting the very world that hates and kills them ….The world is in the wrong. They murdered [Jesus]. In other words, the Spirit reverses the world's verdict against Jesus and pronounces against the world a verdict of guilty. So in putting Jesus on trial, the world put themselves on trial."[46]

John continues the courtroom scenes from his Gospel into the book of Revelation. Scholar Richard Bauckham explains the central theme of legal battle in Revelation as follows.

> The third theme [in Revelation] which is used to characterize Christ's work is that of witness. Jesus himself

---

44 Keener, Craig S., *The IVP Bible Background Commentary New Testament* (Intervarsity Press 1993) John 16:8-11, p. 303
45 Billington, Antony, "The Paraclete and Mission in the Fourth Gospel," in *Mission and Meaning: Essays Presented to Peter Cotterell* (Paternoster Press 1995) prepared for the Web in September 2009 by Robert I Bradshaw, p. 100. Retrieved from https://www.theologicalstudies.org.uk/pdf/cotterell-fs/07_billington.pdf (last accessed January 3, 2022)
46 Gundry, Robert H., *Commentary on the New Testament* (Hendrickson Publisher 2010) John 16:4d-6, p. 438

is 'the faithful and true witness' ([Revelation] 3:14; cf. 1:5).[47]

Jesus' work as witness is continued by his followers, who are ... called his witnesses ([Revelation] 17:6; cf. 2:13) .... It is primarily Jesus' and his followers' witness to the true God and his righteousness, which exposes the falsehood of idolatry and the evil of those who worship the beast. The theme of witness is connected with Revelation's dominant concern with truth and falsehood. The world is a kind of court-room in which the issue of who is the true God is being decided. In this judicial contest Jesus and his followers bear witness to the truth. At the conclusion of the contest, their witness is seen to be true and becomes evidence on which judgment is passed against those who have refused to accept its truth: the beast and his worshippers.[48]

Bauckham's explanation helps us grasp the true significance of the work of Holy Spirit as our Advocate. What's ultimately at stake is, "Who is the true God?" As *talmidim* our lives are to be living witnesses to the truth of who He is. One of the primary roles of Holy Spirit is to assist us in developing a Christ-like nature so that every single time the enemy brings accusation against us in God's courtroom our Advocate is able to successfully defend us based on the shed blood of Christ and our Kingdom citizenship! Ultimately the witness of obedient righteousness in our lives should be strong evidence on which judgment is passed on the unrighteousness of the kingdom of darkness.[49]

---

47 Bauckham, Richard, *The Theology of the Book of Revelation* (Cambridge University Press 1993) p. 72
48 Bauckham, Richard, *The Theology of the Book of Revelation* (Cambridge University Press 1993) pp. 72-73
49 John 16:10, a role of the Paraclete is to convict (prosecute) the world of its unrighteousness. See Keener, Craig S., *The Gospel Of John: A Commentary*, Volume Two (Hendrickson Publishers 2003) The World's Prosecutor ([John] 16:8-11) under *3. The Charges*, p. 1034

In our last lesson, we'll look at God's plan to test us through need and struggle to provide the opportunity for first-hand experience of His faithfulness. We'll learn that God's Spirit is the creative power behind the life led by those who usher in the *new* heaven and earth.

Hear What The Spirit is Saying to the Church: *Will you receive, indeed will you actively seek, the assistance of the Advocate I sent you. Stop trying to live life on your own terms. Look to me, look to My Spirit for His power will enable you to do all that your flesh is too weak to do. By Him the world stands condemned. But by Him you will have life more abundant and be blessed beyond measure.*

LESSON 12:

CREATING THE NEW HEAVEN AND NEW EARTH

"Then I saw a new heaven and a new earth; for the first heaven and the first earth passed away, and there is no longer any sea. And I saw the holy city, new Jerusalem, coming down out of heaven from God, made ready as a bride adorned for her husband. And I heard a loud voice from the throne, saying, 'Behold, the tabernacle of God is among men, and He will dwell among them, and they shall be His people, and God Himself will be among them… the first things have passed away.' And He who sits on the throne said, 'Behold, I am making all things new.'" Revelation 21:1-5a

IN LESSON 3 we looked at God's power working through His Holy Spirit to create and then de-create the visible world in which we live. In this lesson, we will pick up where Lesson 3 left off as we turn to the power of God's Spirit to create the *new* heaven and *new* earth. In ancient Hebrew thought the same Spirit of God who was active in the creation of the cosmos was expected to have an active creative role in the messianic era and the eternal Age to come.[1]

As we will see, "Eternity—and the way we'll live in it—is … being [supernaturally] shaped by our moment-by-moment

---
1   Hill, David, *Greek Words and Hebrew Meanings: Studies in the Semantics of Soteriological Terms*, Society for New Testament Studies Monograph Series 5 (Wipf and Stock 2000, previously published Cambridge University Press 1967) pp. 227,232,253

responses to the life we have before us to live right now."² Before we move on, let's contemplate that last statement a bit more. God's design for eternity is that His Kingdom is the *only* ruling Kingdom on a newly created earth. Establishing His rule on earth does not take place by the force of a conquering human army. God advances His Kingdom by speaking truth.³ People choose to participate in His rule by welcoming the truth He speaks into their lives immediately, deeply and exclusively. This type of hearing leads to being a doer of the Word in every aspect of life. The fruit Word-doers bear as disciples of Christ (Kingdom subjects) comes from obeying Him.⁴ By their obedience God's rulership on earth increasingly conquers the kingdom of darkness, replacing it with the Kingdom of Light. Holy Spirit is "the source of Christian morality"⁵ and is therefore intimately involved in every aspect of this conquering advancement.

We have considered at length how the *dunamis* power can effectively work in a Christ-follower's life and ministry. On the other hand, Paul warned that there will be false teachers and their followers who profess to know Christ but refuse to die to the desires of their flesh and be led by the Holy Spirit. As a result, they become self-loving and self-indulgent in every way imaginable.

> But realize this, that in the last days difficult times will come. For men will be lovers of self, lovers of money, boastful, arrogant, revilers, disobedient to parents, ungrateful, unholy, unloving, irreconcilable, mali-

---

2 Tada, Joni Eareckson, *A Place of Healing: Wrestling with the Mysteries of Suffering, Pain, and God's Sovereignty* (David C Cook 2010) p. 108
3 The spiritual battle we are in is a truth war (God's truth vs Satan's lies), not a power struggle.
4 Gundry, Robert H., *Mark: A Commentary on His Apology for the Cross* (Eerdmans 1993) pp. 206-207,218
5 Hill, David, *Greek Words and Hebrew Meanings: Studies in the Semantics of Soteriological Terms*, Society for New Testament Studies Monograph Series 5 (Wipf and Stock 2000, previously published Cambridge University Press 1967) p. 269

cious gossips, without self-control, brutal, haters of good, treacherous, reckless, conceited, lovers of pleasure rather than lovers of God, holding to a form of godliness, although they have denied its power; Avoid such men as these. 2 Timothy 3:1-5

By way of contrast, Paul taught that the lifestyle that accurately RE•presents Christ permits the Holy Spirit to have His way so that we will be lovers of others and our relationships will reflect that love. He knew that God expects *every* Christ-follower to become the visible image of a presently invisible Jesus. As we discussed in Lesson 9, one of the primary ways in which Christ's image manifests itself in the life of a Christ-follower is through the fruit of the Spirit. Because the fruit produced by Holy Spirit "is the antithesis of the ... works of the flesh"[6] it will be beneficial to unpack Paul's warning about these false teachers.

The Greek term translated as "holding" in 2 Timothy 3:5 is *echo* {ekh'-o} which can mean to hold fast to something. Because Paul employed the word in the Greek present tense he is indicating that the spiritual masquerading of these false teachers is not sporadic, it is their fixed lifestyle![7] Two Word Studies will help us more fully understand Paul's concern.

WORD STUDY

*The Greek word translated as **form** in 2 Timothy 3:5 is morphosis {mor'-fo-sis}. It derives from morpho {mor-fo'-o} which refers to form or shape.*

---

6 Harmon and Sloat, *Galatians: A Commentary By Matthew Harmon and John Sloat*, Galatians 5:16-26. Retrieved from https://www.thegospelcoalition.org/commentary/galatians/#section-32 (last accessed December 8, 2023)

7 *2 Timothy 3:3-5 Commentary*, Precept Austin under *The Hypocrisy Of Holding To A Form Of Godliness, Holding*. Retrieved from http://preceptaustin.org/2_timothy_33-5 (last accessed January 7, 2022)

> *In this context morphosis is employed in the sense of façade or external appearance which is a shame not the real thing.*[8]

These false teachers willingly observed external forms of the Christian faith, but they have refused to give the Holy Spirit power and influence over their heart and their life. "Those who practice such religion find the external forms and expressions of evangelical worship to be amenable to their lifestyles but they are violently at odds with the gospel's internal effects of subduing sin and nurturing holiness."[9]

The word "power" Paul used is *dunamis* which is commonly associated with the Holy Spirit. If you need a refresher, look back to Lesson 5 for the *dunamis* Word Study. Paul goes on to explain what is causing these people to lack the *dunamis* power necessary to die to self and become like Christ. They *deny* it!

WORD STUDY

The Greek word translated as **denied** *is arneomai {ar-neh'-om-ahee}. It can mean to reject something offered, refuse to be identified with, or to disown (renounce).*[10]

---

8 Zodhiates, Spiros, *The Complete Word Study Dictionary: New Testament* (AMG Publishers 1992) word #3446, p. 998
9 Zodhiates, Spiros, *The Complete Word Study Dictionary: New Testament* (AMG Publishers 1992) word #3446, p. 998
10 Zodhiates, Spiros, *The Complete Word Study Dictionary: New Testament* (AMG Publishers 1992) word #720, p. 254; Hill, Gary, *The Discovery Bible*, HELPS Ministries, Inc., [G]720 *arnéomai*

> *This type of denying always involves action. It is more than an intellectual act, arneomai means the thought is clothed and put on display by practice.*[11]

Again, Paul employed the word *arneomai* in the Greek perfect tense meaning this denial happens continuously. The *Theological Dictionary of the New Testament* states that the main thrust of *arneomai* in the New Testament is "that of denying a *person* ... rather than a thing."[12] But what "person" is Paul referring to whose rejection results in a mere form of godliness? Jesus told His disciples that they would receive power (*dunamis*) when the Holy Spirit came on them (Acts 1:8). Scripture clearly identifies both the person and the power available to every Christ-follower as the Holy Spirit. Paul's warning to Timothy about these men and their followers is that they had an appearance of godliness, but denied Holy Spirit the opportunity to be at work *in* them. In today's terms these men might be labeled "nominal Christians." That is, as we recognized in Lesson 9, they are Christian in name only.

Their rejection of Holy Spirit meant God could not work *in* them, but neither could He work *through* them. In fact, denying Holy Spirit's power meant that these men did not even have *the will* to do the work God had prepared for them to do. It's worth our time here to support my last statement with Scripture. To do so we'll turn to what Paul wrote to the church at Philippi.

> So then, my beloved, just as you have always obeyed, not as in my presence only, but now much more in my absence, **work out your salvation** with fear and trembling; for it is God who is at work in you, both to will

---

[11] *2 Timothy 3:3-5 Commentary*, Precept Austin. Retrieved from http://preceptaustin.org/2_timothy_33-5 (last accessed January 7, 2022)

[12] Bromiley, Geoffrey W., *Theological Dictionary of the New Testament* (Eerdmans Publishing Co. 1985) entry for *arneomai* under *a.2.*, p. 79, italics added

and to work for *His* good pleasure. Philippians 2:12-13, italics in original, bold added

First of all, let's be very clear on what Paul is *not* saying. When he instructs the Christ-followers at Philippi to "work out your salvation" he is not advocating a works-based salvation. The fact that Paul addressed the Philippians as "his beloved" makes clear that he is writing to those who were already saved and part of the community of Christ-followers. *Work out* "means to carry the work through to its conclusion."[13] Paul is exhorting them to implement what they have already received as a free gift of grace.[14] Because "the nature of the Christian life does not lie in what one has become but in what one is becoming," salvation is a paradox.[15] Recall that we learned in Lesson 8, for Christ-followers, everything that is a spiritual reality also entails spiritual responsibility. Salvation is received as a gracious gift from God, but once it is received it then requires effort on our part.[16]

In the days of the early church it was common to assume that anyone "who was persuaded of a particular philosophy or religious claim expected at the same time to follow that group's way

---

13 Garland, David E., "Philippians," in *The Expositor's Bible Commentary: Ephesians – Philemon*, Vol. 12, Revised edition, edited by Longman III and Garland (Zondervan Academic 2006) Philippians 2:12, p. 225

14 Gundry, Robert H., *Commentary on the New Testament* (Hendrickson Publishers 2010) Philippians 2:12-13, p. 787. "But why work at salvation if it's not by your working? Because if you don't, you'll [reveal] that God isn't working in you. But if you do, you'll show that he is in fact working in you....All in all, then, God's working in you doesn't *relieve* you of working; it gives you *reason* to be working." Ibid., italics in original

15 Garland, David E., "Philippians," in *The Expositor's Bible Commentary: Ephesians – Philemon*, Vol. 12, Revised edition, edited by Longman III and Garland (Zondervan Academic 2006) Philippians 3:12-13, p. 245, citing Martin Luther

16 Garland, David E., "Philippians," in *The Expositor's Bible Commentary: Ephesians – Philemon*, Vol. 12, Revised edition, edited by Longman III and Garland (Zondervan Academic 2006) Philippians 2:12, p. 225

of life."¹⁷ As members of God's family, Paul was encouraging his audience to grow in ways that would enable them to be more like Christ. In Romans 8:29-30 Paul said that those called by God were predestined to be conformed to the image of His Son and those He called "He also glorified (Romans 8:30)." Paul was referring "to perfect conformity to the image of Christ, the ultimate state of [Christ-followers] when they become like Christ."¹⁸ In fact, Paul was so certain that God's plan and purpose included this glorification of every follower of Christ that he actually used the word "glorified" in the past tense.¹⁹

The NET and NLT translations bring a little more clarity to the second portion of the Philippians 2:12-13 which I want to highlight next.

> for the one bringing forth in you both the **desire** and the effort – for the sake of his good pleasure – is God. Philippians 2:13 NET, bold added

> For God is working in you, giving you the **desire** and the power to do what pleases him. Philippians 2:13 NLT, bold added

Paul is intentionally shining a spotlight on God's role.²⁰ He emphasizes the truth that all credit belongs to God because *He* is the one working in us. The word "desire" in bold text is the Greek word *thelo* {thel'-o}. It implies "active volition [desire] and

---

17 Cohick, Linn H., *The Letter To The Ephesians*, The New International Commentary of the New Testament (Eerdmans 2020) Ephesians 1:4-5, p. 98
18 Patterson, Dorothy Kelley, general editor, *The Study Bible for Women* (Holman Bible Publishers 2015) *Word Study Roman 8:29-30* under *Glorified*, p. 1784
19 Patterson, Dorothy Kelley, general editor, *The Study Bible for Women* (Holman Bible Publishers 2015) *Word Study Roman 8:29-30* under *Glorified*, p. 1784; In both the Hebrew and Greek language, the use of a word in the past tense could highlight the fact of certainty. The author is so convinced of the outcome that he can speak of it as already having been achieved.
20 Gundry, Robert H., *Commentary on the New Testament* (Hendrickson Publishers 2010) Philippians 2:12-13, p. 787

purpose."²¹ *Thelo* can mean to will something in the sense of having a purpose and seeing that purpose fulfilled.²² When Paul used the word *thelo*, he was referring to God's deliberate, purposeful intent which would lead to the fulfillment of His plan for a new creation.²³ We have learned that God takes the initiative to enable, equip and empower every plan He has for us. From Philippians 2:13 we see that it is "God's power [that] makes His church *willing* to [be transformed and] live godly lives."²⁴ That means, when He is permitted to do so, God not only initiates empowerment, He also initiates every Christ-follower's motivation to do those things He has planned for them.²⁵

> We know that there is often a great gulf between the will and the deed. Even when God has endued [provided] the willing, the doing does not always come at once. But it will come whenever a man surrenders himself to the will which God has wrought and openly expresses his consent in the presence of God.²⁶

Notice that consent is necessary. When Christ-followers permit the Holy Spirit to impart to us the desire and the power to do God's will, "then that desire and power becomes [ours] by His gift, and [we] do His will 'from [our] heart.'"²⁷ Joni Eareckson Tada,

---

21   Zodhiates, Spiros, *The Complete Word Study Dictionary: New Testament* (AMG Publishers 1992) word #2309, p. 727
22   Zodhiates, Spiros, The Complete Word Study Dictionary: New Testament (AMG Publishers 1992) word #2309, p. 727
23   MacArthur, John, *The MacArthur Study Bible* (Thomas Nelson 2006) study note Philippians 2:13 under *to will and to work*, p. 1793
24   MacArthur, John, *The MacArthur Study Bible* (Thomas Nelson 2006) study note Philippians 2:13 under *to will and to work*, p. 1793, italics added, citation omitted
25   *Holman Christian Standard Bible*, Study Bible edition (Holman Bible Publishers 2010) study note Philippians 2:12-13 under *God ... is working*, p. 2046
26   Murray, Andrew, *Experiencing The Holy Spirit* (Whitaker House 1984) p. 66
27   *Philippians 2:13 Commentary*, Precept Austin, quoting F. F. Bruce. Retrieved from https://www.preceptaustin.org/philippians_213 (last accessed January

who has been a quadriplegic since 1967, explained in her own words this exchange of desires that takes place when we delight ourselves in God alone.[28]

> In the process of my pursuit, I just ate God up. I made it my goal to simply delight myself in *Him*. And not with the purpose of holding back on a couple of desires I'd hoped He would quickly fulfill once I delighted myself in Him. No. I didn't center on what God could do for me. Not how He could please me, but how I could please Him. I kept putting my wants and wishes in check and, instead made certain my goal was simply to enjoy the Lord being ... the Lord! And you'll never guess what happened! .... God gave me the desires of my heart! ... It's true ... He really did. The thing was, because I had delighted myself in God, He miraculously replaced my little private lists of wants and wishes with a list of His own. *His desires became mine.* And what are His desires? That the gospel go forth, that the kingdom be advanced, that the earth be reclaimed as rightfully His, that the lost get saved, that His glories be made known.

As we refocus our heart to find our satisfaction in God alone, He reshapes our heart so that the desires of *His* heart become the desires of our heart.[29] That's true heart transformation and it is a death knell to Satan's power. That may sound radical. However, in reality, it is the very essence of our Covenant relationship with God. This is the process of heart transformation which was

---

11, 2022).

28 Tada, Joni Eareckson, *A Place of Healing: Wrestling with the Mysteries of Suffering, Pain, and God's Sovereignty* (David C Cook 2010) p. 49, italics in original

29 For a better understanding of how we cultivate a heart of desire-based obedience, see Roeger, Deborah L., *The Power of Obedience: Reading Scripture Through The Lens Of Obedient Discipleship* (Energion 2022) Lesson 11

depicted through the prophet Jeremiah as God writing His laws on our heart![30]

Unless we cooperate with Holy Spirit and stay completely open to Him and His power at work in us, His hands are tied and He cannot do God's work through us. Because His power fuels the desire and willingness to permit His work in our lives, without the flow of His power we can be absolutely oblivious to what we lack! As we will see, this is no minor matter. Turning to our Key Scripture for this lesson will help us better understand why remaining open to the work of the Holy Spirit is vitally important. We will begin by restating our Key Scripture.

> Then I saw a new heaven and a new earth; for the first heaven and the first earth passed away, and there is no longer *any* sea. And I saw the holy city, new Jerusalem, coming down out of heaven from God, made ready as a bride adorned for her husband. And I heard a loud voice from the throne, saying, "Behold, the tabernacle of God is among men, and He will dwell among them.... [T]he first things have passed away." And He who sits on the throne said, "Behold, I am **making** all things new." Revelation 21:1-5a, italics in original, bold added

I have highlighted the word "making" in bold text. We will use a Word Study to see how that word relates to God's creative activity.

---

[30] "But this is the covenant which I will make with the house of Israel after those days," declares the Lord, "I will put My law within them and on their heart I will write it; and I will be their God, and they shall be My people." Jeremiah 31:33

> ## **WORD STUDY**
>
> *In Revelation 21:5 the Greek word translated as* **making** *is poieo {poy-eh'-o} which refers to action. Basically, this verb means "to make" or "to do" and can express either continued action or completed action.*[31]
>
> *Among other uses, poieo can express "any external act as manifested in the production of something tangible, [physical], obvious to the senses, completed action."*[32]
>
> *The Greek Old Testament employs poieo to translate the Hebrew word bara' in the Genesis account of God "creating" the first heaven and earth and His act of "creating" man.*[33] *(Refer back to bara' Word Study in Lesson 3).*

Thelo ("desire" in Philippians 2:13) and *poieo* ("making" in Revelation 21:5a) may be used side-by-side in Greek to speak of desire that is implemented.[34] The fulfillment of God's desire results in all things being made new. In the present age, God fulfills His desire one individual at a time as they permit Holy Spirit to transform them into a mature new creation. God is the author of this new creation which begins when someone is born again

---

[31] Zodhiates, Spiros, *The Complete Word Study Dictionary: New Testament* (AMG Publishers 1992) word #4160, p. 1188
[32] Zodhiates, Spiros, *The Complete Word Study Dictionary: New Testament* (AMG Publishers 1992) word #4160, p. 1188
[33] Bromiley, Geoffrey W., *Theological Dictionary of the New Testament* (Eerdmans 1985) entry for *poieo* under *A. II. The LXX*, p. 895
[34] Wenstrom, William E., Jr., *Greek Word Studies* (Wenstrom.org ©2016) entry for *Poieo*. Retrieved from https://www.wenstrom.org/downloads/written/word_studies/greek/poieo.pdf (last accessed May 21, 2024)

(born from above).³⁵ That is to say, "Whenever a person comes to be part of the body of Christ by faith, there is a new act of creation on God's part."³⁶ In Lesson 3 I included a quote from scholar Murray J. Harris that nicely summarized the act of new creation in the life of a Christ-follower. It is worth restating here because it so aptly states the basis for the maturing process that is expected to take place in every Christ-follower.³⁷

> When a person becomes a Christian, he or she experiences a total restructuring of life that alters its whole fabric—thinking, feeling, willing, and acting. Anyone who is "in Christ" is "Under New Management" and has "Altered Priorities Ahead" ….

The work of conquering the kingdom of darkness which Jesus began won't be complete until His second coming. "The purchase of salvation was complete and the outcome was settled with certainty …. But the *application* of salvation to God's people was anything but finished."³⁸ The day is coming, however, when there will be complete and perfect fulfillment of all that God desires and the person-by-person transformation that has been occurring since the first coming of Christ will culminate in transformation on a cosmic scale. A totally new creation will replace the first creation which has been tarnished by sin.³⁹

---

35 In John 3:3 Jesus explains, "unless one is born again he cannot see the kingdom of God." The word translated as "again" is the Greek term *anothen* {an'-o-then} which can mean *again* or *from above*.

36 Harris, Murray J., "2 Corinthians," in *The Expositor's Bible Commentary: Romans - Galatians*, Vol. 11, Revised edition, edited by Longman III and Garland (Zondervan Academic 2006) 2 Corinthians 5:17, p. 481

37 Harris, Murray J., "2 Corinthians," in *The Expositor's Bible Commentary: Romans - Galatians*, Vol. 11, Revised edition, edited by Longman III and Garland (Zondervan Academic 2006) 2 Corinthians 5:17, p. 481

38 Tada, Joni Eareckson, *A Place of Healing: Wrestling with the Mysteries of Suffering, Pain, and God's Sovereignty* (David C Cook 2010) p. 65, italics in original

39 Mounce, Robert H., *Revelation*, The New International Commentary on the New Testament (Eerdmans 1998) Revelation 21:5. p. 385

Let's return to our Key Scripture for this lesson and zoom in on the word "new" as in the *new* heaven and *new* earth and the *new* Jerusalem. We looked at this word in Lesson 3, but we'll do a quick review here.

> **WORD STUDY**
>
> *In Revelation 21:1,2,5 the Greek word which is translated as* **new** *is kainos {kahee-nos'} denoting new in quality. Kainos means recently made, fresh because it is something "not found exactly like this before."*[40] *In sum, kainos conveys what is new (advanced) in development with the implication of progress.*

Just as in Lesson 3, our understanding of *kainos* will be strengthened by contrasting it to the word *neos* {neh'-os} which is also translated as "new." *Kainos* refers to the *quality of the new* suggesting an innovation or advancement while *neos* refers to the *timing of the new* (being "new on the scene").[41] *Trench's Synonyms of the New Testament* succinctly distinguishes *neos* and *kainos* in this way, "Contemplate the new under aspects of *time*, as that which has recently come into existence, and this is νέος [*neos*] .... But contemplate the new, not now under aspects of *time*, but of *quality*, the new, as set over against that which has seen service, the outworn ... or marred through age, and this is καινός [*kainos*]...."[42] By under-

---

40 Hill, Gary, *The Discovery Bible*, HELPS Ministries, Inc., [G]2537 *kainós*
41 Hill, Gary, *The Discovery Bible*, HELPS Ministries, Inc., [G]2537 *kainós*
42 Trench, Richard C., *Synonyms of the New Testament* (Kegan Paul, Trench, Trübner 1901) entry for *lx. νέος, καινός*, italics in original. Retrieved from https://www.blueletterbible.org/lang/trench/section.cfm?sectionID=60#:~:text=But%20contemplate%20the%20new%2C%20not%20now%20under%20aspects,signs%20of%20decay%20and%20dissolution%20%28Heb.%201%3A11%2C%2012%29 (last accessed January 8, 2022)

standing *kainos*, we learn that when John sees the new heaven and new earth he is seeing something that is *qualitatively different* than the former heaven and earth. The new universe was distinguishable somehow to John based on its *quality* not its newness in time.

Now buckle your seatbelt for our whirlwind review of biblical history. Let's see what significant truths God has preserved for us that can inform us about the nature of this *new* universe and how it is created. We'll begin with Adam and Eve in the Garden.

God, through His Spirit, created the perfect environment to dwell among His creation and He placed Adam and Eve in the midst of that temple/garden with the authority to rule as His vice-regents over all of creation. We know the story. They chose Satan's deceptive scheme rather than God's truth and were expelled from the garden. Through this earthly transaction, Satan gained legal right to set up his kingdom on earth and all of Scripture then records the rest of the story. God's redemptive plan as Kinsman-Redeemer begins to unfold in the Old Testament and continues into the New Testament. After Adam's sin, "[e]ach generation would now have to demonstrate its own faithfulness to the Lord in a hostile environment."[43]

So, we read of Abraham's descendants who had been brought out of Egyptian slavery by God into the wilderness where He would test them – just as He tested Adam and Eve. God would permit a need to arise so that through His provision He could demonstrate His Covenant faithfulness. That faithfulness would then become a personal reality to Israel as He built His track record of Covenantal faithfulness experience by experience. He had created a people for Himself[44] and His desire was to motivate them to choose Him above all else.

---

43 *Holman Christian Standard Bible*, Study Bible edition (Holman Bible Publishers 2010) study note Judges 2:20-23 under *test*, p. 394

44 "Is this how you repay the LORD, you foolish, unwise people? Is he not your father, *your creator*? He has made you and established you. (Deuteronomy 32:6 NET, italics added)." Deuteronomy 32:6 pictures Israel becoming the people of Yahweh as an act of creation. McConville, J. G., *Deuteronomy*,

In the period of the Judges we take note that God did not remove *all* the ite-enemies from the land.[45] They were there to test each subsequent generation.[46] The Lord allowed these "ites" to remain in the Land to enable His people to learn warfare and to see His faithfulness first hand, He was testing their commitment to serve Him alone. Moses had warned them that experiencing prosperity in the land would be a snare to them.[47] He had also warned them that the inhabitants of the land would be a snare to them.[48] Both warnings proved to be true. These warnings were not idle threats, they were intended to put Israel on high alert so she would not be complacent and be easy prey for Satan's schemes!

Chapter 10 of 2 Chronicles begins to tell the story of the kings who reign after Solomon, those who ascended to the throne in the divided kingdom of Israel. Biblical history records the northern tribes were never ruled by a king who honored God. Eventually God permitted Assyria to conquer them. In 2 Chronicles 12, we read that "when Rehoboam [King of Judah] had established his sovereignty and royal power, he abandoned the law of the LORD – he and all Israel [Judah] with him."[49] When war broke out against Judah, Rehoboam heard the message of the prophet Shemaiah and he repented. In response, God sent His word to Rehoboam that He would not destroy Judah but "they will become [Egypt's] servants so that they may recognize the difference between serving [Him] and serving the kingdoms of other lands."[50] And this was the recurring pattern throughout the period of both Israel and

---

Apollos Old Testament Commentary 5 (IVP Academic 2002) Deuteronomy 32:5-6 under *Comment*, p. 453

45 At that time the Promised Land was inhabited by the Kenites, the Kenizzites, the Kadmonites, the Hittites, the Perizzites, the Rephaim, the Amorites, the Canaanites, the Girgashites and the Jebusites (Genesis 15:18-21). Here I summarily refer to them as the "ites."
46 Judges 3:1-6
47 Deuteronomy 8
48 Deuteronomy 7
49 2 Chronicles 12:1 HCSB
50 2 Chronicles 12:8 HCSB

Judah's kings. Judah's exile to Babylon came in the form of punishment. They would be exiled from the land because of their repeated rejection of Yahweh's sovereign rule over them. However, God's Spirit went with them (Ezekiel 11:16) and the exile in Babylon also provided a classroom experience to teach Judah anew the ways of her true God and King. Through the prophet Isaiah God reminded Israel He had created (*bara'*) her as a people for Himself. In fact, He had not only *created* her, He had *formed* (*yatsar*) her[51] denoting His "painstaking care whereby every circumstance of life is weighed and measured to give exactly the right pressure of the potter's hand so that the finished vessel will match his specifications."[52]

In the times of the early church we see the pattern continue. Why did God decide to leave the first-century *talmidim* in the turmoil of the Roman Empire? Certainly, one reason was to teach them – to test them – to allow them to experience His grace, His provision and His faithfulness in the midst of a hostile world. It was their *wilderness* experience. It was their testing in the Promised Land living among the "ites." Every generation passes this way! It is the perfect plan that the creator God has chosen. Recall that in our Word Study of *bara'* we learned that the idea of God creating *de novo* as a sole and free act of His own "determination that it should be so" is inherent in the meaning of *bara'*. "In creation itself, the Lord originates, maintains, controls [and] directs," the same is true of His relationship with His people.[53]

---

51 "Now this is what the LORD says—the One who created (bara') you, Jacob, and the One who formed [*yatsar* {yaw-tsar'}] you, Israel—"Do not fear, for I have redeemed you; I have called you by your name; you are Mine. (Isaiah 43:1 HCSB)." Isaiah chapters 40 and 41 are dominated by the theme that God is the one who created the heavens and earth. In Isaiah 43 attention then turns to Israel as the focus of God's creative power.

52 Motyer, J. Alec, *The Prophecy of Isaiah: An Introduction & Commentary* (InterVarsity Press 1993) Isaiah 43:1, p. 330

53 Motyer, J. Alec, *The Prophecy of Isaiah: An Introduction & Commentary* (InterVarsity Press 1993) Isaiah 43:1, p. 330

The witness of the Bible is that from the very outset of creation God's desire is that His Kingdom be filled with those who have chosen Him as King. They are the ones who have decided to obey His commands and to live life in a way that glorifies Him. That means, as we said at the beginning of this lesson, the way we will live in eternity is being supernaturally shaped by our moment-by-moment choices in our present life. Knowing what God has in store for our future ought to impact the way we think and act here and now.

In preparation for the *new* heaven and earth, for the coming of the New Jerusalem which will be the eternal dwelling place of God with His people, God provides ample opportunity for everyone to choose their eternal kingdom. "[T]the kingdom of God is manifested in saving power and right relationships, and ... those who truly please God live in such a transformed way."[54] On the other hand, those who insist in indulging their sinful nature rather than permitting Holy Spirit to lead them "are in danger of being left out of the inheritance of the kingdom of God, which is essentially ethical (cf. Ro 14:17-18)."[55] Those who reject the transforming, enabling and equipping power of Holy Spirit live the only life they can, a life contrary to the kingdom of God.

So, what is the qualitatively *new* heaven and *new* earth? The period of testing is over! There is no more need to learn war. The choices have been made – the sides have been permanently decided for all eternity. God has His kingdom and sadly Satan has his.

For those whose lives have exhibited single-minded, undistracted devotion to Christ, "righteousness has settled in and taken up permanent and exclusive residence" and the result is that the

---

54 Schreiner, Thomas R., *Romans*, Baker Exegetical Commentary on the New Testament, 2nd edition (Baker Academic 1998, 2018) 2. Do Not Cause a Brother or Sister to Fall (Romans 14:13-23) p. 704

55 Rapa, Robert K., "Galatians," in *The Expositor's Bible Commentary: Romans - Galatians*, Vol. 11, Revised edition, edited by Longman III and Garland (Zondervan Academic 2008) Galatians 5:20-21, p. 630

entire universe is new in quality.[56] And what is the Spirit's role in making this *new creation*? It's simple. He is the power behind every life which fulfills God's desire. Those of us who have fully yielded our lives to the leading of the Holy Spirit become the manner and the means by which God ushers in the *new* universe. We are the ones who live to enjoy it for all of eternity. Thank you, Holy Spirit!

Hear What The Spirit is Saying to the Church: *Behold I create all things new. Like Adam and every generation thereafter I have given you choice. Will you choose the deceptive scheme of your adversary or will you choose my Truth? Your choice is the very essence of life so choose wisely. This is no momentary choice; it is for all of eternity. Your very life depends on it.*

---

56 MacArthur, John, *The MacArthur Study Bible* (Thomas Nelson 2006) study note to 2 Peter 3:13 under *righteousness dwells*, p. 1930

APPENDIX

HOW TO DO BASIC WORD STUDIES WHEN YOU DON'T READ HEBREW OR GREEK

To understand why Word Studies are important refer to "Preface: About Word Studies."

BEGIN WITH PRAYER

The best counsel I have seen from anyone about how to do Word Studies on the internet comes from the Precept Austin website, "And so as you begin your word study, remember to begin with prayer beseeching our Father to grant that our Teacher, the Holy Spirit might guide us into all truth (Jn 16:13), for spiritual truth is spiritually revealed by the Spirit."[57]

There are multiple ways to do word searches using internet reference tools. As you become proficient at using these tools you will develop your favorites and find shortcuts to locating the information you are seeking. I am providing a basic starting point here for those just beginning.

As an initial matter, don't forget to check the English Dictionary for how your word of interest is defined in the English language. You may not be aware of all the nuances of a given English word. As a result, sometimes that research alone provides greater clarity to a word's usage.

Next, read your targeted Scripture in multiple Bible translations. Reading your passage in several translations may provide you with all the information you need.

---

[57] *How to Perform a Greek Word Study*, Precept Austin. Retrieved from https://www.preceptaustin.org/greek_word_study#web (last accessed January 24, 2022). Note, as with the other materials on this website, this is an overall helpful article regarding Word Studies.

As a general rule of thumb, I "over research" my word of interest to be as assured of accuracy as I can possibly be. When I am in doubt I check with someone more knowledgeable than I am.

Strong's Numbers are the starting point for your research

When you've decided to proceed with an internet search the Strong's number associated with your word of interest is a must! A Strong's Number is the unique number that has been assigned to a word used in the Bible.[58] For example: the Hebrew word יָשַׁע *yasha`* {yaw-shah'} has been assigned the number: 03467. The Greek word δοῦλος *doulos* {doo'-los} has been assigned the number: 1401. Each number links the root meaning of the word back to the original meanings in the Hebrew and Greek manuscripts from which they were translated. *NOTE: When you use this number in internet searches you will generally need to add a "H" before the number for a Hebrew word or a "G" before the number for a Greek word.*

Caveat: Strong's concordance, keyed to numbers for roots in the original languages, is a valuable resource. Users need to be aware of some issues: 1) Strong's is old enough to almost be outdated. Because it is keyed to the language of the KJV it is advisable to check your results against more modern commentaries and other Bible translations. 2) Strong's provides glosses (words or phrases proposed as possible translations of a particular Greek or Hebrew word) rather than definitions.[59] That's because those Greek and Hebrew words have many potential meanings in differ-

---

58 Strong's Numbers originate from a reference book known as *Strong's Exhaustive Concordance of the Bible.*
59 When a Greek student is taught that *"pistis"* means "faith" what he is learning is a "gloss." Contrast that with the following from the *Greek-English Lexicon of the New Testament Based on Semantic Domains*: "that which is completely believable—'what can be fully believed, that which is worthy of belief, believable evidence, proof'" [Louw, J. P., & Nida, E. A. (1996, c1989). *Greek-English lexicon of the New Testament: Based on semantic domains* (electronic ed. of the 2nd edition.) (Vol. 1, p. 370). New York: United Bible societies)].

The Power of My Spirit   253

ent contexts. It is imperative that you check carefully which word definition works best for the passage you are studying.

HOW TO LOCATE A STRONG'S NUMBER ON THE INTERNET USING FREE RESOURCES:

1. Go to https://biblehub.com.

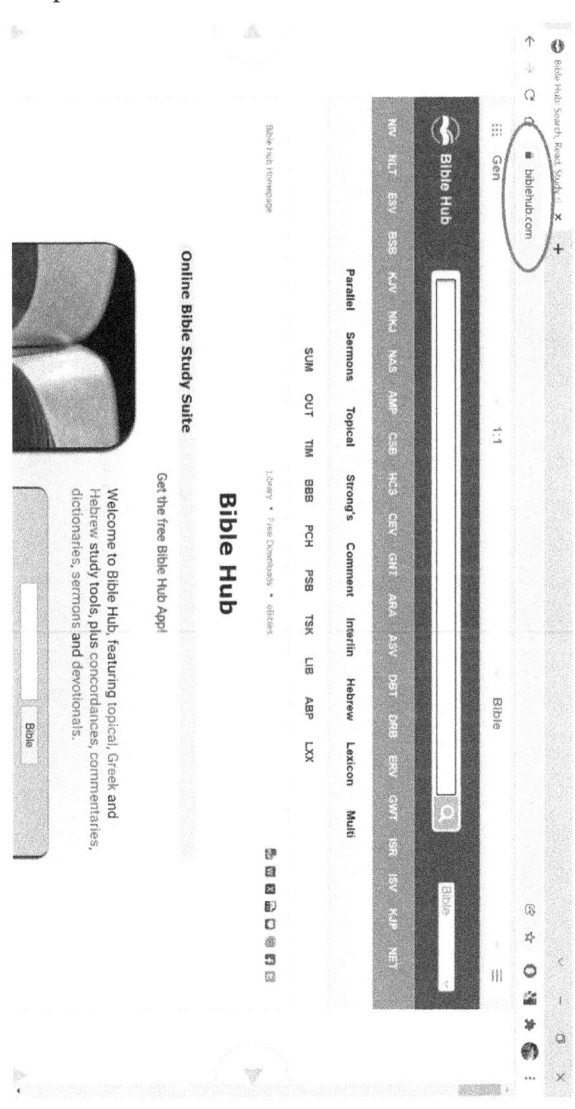

254How to do basic WORD STUDIES when you don't read Hebrew or Greek

2. Across the tool bar find the header for "Interlin."

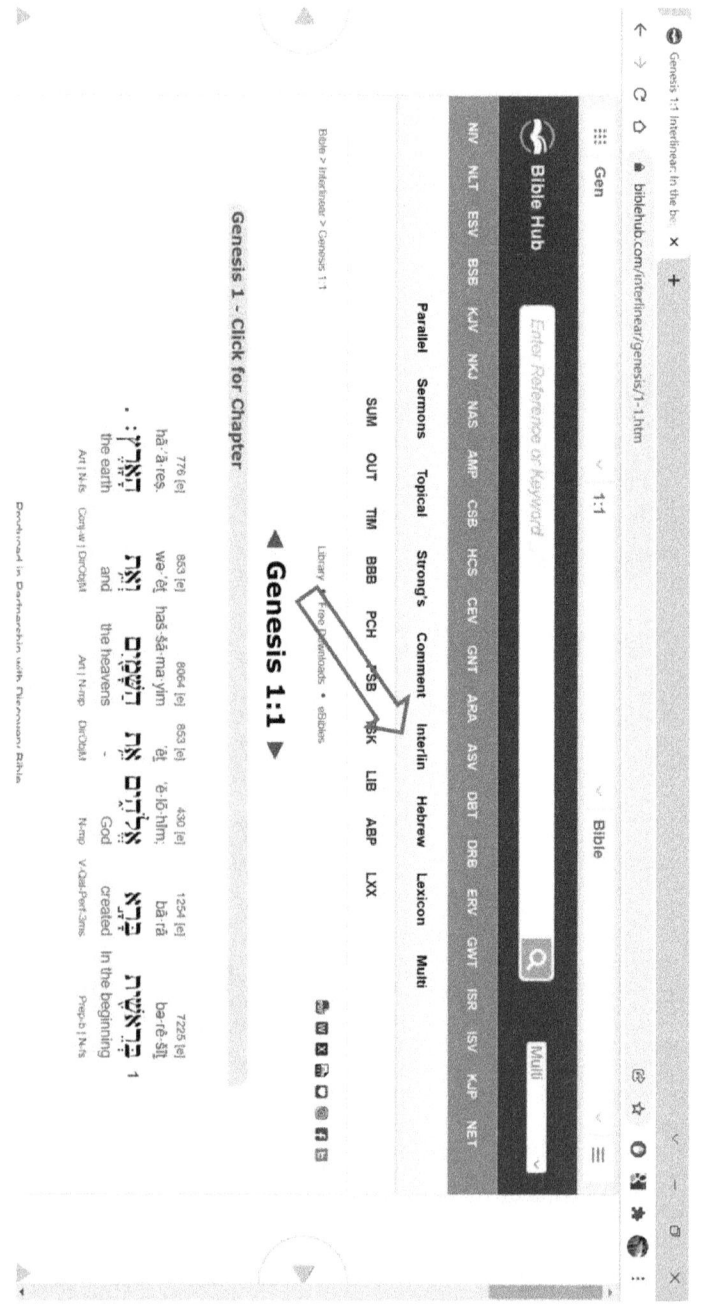

The Power of My Spirit   255

3. When you click that header, it will take you to the Interlinear page for Genesis 1:1. Find the search box at the top of the page and enter the verse address containing your word of interest. The search engine will take you directly to the Interlinear entry (either Hebrew or Greek) for that verse.

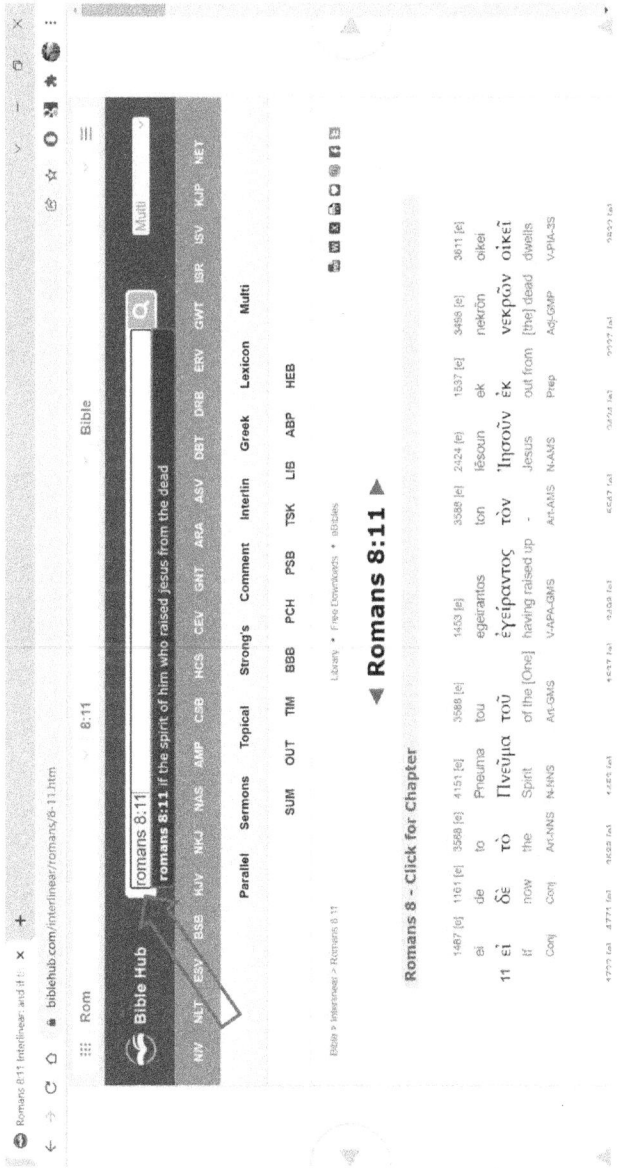

How to do basic WORD STUDIES when you don't read Hebrew or Greek

4. The numbers in blue across the top of each word is the Strong's number. You can click on that blue number and it will take you to a page with the Strong's Concordance information and other Bible Dictionary entries for that word. However, once you have the Strong's # you can research in a wide variety of other reference sources as well.

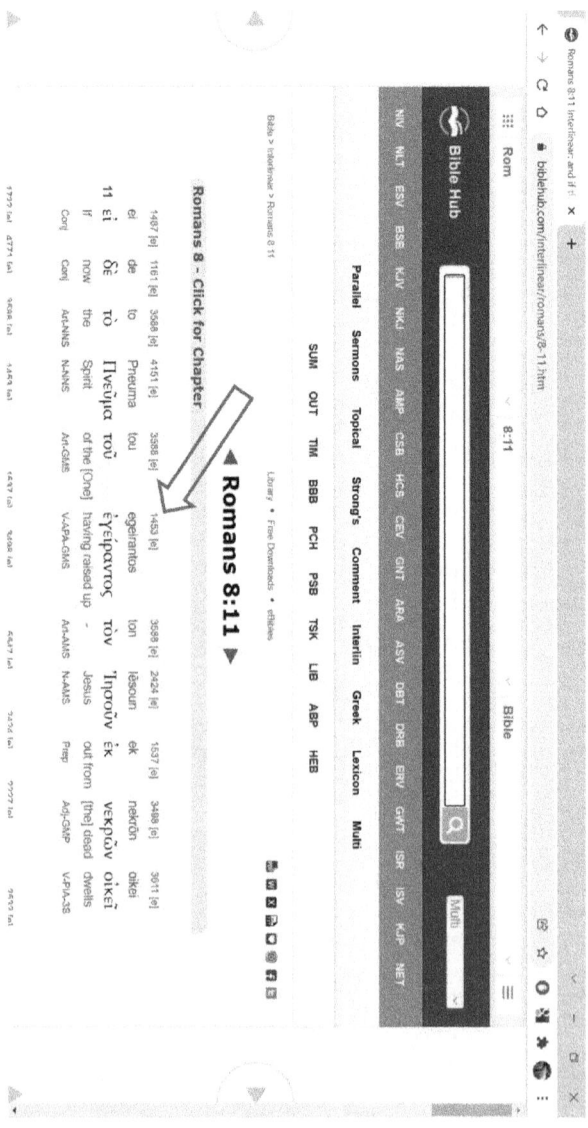

COMMENTARIES CAN BE A GREAT SOURCE OF INFORMATION IN UNDERSTANDING HOW A WORD IS USED

Often the Commentary will define the word itself, but even if no definition is provided checking a variety of Commentaries for that particular verse/section of Scripture is a good way to gain additional understanding regarding the context surrounding your word of interest.

Bible Dictionaries and Bible Encyclopedias are another free resource worth searching to view any entries that might be available for the word you are studying.

Caveat: As you consider broadening your internet search a quote from Yale University Library helps us place the usefulness of internet resources in their proper context.[60]

> 1. Searching on the Internet. Care must be taken in searching for information on the Internet …. [F]reely available Internet resources have not necessarily been published by reputable academic publishers nor have they been selected by librarians with expertise in their subject area. Nearly anything can be posted on a website, and just because it is available online does not mean it is valid or authoritative. **However, this does not mean that you cannot find good resources on the Internet; the key to doing so is to carefully evaluate what you find on the web.** If you use web resources, be sure to ask these questions:
>
> - Who is the author of the website? Are the author's credentials listed?
> - What institution or organization is behind the website?

---

60 Yale University Library, *Biblical Studies Guide: Websites*, Yale University Library Research Guides at Yale University, bold added. Retrieved from https://guides.library.yale.edu/c.php?g=295834&p=1972575 (site last updated Ap. 30, 2021 1:08 PM) (last accessed January 24, 2022)

- When was the website created or last updated?
- Who is the intended audience for the website?
- Is the information provided objective or biased?
- How does information provided by the site compare to other works, including print works?

There are times when a website you are viewing provides you with the opportunity to view the beliefs and doctrines behind those who post articles on that particular site. Taking the time to read that information can provide valuable insight about the biases the author(s) may have about biblical points of view. Understanding the framework (lens) though which the author is operating may explain cases where their viewpoint is radically different than others you have read in your research efforts. It helps you evaluate the weight you may want to give to their characterization of your word of interest or its biblical context.

A Caution Regarding Commentaries: The advice provided by the Yale University Library quote above concerning internet searches is equally wise counsel when using Commentaries.

A Few Remaining Observations

Words can have multiple meanings. As an example, the word "dig" has a wide range of meanings in the English language. It can refer to excavation (for archaeological or other purposes); an insult, taunt or sarcastic remark; a jab or nudge; to tunnel, to burrow or mine; or to plow a field. Dig can imply using large commercial equipment, a simple hand trowel or shovel; or it can refer to words that come out of your mouth. The same is true in Greek and Hebrew. However, generally speaking a word only carries one specific meaning at a time.

Caveat: Without getting too complicated, let me add one quick caveat to my last statement. The Apostle John is well known for using a word to mean two things at once (known as double entendre).[61]

The goal in a Word Study is to determine the author's originally intended meaning. It is a fundamental principle for Word Studies that the author's usage determines the word's meaning. In other words, the author's original intent, as determined by context, must be the guide you use to choose the most applicable meaning from the range of possible word meanings. The goal of your research is to find a working definition that fits precisely in the specific context. As my Publisher warns, "Most errors in interpretation come from focusing too narrowly on a single verse or even phrase. If you come up with an understanding of the meaning of a particular word that contradicts the teaching of that author in the rest of his writings, you might want to reconsider. Who is more likely to have made a mistake?"

A research technique I often use in Word Studies is to locate the first use of that word in the Bible. Let me first explain why I do that and then I'll provide an easy way to locate that first biblical usage for your word of interest.

---

61 Keener, Craig S., *The Gospel Of John: A Commentary*, Volume Two (Hendrickson Publishers 2003) John 19:30b, p. 1148; Levison, Jack, *Filled with the Spirit* (Eerdmans 2009) p. 245. "One of the unique devices used by the author of the Fourth Gospel is that of double meaning. The author uses two meanings of a word, both of which are distinct enough that they could not convey one aspect of thought. He probably did not intend to present an either/or situation wherein a Christian must make a choice of meaning. More likely he was following a pattern of usage found in Qumran and the Old Testament wherein two meanings were intended to be conveyed through one expression." Wead, David W., *The Johannine Double Meaning*, Restoration Quarterly, 13 no 2 1970, pp. 106-120. Language: English; Publication Type: Article; (AN ATLA0001588405), citing 1. S. Cohen, "The Political Background of the Words of Amos," Hebrew Union College Annual 36 (1965) pp. 153-160

REASON FIRST OCCURRENCE CAN BE IMPORTANT

The first time a key word or concept is mentioned in the Bible "gives us important details or facts regarding the subject, which will, of course, help us understand the person or thing introduced."[62] It is notable that "ancient Jewish commentators call special attention to [first mentions in Scripture], and lay great stress upon them as always having some significance. They generally help us in fixing the meaning of a word or point us to some lesson in connection with it."[63]

AN EASY WAY TO LOCATE FIRST USAGE

Using https://www.blueletterbible.org/lexicon/index.cfm enter the Strong's number for your word of interest, remember to use the "H" before the number for Hebrew words or the "G" before the number for Greek words. The search will take you to the Lexicon entry for that word. Scroll down past the definitions and reference section to the header: Concordance Results Shown Using the KJV. The first text box under this heading will show you how many times that particular word was used in WLC (Westminister Leningrad Codex) Hebrew. Following that entry will be a list of the verses where that word is used. You will be able to identify your word of interest by the superscript Strong's number next to the word. The first verse listed is the first instance of that word's biblical use.

---

62 Sheets, Dutch, *A Serpent In The Garden*, GiveHim15, February 20, 2021. Retrieved from http://gh15database.com/2021/02/february-20-2021/

63 Bullinger, E. W., *Number in Scripture: Its Supernatural Design and Spiritual Significance*, 4th Ed. (Eyre & Spottiswoode (Bible Warehouse) Ltd. 1921) Part II Its Spiritual Significance, One under *First Occurrences of Words*. Retrieved from https://www.levendwater.org/books/numbers/number_in_scripture_bullinger.pdf (last accessed January 25, 2022)

Some online sources of commentaries (and other valuable research resources) are:

Biblehub.com Retrieved from https://biblehub.com/ (last accessed January 24, 2022). From the Home Page, find the tool bar that lists resources. Select the header for "Comment" which will open a page containing Commentaries for Genesis 1:1. You can enter your verse in the search box on that page and it will take you to the available Commentaries for that verse.

BibleStudyTools.com Bible Versions and Translations Online (biblestudytools.com). Retrieved from https://www.biblestudytools.com/bible-versions/ (last accessed January 24, 2022). From Home Page, locate study menu, drop down menu lists available resources such as: Commentaries, Concordances, Dictionaries, Encyclopedias, and others.

BlueLetterBible.org Bible Search and Study Tools - Blue Letter Bible. Retrieved from https://www.blueletterbible.org/study.cfm (last accessed January 24, 2022). This page lists Bible Commentaries, Bible References, Topical Indexes, among other resources. Blue Letter Bible also permits you to research a specific Hebrew or Greek word if you know the Strong's "G" or "H" number. By the way, this site provides you with the opportunity to hear how the word is pronounced. It's a great tool if you are planning to teach and need to say the Greek or Hebrew word.

NETBible.org NET Bible Translation with Notes. Retrieved from https://netbible.org/ (last accessed January 24, 2022). The NET Bible is a Bible translation containing almost 61,000 translators' notes from over 25 scholars. The translator's notes (identified with a number followed by the letters "tn" like this, [175] **tn)** document the decisions and choices they made for how/why they translated the original text. The notes make the original languages accessible to the reader who does not know Greek and Hebrew. Study notes (identified with a number followed by the letters "sn" like this, [2] **sn**) are often added to the notes section providing an additional layer of helpful information.

PreceptAustin.org Retrieved from https://www.preceptaustin.org/ (last accessed January 24, 2022). Home Page tool bar contains drop down menus for Commentaries, Verse By Verse (Commentaries), Study Tools with options for Greek or Hebrew Word Studies, among other resources. On the Home Page there is a search box that allows you to search for a particular Hebrew or Greek word using the common form transliteration (without markings) and/or search for a particular Bible verse. When you locate the verse you are studying, it will often have word study links to a particular Greek or Hebrew word used in that Scripture. You will also find a treasure trove of quotes from various Bible Dictionaries and Commentaries related to that verse.

Note: A transliteration is the form of a Greek or Hebrew word translated into letters in the English language making the word readable to one who does not read Hebrew or Greek. When you locate the Strong's number you will see your word of interest in its original language form and you will also see the common form transliteration for that word. It is important to point out that occasionally a given word has more than one acceptable transliteration. In those cases, you may need to research the alternate forms of transliteration. To be clear, let's use the examples I used above.

Hebrew word יָשַׁע *yasha*` {yaw-shah'} has been assigned the Strong's number: 03467. In this case "*yasha*`" is the transliteration; while {yaw-shah'} provides the reader with a key to pronunciation.

Greek word δοῦλος *doulos* {doo'-los} has been assigned the number: 1401. In this case "*doulos*" is the transliteration; while {doo'-los} provides the reader with a key to pronunciation.

StudyLight.org Retrieved from https://studylight.org/ (last accessed January 24, 2022). From Home page, the tool bar contains an option for "Bible Study Tools" that will take you to a list of available Bible Commentaries, Concordances, Dictionaries and Encyclopedias.

If you plan to do word studies often and have the ability to invest in a few published resources my recommendation for Greek words: Geoffrey W. Bromiley, *Theological Dictionary of the New Testament*, Abridged in One Volume (Eerdmans 1985)[64] and Hebrew words: Harris, Archer, and Waltke, editors, *Theological Wordbook of the Old Testament* (Moody Press 1999).[65] Additional valuable resources for your personal library include: Baker and Carpenter, *The Complete WordStudy Dictionary of the Old Testament* (AMG Publishers 2003) and Spiros Zodhiates, *The Complete Word Study Dictionary: New Testament* (AMG Publishers 1992) – both are keyed off of the Strong's Number. Suggestion: Search Amazon or eBay for used copies in very good / good condition to purchase these materials at a lower cost.

---

64 When you know the Strong's word number you can enter it in the search box on BlueLetter Bible website. You will have to inform the search as to whether you are looking for a Hebrew Strong's number or a Greek Strong's number. To locate a Greek # place a "G" in front of the number with no spaces. The TDNT Reference (if applicable) will be provided under the header "Dictionary Aids." For example, G42 will be listed as: TDNT Reference 1:114,14. In this case, you would go to page 14 of the Abridged Volume to find the TDNT entry for your word. Note: the first part of the TDNT Reference [1:114] is given for the unabridged volumes of *The Theological Dictionary of the New Testament*.

65 When you know the Strong's word number you can enter it in the search box on BlueLetter Bible website. You will have to inform the search as to whether you are looking for a Hebrew Strong's number or a Greek Strong's number. To locate a Hebrew # place a "H" in front of the number with no spaces. The "TWOT" (*Theological Wordbook of the Old Testament*) Reference (if applicable) is listed under the header "Dictionary Aids." For example, H3467 is listed as: TWOT Reference:929. In this case, you turn to word #929 on page 414 of *The Theological Wordbook of the Old Testament*.

INDEX TO THE WORD STUDIES

Note: Words are alphabetized according to their transliterations under the English alphabet.

Greek
allos 215
anthistemi 161
arneomai 236
charismata 194
diabolos 153
dunamis 101
eleutheroo 131
heis 51
hupotasso 159
kainos 65, 245
kairos 83
ktisis 66
morphosis 235
parakletos 217
pneuma 19
poieo 243

Hebrew
bara' 54
ruah 6
vayyoshi'an 139

Meet the Author: Deborah L. Roeger

I confessed Christ as my Lord and Savior in 1962 when I was 9 years old. I was baptized the same day and I can still visualize that experience clearly in my memory. When God knit me together He did so in a way that blessed me with a deep love for research. It is one of the reasons I excelled in academic study resulting in a Bachelor's degree in Business Administration, Master's in Human Resources Management and Juris Doctor – all with highest honors. All glory belongs to God that my research skills and giftedness as a quick learner brought me out on top in every academic environment and led to an extremely successful professional career.

In the months leading up to February, 1999 God was drawing me closer and closer to Him through worship and His Word. That season culminated in an earnest prayer to *know* Him more. On my knees I offered to *go wherever* He sent me or *do whatever* He asked me to do that I might truly *know* Him. God answered that prayer in a most unanticipated way. Seven months later He shockingly led me to resign from my job with a large wireless phone carrier. At that time, I was employed as a regional Senior Counsel, overseeing the company's legal resources for the Eastern region of the United States. Little did I know that at only 46 years old I had just *retired* from the professional work world. Before a full year elapsed God had unexpectedly reconnected my heart to something He had buried deep within me when I had visited a men's medium security prison as a young college student. He then divinely arranged an invitation from the Christian Warden of that same prison to serve there as a volunteer working with both inmates and staff.[66] Nine years later God called me to lay down the prison ministry work which had by that time expanded into other men's prisons, the women's prison and Ohio's juvenile correctional facilities. His astonishing instruction was that I begin teaching Bible studies in our local church. It was an extremely challenging transition for me to make. However, looking back I see that my love for learning, commitment to advance on my knees in prayer and my well-developed research skills gave me a jump start on lesson preparation.

I cut my teeth on facilitating DVD-driven Bible studies others had written, supplementing those lessons with historical and cultural background information. From there God began to give me assignments to teach various books of the Bible verse by verse. The next step was to instruct me to begin writing Bible studies I would then teach. Eventually teaching assignments grew to include an international teaching ministry. From the rearview mirror, I can see that the progression was a natural one. Each step along the way was undertaken cautiously and prayerfully – undergirded by my own prayers, times of prayer with my husband and the prayer covering of our faithful prayer partners.

At the Lord's direction, my husband and I co-founded Hope of the Nations International Ministry, Inc. a nonprofit ministry with a goal to disciple others. Our earnest desire is to see the body of Christ mature by growing up in the grace, knowledge and love

---

66 In my first meeting with the Warden she asked me if I knew anything about mediation. I was in fact an experienced mediator and was presently mediating disputes for the Equal Employment Opportunity Commission. That began our working relationship which blossomed into a wide variety of ways in which God enabled me to serve both inmates and staff.

of God through the study and application of His Word. Every Bible Study I've written is well researched and profits from the fact that I whole heartedly embrace the goal of being a life-long learner who seeks to apply the truth I teach others. I love drawing fellow Christ-followers into the biblical text for the purpose of life transformation.

My husband and I presently reside in Florida. We have celebrated over 50 years of marriage and are blessed with two married children, Jeremy and Kimberly, daughter-in-law Jennifer, son-in-law Nathan and six amazing grandchildren: Jordan, Jackson, Hannah, Caleb, Jacob and Abigail.

www.ingramcontent.com/pod-product-compliance
Lightning Source LLC
Chambersburg PA
CBHW032036150426
43194CB00006B/300